TRUE NRTH

TRUE NRTH

The Shocking Truth about "Yours, Mine and Ours"

An inspirational story of survival and hope

TOM NORTH

For my wife, Connie, the joy of my life
Whose love and patience inspire me every day.

"In his book, *True North*, Tom North takes his readers on the painful journey of child abuse with honesty, candor and even humor. He reveals the shame, sense of betrayal and outrage, as well as the inevitable poor life choices that are a young person's response to persistent and often cruel maltreatment. While the reader might wish child abuse were not part of our world, North bravely tells the truth; the very thing that gives way to healing and forgiveness. But as importantly, his story is one about resilience and a young man's determination to heal. He reflects on the power of the individuals who give him a sense of purpose and how spirituality gave him a sense of self and peace."

> — Siobhan Greene, Director, Voices for Children - CASA of Monterey County
> (Court Appointed Special Advocates for Children)

"What a Book! *True North* is AWESOME! I was floored reading what Tom North has lived through, and was moved to tears of both profound sadness and laughter as I read his astute observations and realizations. Well done!"

> — Josie Batorski, Educator,
> Certified Studio Teacher for Kids in Film and Television

"*True North* is a raw, gritty, incredible story of suffering, courage, healing and redemption. It helps us understand that human beings are ever so fragile, and at the same time, remarkably resilient. It will deeply move you, and encourage you to see the shimmering beauty and innocence in everyone, including yourself."

> — Scott Kalechstein Grace, Author of *Teach Me How to Love*,
> and *If Dr. Seuss Studied Eckhart Tolle*

"*True North* is a compelling portrayal of the shadow side of one of America's best known families of the 1960s, but it is also the moving insightful and inspiring story of Tom North's personal journey from domestic hell to emotional and spiritual health."

> — David Rasch, Ph.D., Psychologist and author of
> *The Blocked Writer's Book of the Dead*

"*True North* gave me both the inspiration and encouragement to 'follow my heart' and, by so doing, I am discovering a uniting and loving presence that is always there to guide and nurture me. I want to thank you again for writing this book. It was truly life-changing. May all who read this book experience the joy that it points to and draw ever closer to the Source of life."

> — Shane Murphy, Student,
> Maharishi University of Management

"*True North* is a true story and a very important book. Tom North's memoir shows us what it is really like for children to grow up living in daily fear of parental violence and abuse. Each member of this large family developed complex coping mechanisms. North writes from a clear mind and just tells it like it was. The book is both charming and dark. You won't be able to put it down."

— Sherry Michalske, Office Manager- Law firm

"Tom writes with the grace and ease of a seasoned and accomplished writer. His story is both compelling and deeply troubling. And, yet, through the challenges he faced Tom found a path of healing and transformation. His story is like a flashlight in a dark world, but it is a light that leads us on. This is a lively, interesting, personal story. And, most of all, it is a story of someone who has learned to let go of the wounds of the past. *True North* is a story that we all could learn from."

— Rick Moss, Ph.D., Author, Developer of Pre-Cognitive Re-Education and EssentialPathways.com

"*True North* profoundly affects each and every one of us because as we read this story, we find within it our own story and our connection to those around us."

— Joanne Gimbel, Artist, Writer and Mother of Four Children

"Tom North's memoir, *True North*, is an adventure into darkness, crystallized with clear moments, captured as stepping stones into rebirth."

— Sebastian Siegel, Artist & Actor

"*True North* captures the devastating emotional toll that childhood trauma can have upon us, and how the powerful nature of self-awareness, group healing, and forgiveness can set us free."

— Chris Powell, Celebrity Trainer and *New York Times* Best-Selling Author

"Thank you for writing *True North*. Your book has helped me to better understand my relationship with my father and develop a new perspective around that relationship. This is extremely valuable to me. Thank You!"

— Dan Buffo, MBA, Hands-on Energy Healer.

"I laughed, I cried, I was moved."

— Gary Saint Denis, Entrepreneur, Artist, Surfer

CONTENTS

	Acknowledgements	x
	Forward	xii
	Prologue	xvii
1	An Idyll by the Sea	1
2	Helen North	15
3	The Road to Hell	19
4	The War Zone	27
5	The Public Lie Begins	43
6	Living in Hell	51
7	A Natural Escape	67
8	The Twenty-five Cent Solution	83
9	The Donut Shop	89
10	The Summer of Love	101
11	Down the Rabbit Hole	113
12	The Pathmaker	133
13	Alaskan Adventure – Part 1	141
14	Alaskan Adventure – Part 2	159

15	The Mountain Retreat	183
16	From Dreams to Reality	193
17	A Place to Heal	203
18	Visiting the Southwestern Norths	211
19	Guru U	217
20	The Razor's Edge	233
21	Finding Direction	247
22	From Fairfield to Fairfield	253
23	Path of the Householder	259
24	The Wedding	269
25	Reminders Along the Way	275
26	Healing the Family	293
27	Grendel's Demise	301
28	Mom's Health Breakdown	311
29	The Funeral	321
30	The Burial and the Resurrection	325
	Resources	332

ACKNOWLEDGEMENTS

Many people contributed to the development of this memoir, and helped to convert it from random, chaotic memories into a coherent story. Chronologically, as they touched this adventure are: Gary and Joanie St. Denis. It was in 2003, at their dining room table over a glass of Au Bon Climat chardonnay, and with their encouragement that I made the emotional commitment to write this tale.

Beginnings are often the most difficult part of writing and without the help of Don Huntington, (donwriteforyou.com), I might not have gotten this story going.

Kudos go to Terry Taylor, college classmate, teammate and friend, who led me to my writing-savior-editor-coach, Willy Mathes.

Endless thanks to Willy Mathes, my primary coach, editor, cheerleader and friend, (www.bookeditorcoach.com) who stayed with me and lent his patience and guidance throughout. I can only imagine the cringes he stifled and the grimaces that crossed his face as he corrected my atrocious grammar and punctuation.

My sister, Jeanie, and her husband, Steve Murphy and Shane, their son, who were my first readers, provided the first encouraging words that, as a first time author, I *soooo* longed to hear.

Stephanie Lash not only made an anecdotal contribution for chapter 25, *Reminders Along the Way*, but also provided a swift kick in the pants when I needed one, back in 1984.

Judy Sadlier added not only a wonderful review, but took the time to comb through the manuscript and found items that warranted additional attention.

My daughters, Diana and Elyse, provided encouragement as I wrote, and expressed appropriate emotional support as they learned more about their dad. They also carefully double-checked every paragraph indentation, and then gave me big hugs when they had finished.

Barbara Howard (bhmarketingpr.com) proved that little things can be huge, when she suggested the list of resources at the end of the book. This book would not have been published without her marketing acumen.

Debbie Cohen, (debbiehappycohen.com), helped prepare me for the road to come with her insights and grounded advice.

My second eldest sister, Janette, provided clarification on several items of importance. I wish her success in the writing of her own book, which she is working on now.

Phil, my younger brother, but the oldest of the "little kids," helped me with his extensive knowledge of Alaska and the fishing industry. I couldn't have gotten "Alaska" right without him.

And of course, even though she appears in the dedication, I will spend my entire life acknowledging the ongoing contribution made to my success and my wholeness by my wife, Connie, without whom I would still be lost, wandering in the desert.

To all of you, and to everyone who touched this book in it's making, my most heartfelt thanks.

FORWARD

In the 45 years since "Yours, Mine and Ours" became the 4th
highest grossing film of 1968, it has not been unusual that I, or one
of my siblings, are asked what it was like to be one of "that big
wonderful family." This book is my answer to that question.

Since that time, the film has inspired adaptations like "The
Brady Bunch," and has been shown on television so often that it is
common for someone at the office to comment that, "Your movie
was on TV last night." Having seen the film many, many times, I
must agree that what became known among my family members
as "the big lie" was actually a very charming film and a well-told
story. Would that it had only been true!

During the 1980s and '90s, I received several phone calls from
Mormon housewives who were having trouble managing their
brood of 5 or more kids. I learned at the time that Mormon's revere
large families and that within the Mormon community, the original
version of "Yours, Mine and Ours" had become something of a cult
film. These beleaguered moms wanted to know how my mother
managed to create such a magnificent household with what
eventually became twenty children, when they couldn't do it with
a fraction of that number.

I listened to them patiently, opened my heart, and
compassionately assured them that they were not necessarily
bad mothers. Apparently, it hadn't dawned on them that what
they saw on the silver screen starring Lucille Ball was a fiction;
a comedy, written to entertain. I reminded them that they should
believe none of what they hear and only half of what they see
(attributed to Benjamin Franklin). These mothers, who thought
of themselves as failures at domestic management, were relieved
to hear that Helen North-Beardsley was not the perfect wife and
mother the film portrayed her to be, and that her book, *Who Gets the
Drumstick*, was as much a fiction as the movie.

During and after the family healing sessions (Chapter 26), it was
agreed by many of the family members to never again support the
lie promoted by the film. I personally resolved to tell the truth

as I knew it, about my experience in the "Yours, Mine and Ours" household. Subsequently, whenever my connection to the family came up in social conversation, if it was appropriate, I made the effort to correct the misperceptions promoted by the film. When I was done sharing my story, invariably, my listener(s) would comment, "Wow! That's a book! You really have to write a book!" It struck me as interesting that several of the people I shared the truth about "Yours, Mine and Ours" with, called me at a later date to tell me that based on my story, they had gone back to their own families to redress issues they felt were still unresolved. They had reported successes in most, but unfortunately, not all cases. Wondering if there was a need for this topic to be addressed to help victims and survivors of domestic abuse and family violence, I thought it might serve a greater purpose if I did actually write a book about my experience as one of the twenty children in the real family depicted in the film.

My goal in writing *True North* is to reach out to every person who has been victimized, hurt, delayed in development, or in some way, left feeling alone and/or misunderstood in the world. I want to say to you all, YOU ARE NOT ALONE! There is a way; there are many ways, in fact, for you to heal, to take the broken pieces of your life and mend them. You can put your experience to a good and productive use. It is not easy, and it is ongoing. You can, however, be happy in spite of what you were told by those who were supposed to be your trusted guides in early life.

And so, dear reader, here is the book that I have put off writing for so many years, but which has finally found its way into print. *True North* will thrill some and offend others, but my hope is that it will draw attention to the great plague of domestic violence and child abuse in America, and at last set the record straight; now and forever about "Yours, Mine and Ours."

Tom North
Carmel, California

"What's in a name? That which we call a rose
By any other name would smell as sweet."

Romeo and Juliet
Act II, scene ii
William Shakespeare

My dad, Richard Dale North

PROLOGUE

Dick North walked into his squadron commander's office and placed his aviator's wings on his boss's desk. With seven children already, he had just learned that morning he would become a father for the eighth time. The C.O. frowned up at Dick over his bifocal glasses and barked, "What the hell do you think you're doing, Lieutenant North?"

"I have another kid on the way, sir. I've no business flying experimental aircraft." He looked squarely into the commander's narrowing eyes. "I'm turning in my wings and I need you to find me a desk somewhere."

The battle-seasoned C.O. quickly decided to take another tack. Leaning forward he adopted an understanding tone and pled, "I know how it is Dick, but I need you. I need you real bad. We're short as it is and you're the best I've got. Don't do this to me!" Reverting back to his frown and authoritative voice, the commander stated, "Request not granted! If I read this schedule right, you're due to take off on maneuvers in about an hour. Be on that jet, mister! Dismissed!"

A tense pause passed between the two men. "Yes Sir," was all the defeated lieutenant replied. Saluting, he turned and headed for the flight hangar.

Six weeks later, Dick North was dead.

Tom and Nick on a floating log in Penn Cove,
Whidbey Island, Washington – 1959

1

AN IDYLL BY THE SEA

My mother, Helen North, became a Navy widow when she was 30 years old. Her husband, Dick, was killed in the crash of an experimental jet aircraft, leaving her pregnant with their eighth child. At the time of my father's death, I was six years old, the fourth child in the family. My oldest sister was ten.

We lived in Oak Harbor, Washington, a small town on Whidbey Island, which in the 1950s, relied on agriculture and two Navy bases as its social and economic focus. Located about 90 miles northwest of Seattle, Whidbey Island is connected to the mainland by the Deception Pass Bridge and a dozen or more ferry boats. Our home was in what was then a new subdivision called Penn Cove Park which was carved out of the wild green countryside. The houses reflected the modest life styles of their occupants, most of whom were connected to the military.

The great storms of the Pacific Northwest regularly pass over Whidbey and the many other islands in the Straights of Juan de Fuca on their way to the rest of the state. The rain they shed leaves the forests lush with pine and fir trees, rhododendrons, giant ferns and blackberry vines. Mosses and lichens cover the floors of the temperate rain forest that extends from southeastern Alaska through British Columbia and down into Washington. Except for the land cleared for cultivation, Whidbey Island was, back then, a verdant timberland. Today it appears less forested, but still has that rural, isolated feeling found on most of the northwestern islands. Being a small boy in an environment like Oak Harbor was idyllic.

There are boys who cling to their mother's skirts and there are boys who launch themselves into the world seemingly from birth. I was the latter. From the time I could walk, my poor mother seldom knew where I was. However, mothers know which of their children are needy and which are self-sufficient. With a gaggle of children, Mom knew she could cut me loose and I'd be fine. I'd check in when I needed or wanted some attention, and if she had a moment, I'd get some. If not, I'd have to create a crisis- like a bee sting.

During the first spring I can remember, at the age of three, I stood in the clover of our front lawn. I was watching the bees collect nectar from small white flowers, listening to the buzz of their wings. There were so many I could not only hear, but feel their humming vibrate the air. I knew that bees sting when bothered, and I was curious what that felt like. I reached down and wrapped my hand around a honey bee. Its buzz became louder and its wings beat faster, as it warned me to let it go. I sensed that it really didn't want to sting me, but I squeezed it, and sting me it did. The stinger was in the middle of my palm, but I felt the intense heat and ache of it all the way up my arm. If pain is the body's way of telling us we're alive, I was getting the message. I ran to Mom, who was sitting on the front step to the house with my infant sister Jeanie in her lap. Pointing at the stinger embedded in my tiny palm, I cried, "The bee stung me!" I knew I had brought it on myself, but I was outraged nonetheless and acting the innocent victim, not wanting to admit it was my own fault. Still, a little motherly sympathy goes a long way, and it was a great way to focus her attention toward me and away from the four other children in the yard. With Jeanie on her lap, Mom told Collien, my eldest sister, to go into the bathroom and get the bottle of Bactine antiseptic and a pair of tweezers.

Collien was only eight years old, but already her mother's right arm. She delighted in being the eldest and Mommy's little helper.

She ran into the house, returning a moment later with the bottle of antiseptic and the tweezers. Proudly she gave them to Mom and took Jeanie from her lap.

Mom removed the bee stinger from my hand and swabbed some of the liquid on it. It felt cold and actually stung again. She patted me on the bottom, sending me back out onto the lawn, and said, "There you go. Now leave the bees alone."

Throughout my life, I was devoted to my mother. I saw her as a loving, caring person whose attentions were simply stretched too thin. At the same time, as the self-sufficient one, I received less of her notice than my siblings. It was the trade-off for my freedom, I suppose. On occasion, she would take me to task for being gone without permission, but normally she was too busy attending to the other children to pay attention to all of us, which usually suited me just fine.

Our home was two blocks from Penn Cove Beach, a small public recreation area, where the low tides exposed sand and rocky shore going out a hundred yards or more. I was drawn to explore the beach's natural treasures, as if each find was a nugget of pure gold. Clams, oysters, prawns and crabs abounded. Every discovery I made was a moment of wonder. It was on these walks at the seashore that I remember having reveries, indulging in the excitement of just being alive.

I believe we all have this sense of the magic of life itself when we are children. On a bright, cloudless day, I turned my face in the direction of the sun, feeling its warmth and the intensity of the light on my eyelids. I was wondering what came before. As in, what came before this life I'm now living? I had closed my eyes and looked back in my memory and all I could see was light, bright golden light, all around. Maybe it was just the sunshine. I couldn't make sense of my experience, but it felt wonderful. I smiled, and then giggled. As I focused my attention inward to see further, a voice somewhere within me said, "No, you can't go back." I wasn't happy with that answer to my question, but quickly opened my eyes to the sound of a flock of seagulls screaming and diving on something down the beach from where I was standing.

Occasionally, the receding tide strands spiny dog sharks in tidal pools, and when the water drains out of the pool, the shark is left to die. Before it does, the seagulls peck its eyes out. I ran down the sandy shore in the direction of the big white and grey birds, arriving after they had done their damage. The small shark, about two feet long, was in its death throes, wiggling and writhing on the sand, its gills opening slightly as its mouth opened and closed in gasping attempts to breathe. Staring at its empty eye sockets, I was neither shocked nor repulsed. This was a part of my education and training, teaching me that nature is creative and destructive, kind and cruel.

The tides changed quickly down at the beach, and the swirling incoming rush of the ocean created treacherous little islands of sand cut off from the main beach in the blink of an eye. I seemed to have a sixth sense for these dangers, and only once got caught on the wrong side of the knee deep current that "wasn't there and then it was." That one time, I knew, even at the age of 4, that I had to wade across or drown, so I went home soaking wet and a little shaken. I didn't know if I would be in trouble or not. When I told Mom what had happened, she thought nothing of it, being too busy with the other children. She told me to go change clothes and that was the end of it.

Oak Harbor's beaches provided other natural wonders, and not just for me. During the spring, the smelt runs were a community event. The church bells would launch into an extended ringing, signaling the arrival of the smelt, a small, slender silver-brown fish about four inches long that schooled and spawned by the millions along the shore. Townsfolk would drop whatever they were doing, leave the shop or jump off the tractor and head for the bay, smelt rake in hand. Using a stiff pole eight or ten feet long, with a curved wire-mesh net at the end, people would thrust their rakes out into the shallows and drag them back up onto the shore, bursting with smelt. Children, adults, teens, all laughing and excited, grabbed the fish with their hands and filled every conceivable container with wriggling, shiny smelt. We ate them whole, battered and deep fried. In addition to the fact that the fish were crunchy and delicious, the annual smelt run always seemed to make for a wonderful family adventure.

Our home was one of only a few on our street, which angled slightly down to a white wooden barrier with reflectors on it that blocked through traffic. At the other end of the street was a ravine through which a creek flowed that was home to trout, frogs and dragonflies. As lots were cleared for new homes, brush piles would appear. Within a few days, as I explored the new project, I often found garter snakes by the dozens, weaving in and out of the tangles of dead branches, feasting on grasshoppers and other insects disturbed by the clearing. Cottontail rabbits were everywhere. Our beagle, Troubles, led us on many a chase through wood and meadow, after those fluffy white rumps. The lot next to our house was choked with pine trees so thick that sunlight could barely penetrate. Most of the saplings died of overcrowding, poor light and from a certain little boy who pulled them out by the roots, pretending to be Hercules. On a corner of the lot, my father chopped wood for exercise and built long rows of firewood, little of which ever made it to the fireplace. It seemed that he just enjoyed chopping trees into firewood. He brought driftwood logs up from the beach and chopped those, too. Once I watched him break an ax on a fat log. He cursed the log. Or maybe it was the ax. I can't remember which. I didn't really care that he chopped so much wood. I just wanted to be with him. If he wanted to chop wood, that was fine with me.

My dad had been a hunter from a long line of hunters. When his oldest four children were five to nine years of age, he began teaching us firearm safety and how to shoot a small-caliber rifle. He set up a fruit crate in the backyard. Laying the rifle across the crate, he taught us to sight down the barrel of the gun at the paper target he had tacked to a tree. Collien, the eldest, was the best shot. Janette, a year younger than Collien, had to be helped by Dad, who steadied and guided her as she held the gun and aimed it. Janette was a whimsical, mischievous child. Subject to flights of fantasy, she would often giggle or laugh out loud at a joke that, apparently, only she was privy to. She also could be a problem for Mom. One day she was scolded for writing on the wall with a blue crayon. Grandma Brandmeir, Mom's mother, who was visiting at the time, warned that she should not have told Janette not to write on the wall with blue crayon.

Grandma said, "Not with this child. She'll be back in no time with a red crayon."

Mom scoffed at the suggestion. Sure enough, Janette was immediately back at the wall with a red crayon.

When questioned why she disobeyed, she insisted that she hadn't. "Mommy, you said not to use a blue crayon."

Mom, being overwhelmed already, had no patience for this kind of subtlety. She handled it with a spanking.

Nick was an excellent shot for his age, which pleased Dad. I was not to be outdone, though, and also hit the targets at will. We were small, so it was easy to lie prone, crouch, kneel, or sit behind the crate, plinking at cans and shooting at the hanging targets. The younger children, Jeanie, Phil and Gerry were too small yet to learn to shoot. Jeanie, at age four, was already known as "Mary Sunshine," due to the fact that she was always smiling. Phil, a quiet and subdued little boy, had been born with bowed legs and had spent his first year with both of them in casts. Gerry, a roly-poly baby at just under two, was nicknamed "Buddha."

After our lesson, we went out with Dad to hunt rabbits. We piled into the old Oldsmobile sedan and drove to our neighbors, the Muzzals, who owned a dairy farm about a mile away. Dad opened the door of the car and Troubles jumped out already baying. She hit the ground running and the chase was on! The rabbits tended to run in wide circles. If my dad didn't shoot them on the run with his rifle, Troubles would hole them up in a rock pile or in a thick section of berry bush. We watched our dad take out his .22 caliber pistol from its holster, peer down the hole in the rocks or brush, and POP! Then he'd drag the dead rabbit out by the hind feet and tell Troubles what a good dog she was. On one occasion, we lost sight of the rabbit and so did the dog. We looked all around us for the rabbit only to find that it was sitting between Collien's feet. We laughed so hard that my dad let the clever little bunny go. When we came home, we watched my dad skin and clean the rabbits. It became an immediate anatomy lesson for all of us kids.

My mother, knowing that rabbit for dinner was just about a sure thing, had been prepping vegetables for rabbit stew with dumplings. I remember fondly that we were all allowed to eat as much as our little tummies could hold. Mmm-good! Tasted just like chicken!

The dairy farmers who allowed us to hunt on their land became family friends. Dad would help them with their hay harvest in the summer, and they allowed him to hunt on their property. The sights and smells and sounds of a dairy farm were magnetic to a young adventurer like me. Occasionally, my older brother Nick and I were allowed to walk from our home after school to the farm to help with the evening milking. We were small children, but we could help by climbing up the narrow stairs in the milking shed to the second level where the grain was stored.

As each cow took its turn in a milking stall, we would measure the amount of grain Mr. Muzzal had shown us into a chute, pull a thin chain, and watch the grain slide down into a feeding bin. The cow chewed contentedly as it was milked.

When a young heifer wouldn't give milk, she was either pregnant or just a poor producer. At the tender age of five, I saw what happens to non-producers. Once it was determined that a cow was not giving milk, the veterinarian was called to examine her. The vet wore a latex glove that extended right up to his shoulder. He put his arm into the cow's rectum and reached all the way to where he could feel the uterus and check its size. I watched the vet, who, from my vantage point, seemed incredibly tall with very long arms, put his entire arm into the cow's rectum. When the examination was over, the vet removed his arm, covered with manure up to his shoulder. Eyes wide, I stared at it, my mouth agape. He turned to me, grinned and extended his hand for me to shake, saying, "Put 'er there, pardner."

If the cow was pregnant, she went to a special pen until she gave birth. If not, she was isolated in a corral away from the other cows. On a sunny Saturday morning in May, Dad drove Nick, Janette, Collien and me up to the farm and parked in the lower lot where the heavy equipment was stored. Tractors with tires six feet tall, harvesters and giant trucks dwarfed our small family car. To the side of the lot was that corral with one lonely looking cow standing at the back corner with her face away from us. Mr. Muzzal who towered above us at 6'8" had a revolver in a holster at his side. After he greeted Dad and each one of us by name, he smiled and said, "Well, let's get to work." He pulled the handgun from its holster. I recall it looking just like the one my dad used for rabbit hunting. Holding it behind his back with his thumb on the hammer and his finger on the trigger, he walked toward the corral. As he approached, he sang out loudly, "Here Bossy! Here Bossy!" The cow, which had been trained from birth to come to that call, turned from the corner and walked over to Mr. Muzzal. It looked to me like he was going to scratch her behind the ear, like Dad did with Troubles; but instead, he leaned over the corral fence, took her right ear in his left hand and with his right hand he brought the gun around, put the barrel in her ear and pulled the trigger. Bang! The sound echoed off the buildings and farm machinery. The cow went down like she was a cardboard cutout in a heavy wind. Our eyes popped out of their sockets and our jaws dropped to the ground. Mr. Muzzal killed the cow! My dad, who had grown up on a farm, was already on the smaller tractor, moving it closer to the corral. Mr. Muzzal opened the gate, then walked over to the cow, and with a big knife cut a slit between the bone and the tendon just above one of the back hooves. He threaded a rope through the incision and made a loop. Wrapping the loop around the big hook that hung from the front of the tractor, he signaled my dad to back out of the corral. Ol' Bossy, the young heifer who didn't give milk, was dragged out into the middle of a concrete area, hoisted into the air and butchered. As I watched the dismantling of this cow, I saw the tongue, heart, and liver, as well as the kidneys, placed carefully in a bucket of water and saved for later. We had eaten a lot of organ meats at home, primarily because they were the least expensive cuts of beef, but it had never occurred to me to think about where they came from. My sense of shock changed to wonder as I connected my meals to this cow.

Nick and I were fifteen months apart in age and we enjoyed much of our free time down at the shore at Penn Cove. Shallow inlets and lagoons could be found along the contours of the shore, some of them clogged with driftwood logs. We walked out on the logs, which barely moved because we were so small. The water beneath the logs was one to three feet deep and crystal clear. We could see the sandy bottom and little silver, minnow-like fishes darting among tufts of green sea grass.

Jumping from log to log we chose the larger ones we knew would support us. Great blue herons and white, snowy egrets stood like lawn ornaments on our logs, patiently eyeing those small fish that hovered beneath the protection of the flotilla of driftwood. Troubles came with us and followed along, from log to log and along the beaches, as we searched for treasures as nascent beachcombers. During an extremely low tide, a geyser of water might squirt out of the sand, signaling a clam beneath the surface. If we were quick, we could dig down about a foot and capture it before it escaped. We'd take them home and our mother would praise us for being good hunter-gatherers.

Even Mom got into the act of hunting and gathering. She once told me a story about how my dad and a friend had gone pheasant hunting one morning. In their absence, four large male pheasants landed in a pine tree in our backyard. When Mom saw them out the living room window she went to the gun locker and grabbed the spare shotgun. She then headed for the backyard. When Dad came home from his hunt empty-handed, he found a brace of cock pheasants on the counter in the kitchen, with a beaming wife standing by.

My feeling as a child was that my parents were very much in love. They laughed a lot, kissed a lot, looked at life as an adventure and generally displayed affection to each other and to their children. Dad was famous for belly raspberries. He would blow on our tummies and we victims would laugh and giggle till we begged him to keep going. Our life was simple, but full of love and fun.

When he was around, which, unfortunately for me and my siblings was not often, he was a great dad. I couldn't get enough of him. Most of the time, he was away as part of a Navy flight crew in the post-Korean War Pacific. It seemed that he came home long enough to get my mother pregnant again and then went back to another tour of duty.

It was especially hard on my older brother. For days and weeks after Dad left, Nick would sit at the corner of the lawn that fronted the street and stare up the road, waiting for his dad's return. Nick was a sensitive, intelligent little boy, who looked just like his father. As the eldest son, he was doted on by Mom.

When Nick didn't like his cereal one Saturday morning, he threw it on the floor. Dad, not liking the attitude he sensed from my brother, wanted to scrape the oatmeal off the floor and have him eat it anyway. Mom thought otherwise. It was the first time I remember seeing her so animated. She was like a mother bear in defense of her cub. She was right up in my dad's face, shaking her finger at his nose, telling him in no uncertain certain terms how this was going to play out. As they argued over whether Nick was going to eat the dusty, dirty, dog-hair oatmeal, I leaned against the door jam in front of the open door to the garage, my thumb between the door and the frame, watching the drama. I was about to take a starring role. Nick tried to interrupt Mom and Dad in their argument which was an exceptionally bad idea. Dad sharply told him to go out into the garage, our makeshift playroom, which he did. Indignant, he slammed the door on his way, separating the top of my thumb from my hand, just above the first digit. The scream I let out was probably heard in the next county. The artery in the thumb was severed, spurting blood all over the door, the wall and me. Dad found the missing digit among the dust bunnies behind the door, wrapped a towel around my hand and off to the emergency room we raced. Once we arrived at the hospital, Dad became larger than life, chasing orderlies around to get a doctor right away. I remember watching him between my injury-induced sobs and being proud of him. It was painful, but for a brief time I was the center of his attention. (And yes, my thumb was successfully reattached.)

Unfortunately for me, attention from my parents generally continued to come as a result of accidents, crises, and/or emergencies. In the dynamic of the family, it was a good thing I was an independent child. Collien, as eldest, was Mom's chief ally. Janette, as chief mischief maker, had to be watched all the time. Nick looked like his dad and had the doting-mother factor going for him. Jeanie was all smiles and followed Mom like a shadow. Phil had physical developmental issues that needed to be corrected, and Gerry, "the Buddha," was still barely a toddler, so he needed watching. Because I was so adventurous, I received the lion's share of the accidents, bumps and breaks… and got my attention that way.

On another occasion, during first grade recess, I climbed to the top of the jungle gym to fly off into space like Buck Rogers. I lost my balance as I jumped, and my sneaker got caught under the bar. The sky was my target, but the gravel became my destination, as I fell headfirst. I was lucky not to have broken my neck! Gravel and dirt were embedded in my bloody skin from forehead to chin. The teacher didn't seem to think it was worth notice, and had me sit at my desk for the balance of the day. I was sent home on the bus, gravel encrusted face and all. She seemed to be taking the military attitude of "get tough or die" a little too far. Mom was furious when she saw and heard what had happened. She put us all in the car, drove over to the school and read my teacher the riot act. It was reassuring to know that Mom could get her dander up when it came to protective instincts.

In hindsight, my life up to this point easily fit into the category of "exciting." I had daily adventures full of wonder and magic that would have made Tom Sawyer or Huck Finn smile in approval.

My dad's tours of duty in the Asian military theatre typically lasted nine to twelve months, punctuated by a few weeks or months at home base. He was a bombardier-navigator on a crew that was assigned to test-flying A-3Ds, which were experimental fighter-bombers designed for aircraft carriers. The Navy wanted a dual-purpose aircraft; however, the two Westinghouse J-57 turbojet engines were so heavy, they vibrated the plane to pieces in mid-air. In order to reduce weight, the Navy engineers eliminated such superfluous things as ejection seats. The later production-model A-3 aircraft were equipped with safer Pratt & Whitney J57 engines, but the plane always carried a reputation as a widow-maker. The Navy called these jets "Sky Warriors" but naval officers gave them the nickname "All 3 Dead," referring to the pilot, navigator, and gunner that each downed airplane would carry to the grave.

In her book, *Who Gets the Drumstick*, my mother begins with the day Dick North died. "It was a morning like a thousand others in our Navy life together…It was good flying weather. Did he want to say something to me then? It is hard to know. He hugged me good-bye; I kissed him. In four hours he was dead."

I was six years old when my father died on June 7th, 1960. For all of us, life took a 90 degree turn in a direction we could not have imagined. As much as I loved being with my dad, I had adapted to his not being around. The only difference was that, this time, I had to reconcile the fact that he was never coming back.

At the funeral, I watched the adults crying, wiping their faces with handkerchiefs. So I cried, too. I didn't want to feel sad, but I sensed that this was the thing to do. I didn't understand death. As a six-year-old-child, it was impossible to articulate the emotions I felt. It took me a while to grasp that I would never see my father again.

One of the difficult questions for adults to address for children when a tragedy strikes is "why?" Whatever answer is provided is certain to be inadequate due to the limited ability children under the age of reason (typically around seven years old) have to see outside of their own little universe. When I asked why my dad died, the adults in my environment told me some variation on the theme of "God wanted your daddy to be in heaven with him." That answer created a cognitive disconnect for me that began to express itself in my body. I began having severe intestinal cramps that ended up lasting for months. I also began having a recurring dream. In it, I was standing on a small promontory overlooking Penn Cove beach. The sky was dark and filled with storm clouds. A pirate ship lay just offshore. The pirates held my dad captive and wouldn't let him come to me. As I reached out and called to him, he reached back for me but was restrained by the pirates as the ship sailed away with him. More than once, I woke up crying and shouting for him, begging him to come back. Not long after, we Norths left Whidbey Island, too.

When I was in my teens and old enough to understand, Mom told me the story about when Dad found out that she was pregnant with their eighth child. He had gone to his commanding officer and put his wings down on the desk. She said he'd told his boss he had no business flying such dangerous jets with seven children and one on the way. He asked for a desk job somewhere. The Captain, she told me, refused to accept his resignation. That was six weeks before my father died. The commanding officer cried at the funeral and told my mother that he would never forgive himself for what he had done to her.

None of that mattered to the children. Our dad was gone.
We were unprepared for dealing with the death of a parent.
We became reactive, adjusting as we could to the confusion and
heightened emotional atmosphere around us. Collien took on
more responsibility, becoming even more of a second mother
than she already was. Mom changed too, becoming more serious
and less lively. She seldom smiled anymore and when she did,
it seemed forced. Who could blame her?

Helen and Dick North's wedding – 1949

2

HELEN NORTH

Helen Brandmeir North was a woman of her generation. Born in 1930, she spent her childhood years in Seattle. As the second youngest of ten children, raised in relative comfort during the Depression years, she went to private Catholic grade schools and then to Holy Names Academy for high school.

Her father, Henry Brandmeir, was a lumber broker who had made his fortune prior to and during the expansive, roaring 1920s. Family legend has it that he was asked to bankroll an aviation company his best friend wanted to start, but his brother talked him out of it. Henry had shrugged and argued that he had lost more money in poker games than his friend was asking for. "It'll never fly, Henry," his brother had said. So Henry didn't bankroll the Boeing Company. In fact, when WWII started, he went bankrupt as the government eliminated middlemen and dealt directly with the lumber mills.

During World War II, Mom tuned into the attitudes and behaviors of the time, which meant conserving materials that were needed in the war effort, like rubber and metals. Even nylon stockings were rationed.

When the war was over, the threat of Communism hung over the world as the next global challenge. The anxiety of the war era was lessened, but not gone. Containing this new geopolitical threat meant ongoing sacrifice for military families around the world.

With her husband on a career track in the Navy, Mom followed him around the globe to his various assignments. Although Dad was stationed much of his career on Whidbey Island, they followed his orders to locations as far away as Okinawa, Japan, Key West, Florida and Kodiak, Alaska. Finally, and fatally, they came back to Whidbey Island.

Helen loved their travel to dramatic, exotic locations, but most of all she loved Dick North. He was tall, handsome, six years older than she and world-wise. He was a gentle, affectionate man, quick to smile and had an air of Errol Flynn about him. My favorite photo of Dad is a pose replete with closely trimmed mustache and flying scarf, which was common among aviators of the World War II era. Having no money meant little to them. They made do on a Navy salary and the love they shared.

The Depression and WWII inspired an attitude of martyrdom that stayed with Mom her whole life. When she married in 1949 at the age of 19, she carried on the prevailing mindset of conformity to social and religious norms, relying more on what was expected of her by outside authorities, than on what she may have thought herself. Hers was a philosophy of selflessness and, like many devout Catholics, she paid less attention to what made sense and more to what was required. Going to church on Sunday and holy days was mandatory. Avoiding meat on Fridays was the rule. Regular observance of the Sacraments was required, and of course, bowing the head when the name of Jesus is spoken was important, too.

This compliance meant among other things, no birth control; so when the babies started arriving, they just kept coming. She loved her husband, and, according to my sisters, reveled in playing the seductress. Taking care of herself was not a priority; and as she gave birth to more children, what little sense of self she had, diminished. My guess is that, as she spread herself thinner and thinner with each new child, she most likely succumbed to some of the complications that modern medicine now identify as postpartum depression.

Perhaps it was depression or fatigue that caused her to slip in the supervision of her children. We lived for a time in Great Lakes, Illinois, while my father studied at one of the several officer training schools he attended over the course of his career. I remember wandering into the furnace room of the apartment we lived in and finding a box of matches on the floor. I had seen my parents light matches and decided I could do this, too. I sat by the furnace and lit every match in the box, one by one, watching them burn down to cinders. I was three years old. Where was Mom? On a cold wintry day, Nick and I were wandering among what seemed to us to be snow canyons. We were walking aimlessly along the sidewalks of the housing complex, with snow drifts towering over us. A neighbor woman found us, asked our names and took us back to the apartment. What were two little boys, ages four and three, doing walking alone in the snow and ice of the Great Lakes winter? How does that happen? Our apartment had a steep stairwell that led to the upper bedroom level. Baby gates were absent, which is why I fell down the stairs and split my chin wide open, requiring several stitches. I sat in a pool of blood at the foot of the stairs crying until my older sisters came along; again, no mother in sight. When we moved back to Whidbey, the days spent exploring the seashore, alone or with Nick, were also unsupervised. As a child, I loved the freedom. As an adult, I would no sooner let a four or five-year-old wander alone on those beaches than I would send them out on the freeway. The tides were much too fast and treacherous. My mother seemed oblivious to these dangers. To this day, I marvel at her inattention to her children's safety. I think it is unfair to measure her (or anyone) by current standards, but it begs the question.

Mom was most happy when Dad was home. She was delighted and, I would think, relieved to share the domestic duties and child supervision. Generally, discipline was kept to a minimum and a feeling of love pervaded the household. She cooked well enough, kept us bathed and dressed in clean clothes. She even made time to hustle the eldest three children off to music lessons: piano for Collien and Janette and violin for Nick. My protestations that I, too, wanted to learn to play some musical instrument fell on deaf ears. She said the money had run out. While I can't know what her real reason was, I believe it's fair to speculate that she just ran out of time and energy.

Helen and Frank Beardsley's wedding,
Carmel Mission, Carmel, California – September 9, 1961

3

THE ROAD TO HELL

When Dad died, Mom had little time for mourning. She was overwhelmed by the magnitude of the disaster and had to get through life one day at a time. That she was pregnant with her eighth child complicated matters beyond control. She had been told early in her adulthood that she should have no more than two children, due to the prevalence of poor blood circulation in her family, which was already manifesting as severe varicose veins in her legs. However, in her mind, that was out of the question. In conversation with Jeanie, many years later, Mom confessed that she had wanted to stop at four children. The aforementioned influence of the Catholic Church in her decision making about birth control, had, however, compounded the catch-22 she found herself in. Here she was, preparing to deliver another child without her husband present; something she had done before, but this time was very different. Dick North would never come home again. Mom wanted to be prepared in case she didn't survive the delivery, so she made out a will listing which relatives would get which children, sadly realizing that the eight of us kids would need to be split up.

Two months later, having survived the birth of her eighth child and fourth daughter, Mom got by only with the help she received from her generous and loving relatives. She later wrote in her book that the advice she had been given in the hospital maternity ward on Whidbey Island, after Dad's death, had been sound. Mom had been told that she was a living reminder to every navy wife of the tragedy that could happen to them. The advice she'd received? "The best thing you can do Helen, is move on."

The delivery of the newest North was very hard on Mom. She lost so much blood that the doctors were not sure she would make it. But she did, and a few months later when her health stabilized, Mom loaded all eight of us in our old Oldsmobile sedan, and began the long drive to California. She had a brother and two sisters who lived in the San Francisco Bay area. Her unmarried brother Bob had been a surrogate father for us children during Dad's long absences. Now he was needed more than ever. Her younger sister Kay, also unmarried, had been very helpful as well. Mom had always been close to Bob and Kay, and they had provided the support system Mom could not have done without.

Along the way, we stopped in Seattle to see my mother's second eldest sister, who has asked to be referred to simply as "Auntie" to protect her privacy. Auntie is a wonderful woman with a huge heart. While we were there, she sat each child next to her on the piano bench and sang while playing the piano. "I took Tommy to the circus, the circus for to see. He got stuck in the lion's cage and he wouldn't come home with me. Wouldn't come home with me, wouldn't come home with me. He got stuck in the lion's cage and he wouldn't come home with me." Then she would have me pick a circus animal to get stuck in a cage with, and repeated the verse with that animal. Each child got stuck at the circus with the elephants, giraffes, monkeys, etc. Nodding her head back and forth to the bouncy tune as she sang, Auntie had us laughing forgetfully for the first time since our dad's death.

During the entire road trip I had an illness that no one could identify. I was grasping my belly and doubling over in pain most of the time. The symptoms suggested some kind of intestinal or stomach flu, but without a fever. Mom had me hospitalized twice, but the doctors weren't able to diagnose my illness. I was regularly put to bed with a hot water bottle on my stomach, which seemed to be the only thing that could bring comfort. On the road, I curled up on the floor of the car behind the driver's seat with the hot water bottle clutched to my stomach, while the other kids put their feet on me. Looking back, it's likely I was mourning my father's death in a visceral way that allowed my emotional pain to find a physical outlet.

We lived for a time in a house in San Leandro, which is a bedroom community to the cities of Oakland and, across the bay, San Francisco. The place Mom bought was on a main thoroughfare near an industrial part of town. The only thing between the house and four lanes of heavy traffic was a sidewalk and a small front yard. Depending on where you live or grew up, that might seem like a perfectly ordinary environment. For a kid like me, who grew up with few neighbors and endless forests, beaches, and farm land to explore, the transition was a shock.

Behind the old rambling Victorian was a deep gully that was lined with eucalyptus trees. I had never seen a eucalyptus tree. It seemed strange compared to the pine, cedar and fir trees of the Pacific Northwest. With sickle-shaped leaves and bark peeling off in sheets, its pale colors seemed odd by comparison. The leaves of this tree are so acidic that little grows beneath them. This was unlike the great cedars and firs, which support a plethora of shrubs, ferns and mosses that make a forest so green and so magical. To me, this gully seemed sick. I walked down to the muddy bottom of the defile and realized that the entire bed of the oily, smelly creek was concrete. I couldn't imagine who would pave over an entire creek bed! Nothing lived in this brown water; no salamanders, no fish, not even water bugs! Walking back to the top of the gully, I found a chain-link fence around every home that backed up to it. One back yard had an anemic-looking peach tree in it, with tiny peaches the size of crab apples. I didn't like this place at all; to me, it seemed dead.

Mom enrolled the four of us school-age children in a Catholic School. Dad had converted from being a Protestant to a Catholic when he married Mom; and later, she always said that he would have wanted his children educated in a Catholic school. It was late in the school year and the principal had her hands full trying to place four new students. But she was inclined to take pity on our mother. Sister Eleanor shared with Mom that her brother had recently been widowed, leaving him with ten children. To her credit, the good sister empathized with Mom, and promised her that one way or another, she would find room for her children. Mom gave her a prayer card for the bereaved which Navy wives, who were losing husbands in a steady stream, had been passing among themselves. "Give this to your brother," she said to the nun. "It might comfort him." It might have seemed like a small act of kindness to her at the time, but it had implications far out of proportion to the simple gesture that it was.

During this transitional time in my life, I was lost in an emotional netherworld; surviving one day to the next. My emotions were suspended in a place of darkness I could not escape from. Numb from head to foot, I looked at everyone and everything through a new set of eyes that were clouded over with grief and unanswered questions that I could not ask. Why did my dad die? Why did he leave me? The adults in my life didn't think to sit me down and try to explain that there is a certain amount of random influence in life, but as the center of my own immature little universe, I was at a loss to understand the chaotic whirlpool of change that was swirling around me and pulling me down. I employed the same survival instincts that I had used to monitor and avoid the incoming tides; but now they were redirected to avoiding the traffic on the busy streets of the city.

A few months after we had arrived in San Leandro, another Navy wife acquaintance of my mother's lost her husband. Mom realized that she had given her last copy of the prayer to Sister Eleanor. This was before Xerox machines or emails, so she asked the sister for her brother's address so that she might write him and ask for a copy of the prayer.

Sister Eleanor's brother, a man named Frank Beardsley, sent the prayer along with a picture of him by airmail special reply, the equivalent of an overnight mail response today. He requested a picture of Mom, which she sent. They began corresponding, then dating. Just two months after our move to California, before any of us had sufficient time to come to terms with our father's death nine months prior, we were introduced to the man who would replace him.

It was not long afterward that Mom announced to us that she was going to marry Frank Beardsley. We would be moving to Carmel, California to live with him and his ten children, who would become our step-brothers and step-sisters.

It happened so fast that we were left bewildered; and as small children, we had no say in the matter. Collien and Janette protested that they didn't want a new dad. Mom looked at them with fury in her eyes. "I don't remember asking you if you wanted a new dad!" she replied, her voice rising in scorn. There were reasons beyond our comprehension for our mother marrying Frank Beardsley, which, at the time, only she knew and kept to herself.

Most people would consider four children in a family to be a lot. Imagine how it would be with almost five times that many! Actually, it was shaping up to be an unimaginable situation. For all of us, life became a series of bewildering, often harrowing episodes which for us Norths became another giant step down the road to hell.

In the normal procession of events leading up to an American wedding, the assumption is that two people love each other and choose to live their lives together in a socially sanctioned union. However, in the case of the North-Beardsley collision, there were not just two parties and their in-laws to consider, but two parties and their in-laws and...the eighteen children being brought together! Combining two very large families was rare, so the wedding became a major media event. Local and San Francisco Bay Area newspapers and television stations covered it, and sent it out over the AP wire system. Held at the historic Carmel Mission Basilica, it was originally intended to be a small affair; but you know what they say about good intentions. A small wedding just wasn't going to happen. Over five hundred people filled the church! In her book, *Who Gets the Drumstick*, Mom tells a tale of newly kindled love between her and Frank. She recalls explaining her decision to marry Frank in a family conference to the North children. She wrote that all the children were excited about the idea and couldn't wait for the big event. According to her book, we "loved" Mr. Beardsley and were excited to have all sorts of new brothers and sisters. But what really happened is that Mom had squelched any dissent or questioning in her furious silencing of Collien and Janette.

Not much farther along in the book, she comments that in the dressing room before the wedding, she told her sister, Kay, her maid of honor, that she feared that the North kids would spoil the wedding.

When Kay asked if she was nervous, Mom quotes herself saying, "I'm worried that one of the little Norths will ruin the whole wedding. When the priest asks if anyone knows any reason why this wedding shouldn't take place, one of mine, not one of Frank's will say, "Just a minute, Father. The Norths have to hold a family conference… and Colleen, Janette, Nicky and Tommy will all huddle right in the center aisle."

Now, why would she say a thing like that? Was it because she knew she was lying about the family harmony and had a guilty conscience?

In the book, Mom credits Frank with character traits he neither displayed nor even possessed. She wrote, "Frank had an astonishing grasp of the role of the parent. Some of it came from his memories of his own parents; some from the life he spent with Fran…Life in a large family would move effortlessly, with as little friction as possible." The truth of the matter is that Frank had an astonishing grasp of the role of the parent, all right; but as you will see, it wasn't the kind of role that you or I would associate with a healthy place in children's lives.

This was a man who lived and breathed the military, so any care and rearing of the children was done according to military dictates. There was no "thoughtful research" or "endless magazine articles" that formed his knowledge of the care of children.

We were told by Mom and Frank to call him "Sir" or "Dad". My meekly delivered protest that he wasn't my dad was met with a frown and the threat of the back of his hand. He glared as he leaned over me, and, with clenched teeth, menacingly growled, "Well, like it or not, I am your dad now, and you will address me as such. And remember, you're nothing without the other seventeen! Is that understood!?"

My even meeker reply was, "Yes, Sir." If only what Mom had written had been true.

The Carmel Mission Basilica was built by Spanish Padres in the architectural style of the churches of Spain in the 1700s. It is an ornate and imposing edifice, with gilded carvings and statuary of saints and biblical characters rising forty feet from the floor behind a massive marble altar. The Basilica is a spectacular setting for a wedding, and is, in fact, a popular wedding venue. It was in this church that Mom married Frank Beardsley.

After the wedding mass, the newly combined family was gathered for photos on the very steep bell tower steps of the church. This was the first of many times I heard a frowning Frank bark his order, "Don't pose!" How do you not pose a fake smile when you are an unhappy child who has just been yelled at? Frank went from one child to another, admonishing them with his characteristic frown to smile, not pose. Each of them flinched in turn and tried to find a smile that wasn't a pose. Over the years to come, it became increasingly difficult.

Langendorf Bread commercials – 1963

4

THE WAR ZONE

Frank Beardsley was a Chief Warrant Officer in the U.S. Navy and became the Personnel Officer at the Navy Postgraduate School in Monterey in the late 1950s. He ran his household like a military combat unit. Mom and all eight of us North kids moved into the large, two-story Beardsley home on Rio Road, in Carmel, California, near a suburban style neighborhood called Mission Fields. She used the proceeds from the sale of the house in San Leandro to pay for an addition to the house. A third story was added, providing two large bedrooms for the ten youngest children and a large master suite for Frank and Mom.

The North children were thrown together into a social melee not of our making and beyond our repair. Our new home was an unending boot camp run by a savage sergeant with a murderous temperament. My first experience of Frank's temper was on a trip to see a San Francisco 49er football game shortly after Frank married Mom. I had no interest in the football game and have no memory of it. What I do remember was the drive home from San Francisco to Carmel.

There were several children besides me in the back seat of the Oldsmobile station wagon Frank owned. We were supposed to be asleep, but I was awake and listening to the conversation in the front seat between Mom and Frank. He wanted to stop along the way and visit an old girlfriend of his. Mom said that wasn't appropriate now that he was married, but he insisted. She was appalled as he yelled at her and they argued intensely. Mom could not believe that he would be so insensitive to her wishes, and she pleaded with him not to make her visit with his old girlfriend. He told her to shut up and go with him. I wanted to sit up and tell him to stop talking to my mom that way; but he was big and mean, and I was small and afraid.

They parked the car, and went up to his ex-girlfriend's house, leaving us in the back, supposedly asleep. I had a bad feeling about him before this incident, but as of that moment, at the age of seven, I hated this man. I also knew what it was to fear him. I don't recall Mom's sentiment when she came back with Frank from their "visit" with his old girlfriend, but I do remember that she was absolutely silent the rest of the two-hour drive home.

It soon became clear to us that violence was the immediate response for any questioning of Frank's authority or decisions he made on any and all topics. We simply did not talk back to, or question Frank Beardsley if we wanted to keep from being beaten. If he was in a good mood, he only abused us verbally. If he came upon two children arguing, he would intervene, take sides and severely punish the child whom he thought was in the wrong, beatings being the standard punishment.

Frank had a particular grievance with Nick because he looked just like our real father, Dick North. Pictures of Nick and Dad as young men, held side by side made the viewer do a double-take; they were that similar.

One day, Frank arrived in the kitchen just when Nick had been taunting Collien with an empty plastic bread bag that he had blown up and made a balloon out of. Collien was elbow deep in soapy sink water, doing the dishes. Annoyed by his taunting, she snapped at Nick to leave her alone. Frank hated Nick and grabbed the chance to extract his vengeance. Asked what was going on, Collien replied, "Nick hit me!"

It didn't matter that Nick had done so with an empty plastic bag. Frank punched Nick in the head and knocked him to the floor. As a trained fighter, Frank knew not to hit in the face where cuts and bruises would tell the story. He slapped him viciously in the head again and again. He screamed at Nick, "You don't hit girls!"

When Nick tried to explain that he was just playing with a plastic bread bag, Frank hit him again, knocking him back to the floor. He was yelling at Nick, "Don't talk back to me!" I meekly approached and said, "Dad, it was just a plastic bag!"

Frank turned on me and screamed, "Mind your own business, or you'll get the same!"

I wanted to intervene, but I was terrified and powerless and knew I risked serious bodily injury if I did. I wanted to tell Nick to stay down on the floor, but he kept trying to get up, and Frank kept hitting him. The violence and noise brought my mother running. She stepped between Frank and his victim and told Nick to go to his room. God only knows what might have happened if she hadn't come along.

So began a pattern of violence that intimidated me and my brothers and sisters so completely that we were afraid to talk about it with one another. We never knew if Frank was in the vicinity, listening, spying on us, which, all too often was the case.

In order to protect us from such beatings, my mother developed a talent for lying. If lying had been an Olympic sport, she'd have been a gold medal winner. Whatever it took to distract Frank or create a diversion, so a child could escape his wrath, she would employ that ruse. If a bed had not been made properly, or god forbid, at all, he would go on a rant. If the offending child who had been so derelict in duty would be in one part of the house, Mom would send Frank in the other direction, and have the child fix the problem before Frank could exact his punishment. When we children needed something, anything, we always went to my mother. We did not want to have to ask Frank for anything, ever! He seemed to look forward to the opportunity to deny us whatever we asked for.

"NOT GRANTED" was his common, exaggerated reply.

In my turn, I felt like the Cowardly Lion in *The Wizard of Oz* standing before the stern, steam shrouded image of the Wizard, asking for help that never came. Like the Cowardly Lion, I wanted to run down the hall and jump through the glass and out the window.

Birthdays came at the rate of almost one every two weeks. Surprisingly, none of us shared the same birthday, nor did any of us share the same first name. However, the family never developed a consistent process for birthday celebrations, which came to be observed or ignored on an ad hoc basis.

After the merging of the two families, mine was the first birthday to be missed. Birthdays had always been a special celebration and conducted with fanfare in the North household. Initially, it seemed to be the same in the Beardsley home. Frank's birthday came and was celebrated. Two of the other children's birthdays came, were celebrated, and went. However, I was not emotionally prepared for what became a change of procedure.

On my special day, I waited for someone to say, "Happy Birthday," but no one did. As the evening approached, I marveled at how everyone was keeping the celebration a secret from me. I was impressed. They were really good. At dinner when no one looked my way or smiled at me, I was sure they were all in on a surprise. As everyone filed out after the meal, I sat at the table, watching them leave. I sat and sat, and after about 10 minutes, I realized, watching kids walk by the kitchen door going about the evening, that they had forgotten. I got up from the table and walked over to the door that separated the kitchen from the living room. I stood in the doorway and looked at Mom and Frank. Their habit had been to retreat to the corner of the living room where, comfortably seated, scotch and water in hand, they would talk. Children were not allowed in the living room without permission. I meekly asked if I could come in and talk with them.

Frank scowled at me and barked, "What do you want?"

My mother leaned toward him, placed her hand on his knee and said, "Frank, please." Then she turned to me and said, "What is it Tommy?"

I took a few steps in their direction and with my head hanging, said, "Today is my birthday, and you forgot."

Mom put the palm of her hand up to her face to hide her embarrassment at having forgotten and muttered, "Oh, no..."

Frank's scowl deepened as he yelled, "SO WHAT DO YOU WANT ME TO DO ABOUT IT? DO YOU THINK YOU'RE SOMETHING SPECIAL!?" He put his drink down and began to ball his hands into fists while getting up from his chair.

Mom, shocked at his response, stopped him from getting up and coming at me. She turned to me again and said, "Tommy, run along now and I'll think of something."

The commotion with Frank's outburst had attracted attention and quickly word spread around the house that Tommy's birthday had been forgotten. Children began coming to the rescue. My younger sister Jeanie brought me half of a broken pencil. Several other children brought me items that were lying around the house. One of them was a half-used bottle of glue. As I was staring at it in disbelief, a little girl grabbed it out of my hand, shouting, "Give that to me. It's mine!" I think it was the shortest possession of an item I have ever experienced.

Had I the wisdom or perspective of an adult, I might have realized how overwhelmed Mom was in this new house. Perhaps I'd have realized that it might have taken something just short of a miracle for her to have remembered my birthday. But since the wedding in September, three birthdays had been celebrated before mine, and I didn't have the perspective of an adult. It was that of a child who had known a reasonably stable family existence for the first six years of life and who now was struggling to deal with something entirely different.

Whatever solution my mother thought of that evening, she didn't share with me. There was never any cake, ice cream, or celebration. However, a few days later, as I sat on the floor of my bedroom doing homework, Frank showed up in the doorway, dressed in his Navy uniform. He startled me. I looked up into that scowl I was seeing all too often and said nothing, looking back at my book. He had an unwrapped cardboard box about one foot by two feet under his right arm and his white navy hat in the other hand. He threw the box down on the floor next to me, so that I had to scamper out of the way to avoid being hit by it as it scudded toward me.

"Don't say I never gave you anything." he mumbled begrudgingly. Then he walked away.

The box contained a mold and liquid plastic to make toy cars. I plugged in the mold and poured some plastic into the hot frame for a toy car body. I coughed and gasped as toxic fumes began to spew out into the room. I pulled the plug, boxed it back up and threw it away. I knew I was in trouble in this family.

Years later, recalling this traumatizing event to my younger brother, Gerry, he said, "Get over it. That happened to all of us."

I guess it says something about what a self-centered seven-year-old I was; that I could recall so clearly the event of my missed birthday but never noticed that, eventually, it happened to just about everybody else in the family.

After the birthday debacle, I decided to run away. It's easy to plan running away. If you ever want to run away, just do the following. First, you get your backpack down from the closet. Then, put a knife, a fork, and a spoon in the backpack. Next, you take a loaf of frozen bread and a two-pound block of butter out of the freezer and put it in the backpack. Then, you go to the peanut butter and jelly cupboard and get out the 50-pound tin of peanut butter. This is where you may run into problems. It won't fit unless you have a really big backpack. Neither will the 50-pound tin of raspberry jelly. Recognizing this dilemma, you just might panic, like I did. Maybe running away isn't such a good idea. In my case, I began imagining the police catching me hitchhiking and bringing me home to face a scowling Frank, who would surely beat me to death. That image cured me of my plan. But I had already purloined the bread and butter. Instead of taking them back to the freezer, I took them next door and gave them to kindly Mrs. Lang. She looked quizzically at me for a long moment before eventually thanking me.

On my way back over the fence between our homes, I caught a movement in the dark, damp leaves and branches below the hedge that lined the fence. Looking down, I saw a beautiful yellow snake with brown diamond shapes down its back. Having recently shed its skin, the new one was bright, shiny and clean. I quickly noticed that the head of the snake was long and straight, not triangular like a rattlesnake. Glancing down at its tail, it didn't have rattles, either. This was a gopher snake, and a big one. About five feet long, it was flicking its tongue in and out, smelling the air. The snake noticed me noticing it and curled up into a semi-coil, trying to imitate a rattler. I had an affinity for all wild things and knew that this was not a dangerous snake.

I reached down and grabbed the snake behind its head, lifting it off the ground. It was thick and heavy through the middle, its body as thick as my arm. I had caught smaller gopher snakes before, and knew that they are constrictors, instinctively wrapping themselves around an object, either to kill in the case of prey, or to defend itself, if needed. This snake coiled itself around my arm and squeezed until my hand turned dark red. I was amazed at its strength, but not worried that it might hurt me.

Figuring it would make a great pet, I found a cardboard box to keep it in. I put straw from the lot next door in a box with a bowl of water, and, unwrapping it from my arm, put my new pet in its new home, which was the closet in my room. I went out to catch grasshoppers to feed to my snake, and on my return, found it missing. I asked my older brothers and sisters, step-brothers and step-sisters, and my mother, if anyone had seen a gopher snake, and described it for them, not mentioning that I meant in the house. No one had seen such a snake, but I was assured they would let me know if they did.

Several days later, as I came home from school, I was greeted by Mom's very loud voice, "THOMAS!" I ran to the sound, which came from the laundry room. As I arrived, I saw my mother, standing back a few feet from the washer-dryer area, with her hands on her hips, glaring down at a basket of laundry, with a large colorful snake moving slowly through the dirty clothes. It had a bulge in its belly and may have been feeding on mice that lived in the wall behind the washer and dryer.

Mom scowled at me and sardonically inquired, "Is this the snake you were asking about the other day?"

"Yeah, Mom!" I replied, as I moved in to retrieve my lost pet.

"Outside!" she commanded, pointing to the sliding glass door.

This unfunny episode forced me to realize that a wild snake is probably not a reasonable pet anyway. Immediately, as Mom had ordered, I took the snake back to where I had found it, releasing it beneath the hedge. I suppose I was lucky Frank didn't find it.

Mom and Frank, being good and faithful Catholics, gave birth to two more children over the next two years, increasing the total number of offspring to 20. The two additional infants did not seem to significantly increase stress levels in the house, as these were already over the top. Twenty children is a number sufficient for two full baseball teams complete with umpires. We were almost three times the number of the Von Trapp Family, which, in "The Sound of Music" always seemed to be a crowd. In fact, upon their marriage, a mathematician friend calculated that if the North-Beardsley offspring would propagate at the rate of the parents, by the year 2100, every fourth person on the planet would be descended from them!

The military precision with which the household was run seemed to work for Frank and Mom. For the children it was something different, very different. Beds had to be made and clothes put away before we left our bedrooms. Frank made unscheduled inspections of all of our bedrooms at odd times throughout the day and night. He even took to wearing a white glove during his inspections. To have Frank enter my bedroom sent me into a state of panic. He was always looking for a reason, any reason, to demean, embarrass or punish me or anyone in the room. If items of clothing or books or just about anything looked out of place, Frank would one by one, ridicule the owner of that item. "What's the matter with you!?" he would shout, "You born in a barn!? You don't know how to put things away!? What's the matter with you anyway!?" His diatribes became a ritual that set me cringing the moment he walked in the door.

It was not uncommon for him to get himself worked up enough to slap the offending child, knocking him or her across the room or to the floor. We never knew how far he would go. If he was slightly drunk, he was worse. If he was really drunk, he seemed to mellow out a bit. I preferred him really drunk. He got lazy when he was really drunk and his abuse usually stopped at the verbal level.

In the Frank Beardsley household, punishments were frequent. Spankings were conducted in public, with pants down, worsening the humiliation. The preferred weapon was a belt or a brush. I learned quickly that to avoid Frank's wrath, I had to stay away from him, keep to myself, and avoid crowds of kids. I became like a deer drinking at a pond, taking a few sips and then looking around for the predator that could attack at any moment. I retreated farther within myself, believing that I had to be even more self-reliant if I were to survive in this new environment. I handled the regimentation by simply becoming invisible and attracting as little attention as possible.

One morning, not long after the families were merged, I was told by Frank to get dressed in my church clothes and get in the car. When I asked why, he said, "Just get in the car and shut up. I'm adopting you."

There had been some discussion of adoption around the dinner table the night before; but even though I didn't know what adoption meant, I had already learned not to ask questions for which I would be punished. At the courthouse, I filed into the courtroom with the other children, sat down on a bench, and in a few minutes, I walked out, not knowing what had happened. But from that day on, my name was no longer Tommy North, but Tommy Beardsley. There seemed little point in complaining that I didn't want to be a Beardsley. It was already done, and besides, as I had been reminded so often, I was "nothing without the other eighteen." It was now eighteen, because Mom had given birth to the nineteenth Beardsley.

After the adoption, my sense of confusion and bewilderment grew as my connection to the North heritage and identity disappeared. Not having been privy to the conversations that led up to the adoption, I can only wonder how much it was motivated by a desire to bring these two families together and how much it was motivated by Frank's jealousy and intention to eliminate all that was North.

Mealtimes were enjoyable when Frank was absent, but when he presided, they were simply challenges that we just had to get past. Frank had managed to buy a custom-made table for the dining room that could seat all of us at once. It was kidney-shaped, so there was no head or foot of the table. For a time, Frank and Mom sat together presiding over meals that were conducted in almost total silence. I can't speak for my siblings, but I didn't want to speak for fear that Frank would interrupt with a demeaning comment. There was little conversation between the kids and the parents. Scotch and water by his plate, Frank talked with Mom as though we children were not there. He only interacted with us to silence someone with a menacing glance. We had assigned seats at the table. The seating arrangement had the smaller kids packed in on a bench, trapped by the table. Unable to easily push a chair away from the table and excuse themselves, this resulted in frequent requests to go to the bathroom. It was also a way to get out of the uncomfortable atmosphere and take a deep breath, if just for a few moments. Invariably, the bathroom request was met by the excessively loud reply from Frank of, "NOT GRANTED!" He seemed to think this response was funny, but we sure didn't. He would glower at the offending child and in that menacing voice of his ask, "Why didn't you go before you sat down?"

Under normal family circumstances, that might be an entirely reasonable question. But as long as Frank was involved, the stress in the room was already at maximum level and almost any response from him was enough to bring a child to tears. Trying to avoid yet another scene, mom would nod permission to whoever had made the request, and a small head would disappear under the table following Frank's admonition to "hurry up!" Then, a few minutes later, reappear in the same place. It didn't take long for Frank to tire of the family dining experiment. Within a few months he no longer ate with the children, preferring to dine alone, or with Mom, in the living room. She fixed him steak or other meat dishes, while we ate macaroni and cheese or casseroles of one kind or another. Smelling the steak on the broiler or frying in a pan was torture, but there was nothing we could do about it.

With 22 mouths to feed, meal preparation was a big deal. Mom did the cooking with the assistance of the older girls and often the older boys. Breakfast was cafeteria style, most often centering around a large pot of oatmeal.We were able to make and eat all the toast we desired because every week a truck from Langendorf Bread Company would show up with 100 loaves of white bread. This was more than enough for 22 hungry people, and we would regularly throw stale, moldy bread away when the truck appeared for its next delivery.

Langendorf gave us the bread in compensation for an advertising campaign they mounted using our family. An advertising firm named Young & Rubicam spent 12 days taking pictures to get the marketing punch they were looking for. I was featured in several of the sequences, and was excited to "be in commercials." In one particular segment I came out of the storeroom, my arms full of loaves of bread. As I rounded the door, into the glare of the studio lights, I could see Frank standing by the camera. He had not been there when I had gone into the store room while the film crew was setting up the scene, but to my chagrin, there he was. The smile on my face faded. I was sure he would say something to ruin the moment and he obliged.

Frowning through the lights behind and around him, I heard him say, "Don't pose!"

The director asked me to do the scene again, and when I came out of the storeroom, giving my best paranoid smile, Frank was gone. After several more takes, we finished and the director thanked me for doing a good job.

Later, Frank took me aside, and, poking me in the chest with his forefinger, admonished,

"Don't get a big head about being on camera, kid. Just remember, you're nothing without the other nineteen."

We had become twenty because Mom had given birth yet again.

Every Saturday morning, before anyone was allowed to go anywhere, we formed an assembly line with the goal of constructing the many dozens of sandwiches that were needed for school lunches during the subsequent week. With calorie hungry teenagers in the house, and a single menu item of peanut butter and jelly sandwiches, they went quickly. This was before baggies, so each sandwich had to be made, wrapped individually in waxed paper, folded, and taped tight. The sandwiches were put into cardboard boxes and stored in one of the two large chest-type freezers in our utility room. The "taped tight" was more an intention than a practice; so it was common to eat stale sandwiches that were soggy and half-frozen. We made the sandwiches using peanut butter that came from out of the bowels of a semi-trailer that showed up every week with 50 pounds of smooth peanut butter packaged in an enormous copper-colored tin. Jelly also came in 50-pound tins and was strawberry, raspberry, or grape.

Fortunately, I loved peanut butter and jelly; in fact, I still love it. It's best when it's thick and sloppy, with so much jelly that you have to pinch the opposite ends when you take a bite so the stuff doesn't drip down the front of your shirt, which it will often do anyway.

The bulk food we consumed was delivered by the commissary at the military base. The large quantities were designed for cooks in mess halls that often fed hundreds of men or more. The truck from the commissary also brought oatmeal, sugar, powdered milk, and white and brown sugar in 100-pound sacks. Military issue vegetables, which included green beans, lima beans, peas, carrots, and corn, were delivered in gallon cans. Mustard, mayonnaise and ketchup were delivered in 2-gallon containers.

We were assigned on a rotating basis the job of making the milk for a given meal. For the powdered milk to be palatable, it had to be made carefully, with hot water, which allowed the yellow powder to dissolve evenly. It then needed to be put in the refrigerator well ahead of the meal, so it could cool. If the milk wasn't made properly, it became lumpy; and the most irritating thing at any meal was to find those lumps floating in my milk. There were several of us who were particularly inattentive to this assignment. Either we didn't have enough patience to wait for the tap water to get warm, or we didn't care. Regardless, there was a tendency for the milk to be made at the last minute with cold water, which would guarantee those disgusting lumps that we had to chew up after trying to choke down the gelatinous mixture. As a growing boy, I drank a lot of milk; but I found myself gagging on lumps more often than I cared to.

For the children, meat was scarce and potato casseroles were common. From time to time, we would come home to the smell of a roast cooking in an electric frying pan. Mom preferred to use a pan instead of the oven. Occasionally she'd cook a pot roast in the oven. The aroma always set my imagination afire.

Not knowing if this was just another steak cooking for Frank, I would have to ask, "Do we get some?"

When the answer was "Yes," I imagined eating meat until my belly swelled, only to find when the delicacy was parceled out, that my slice was disappointingly small: about four inches long, two inches wide and an eighth of an inch thick. It was all vapors and no substance. I could eat all the white bread and margarine I wanted, but there were no second servings of meat.

A fairly regular delicacy we enjoyed was due to the generosity of one of our neighbors across the street. John, the neighbor, worked for his wife's family on a local artichoke farm. When harvest time came around, there were the marketable, top quality artichokes, and then there were the "seconds," perhaps riddled with worms and the unattractive holes left by the worms that eat through the leaves of the large green thistles. John would show up at the door with a large gunnysack of seconds, give them to Frank, and attempt to go home. But, over the years, a ritual developed where Frank insisted that a drink was in order, (just one, you know); and a couple of hours later, "Generous John" the neighbor, stumbled back across the street, to a furious wife. She often seemed resentful when I went to play in their yard with their children. I could never figure out why she was frowning at me, but I seldom got a smile. Looking back now, I'm guessing it had something to do with the quantity of alcohol Frank encouraged her husband to consume.

As a San Francisco native and life-long 49er fan, Frank often invited John up to the master bedroom where he kept a state-of-the-art television-stereo console to watch 49er games. Frank had Mom serve them t-bone steaks and scotch, which troubled John, because he knew the children were downstairs eating macaroni and cheese. He shared with me many years later that it seemed wrong for Frank to be dining like a king while his children ate like paupers.

Nonetheless, I loved the artichokes, steamed and dipped in mayonnaise. The worms didn't bother me at all. In fact, they were edible, and in my mind, just another source of protein. I tried one and it tasted like the artichoke it had been cooked in.

Treats were a rare occurrence in the Beardsley home. A Rice Crispy square was a joy. A piece of real chocolate was like heaven. While we got plenty of the standard military issue fare to fill us up, we would have to get creative if we wanted additional delights. Nick and I would get a cardboard box and pick up discarded soda bottles from the side of the road, which we would redeem at the local Safeway grocery store for enough money to buy candy. A box full of discarded bottles would get us a buck or two. Back in those days, a regular candy bar was a nickel. Giant candy bars were a quarter. I would usually get one of the giants, like a Hershey's milk chocolate or a Crackle, and savor the whole thing all by myself. Hostess fruit-filled pies were great, too, and Snowballs, yum! And there's just nothing quite like Hostess Twinkies when you're 8 years old!

Every chocolate fix or pastry was important to me, because it might be a while before the street's gutters would yield another box of bottles.

With twenty mouths to feed, it was a foregone conclusion that there would be no allowance. We didn't need to do the math on that one. What was scary to me as a small boy was when I learned that Frank had a reputation for confiscating any money that was earned by the older kids. So before we got caught with money in our possession, we made sure to spend it. All other earnings went into Frank's pockets to "help support the family." That seemed unfair on several levels. For one thing, I never believed that Frank actually needed to get money from us. The government added a bonus onto military pay for each child the employee had, so Frank certainly had some economies-of-scale going on with all those kids. Frank's confiscation of our earnings seemed unfair to everyone and I saw it as just another bully tactic. Mom agreed and finally convinced him to permit the girls in the family to keep their babysitting money. At that time, three of the twelve girls were in their teens and baby-sitting on the weekends; so Frank's leniency with that matter established a pattern of exceptions to his rule that effectively ended the confiscation of money from the kids.

Good thing too, because at the age of ten I started working a paper route, which was too much work to have to give all the money away to Frank.

Lucille Ball and the cast of "Yours, Mine and Ours"
Frank and Helen, as well as Henry Fonda, are in the back row.

5

THE PUBLIC LIE BEGINS

As time went by, the combination of our two large families attracted more media attention and the story was carried on the AP wire across the country. National magazines such as *Time* and *Life* ran articles about the "big happy family" in California. Lucille Ball, who was the queen of comedy in Hollywood, saw the story and called Frank and Mom. Imagine being Mr. and Mrs. Simple American and getting a phone call from Lucille Ball! Lucy suggested that a movie could be made from their story, and asked them to write a book from which a film would be made.

Over the next couple of years, Mom wrote a book called *Who Gets the Drumstick?* I thought it was a great title, but unfortunately, my compliments end there. To be fair, few first-time authors find success, but my mother lacked both the soul and training of a writer; and as a work of literature, the story was appalling. The only thing that made it readable was the work done by two Hollywood ghost-writers who were assigned to the task by Lucy.

Beyond the logistical aspects of managing the household and the chronology of events, the story was pure fiction. With Frank essentially looking over her shoulder, she wrote about him in a most complimentary style, attributing to him character traits that he never displayed and was literally incapable of possessing. She referred to him as "loving, wise and even-tempered." When the book was published and I read it, I wondered who this man Mom was describing could be. He certainly didn't live in the house I lived in!

Social status and public opinion were extremely important to my mother, so I can understand her wanting to make up a story to support her vision (and Lucy's) of a loving combined family with all the attributes she imagined. To Mom, appearances were everything, and she did her best to maintain them. The book simply reflected that because it was impossible for her to reveal the truth of the family situation. But the script she consciously or unconsciously wrote for herself (as savior/martyr of this family) was to save the children from Frank, and in the process, save Frank from himself; because as we have heard so often, "Love conquers all."

When Mom wrote that Frank was great with kids, she said that he had read endless articles about their care. The only way the word "care" fits in that sentence is that he couldn't care less about children. As long as they served his needs, he tolerated them. When things didn't go his way, he was dangerous. In a conversation with him later in his life, he confided in me that he never wanted children. They were simply a consequence of having sex. But Mom couldn't have written that in her book, could she? Random House published it as a coming best-seller, but everyone associated with the project must have cringed. It was not surprising that it didn't sell well.

The book was published in 1965, but the film wasn't released to the public until 1968. During that period, Lucy was busy with her Broadway career, and it wasn't until 1967 that she was able to make time to complete the film project.

Through her own company, Desilu Studios, Lucy negotiated the film contract with Frank and Mom, offering them $25,000 or 5% of the net proceeds of the film. In hindsight, it wouldn't have been a stretch for them to ask for both, since there was not yet a number to measure 5% against. But Frank and Mom consulted with an attorney who advised them to take the cash. That attorney earned exactly what they paid him, which was nothing, and they received value in proportion to the fee. The film turned out to be the fourth highest grossing film of 1968! Frank and Mom went back to Lucy after the film's financial success was apparent and complained that they hadn't received enough compensation. She paid them another $10,000 on the condition they sign away all rights and royalties to future showings, sequels or productions, which they did. That was another dreadful decision, considering that the movie has been shown on television at least 5 times a year since the early 1970s, the countless video rentals of the film, and the remake of the movie in 2005, not to mention international distribution.

While she was researching her role as Helen North Beardsley, Lucille Ball actually came to observe us for a few days, in order to get a flavor for the characters. At the end of Lucy's first day in Frank's presence, she approached my mother and in a serious, almost threatening tone admonished her, "You keep that man away from me." She left and stayed at the Lodge in Pebble Beach for the duration of her visit.

Having seen Lucy in our house, I expected to see Henry Fonda, who was cast to play Frank; but we never saw him. To have had a father figure like the character Henry Fonda played in the film would have been a dream come true for me. His scripted characterization of Frank Beardsley was wise, practical, loving and honest. In short, his character was the farthest thing imaginable from the actual Frank Beardsley!

Lucy impressed me as being an intense person. She seemed to be all business, without a hint of the comedienne she projected through her stage persona. There was never any interaction on a personal level between Lucy and any of us children. No jokes or laughter, and no warming of relations. I had never met anyone who was so alert and so aware of everything that went on around her. She was focused and knew exactly what she needed, gathering information in a methodical fashion. And then she was gone.

When casting the film was discussed, Lucy offered to let any of the children, who had a desire to, play their own part. Our parents, who were mindlessly devout Catholics, believed money and Hollywood was the root of all evil. Not evil enough to dissuade them from taking Lucy's money, mind you, but they were not about to let any of their children be corrupted by their imagined Hollywood lifestyle, or by the money that might have come to us from the roles we might have played. In my teen years, I found it easy to be resentful about this. Looking back as an adult, I can only speculate how I might have handled fame and fortune as a child. However, what's fame without fortune??? If we had to suffer the fame, it would have been great to have found out what fortune was like!

Tommy's character had a minor role in the movie. His (my) most notable appearance was when I entered the house with wet clothes, holding a soaked newspaper and, dripping with both rain and irony, announced, "Twenty percent chance of rain!" The actor who played my part was a boy named Mitch Vogel. After playing Tommy North, he went on to play roles in 81 other film productions, which included a Golden Globe nomination for his role in "The Reivers." After "Yours, Mine and Ours", he spent the next four years on "Bonanza" playing the role of Jamie Cartwright.

When "Yours, Mine and Ours" was released in 1968, it won both a Golden Globe Award and a Golden Laurel Award. Lucy was nominated for a Golden Globe and won a Golden Laurel for her role in the film. The movie's West Coast premiere was held at the Cinema 70 theatre in Monterey, which at the time was the largest theatre in Monterey County. Lucy came to introduce the film, and our family was paraded across the stage as Lucy announced each of our names. There was Frank again, admonishing us "Don't pose!"

I've watched the movie a dozen or more times, as has much of the American movie-going public. I actually still have the original 16 mm copy of the film that was given to Frank and Mom. The movie was cute, funny and entertaining. It got most of the "facts" of our family straight — the number, gender, and names of each of the children (though it did mix up some of the birth dates.) In fact, the invitation used in the movie's version of the wedding invitation was the very one that had been used in Frank and Mom's wedding.

The film also captured the logistical challenges of managing a family of such scale. This is the only area where it followed the book, *Who Gets the Drumstick?* Practical matters such as food, shelter and clothing are easier to visually communicate than personalities and relationships.

"Yours, Mine and Ours" was very much a period film. Made in the decade of "Leave It to Beaver", "Ozzie and Harriet", and "My Three Sons", the film centered its attention on the idealized sitcom of a Caucasian suburban family. Of course, it differed in scale, which was part of its charm. In fact, Fred MacMurray, the central male character in "My Three Sons", was the first choice to play the role of Frank Beardsley. He was not available, so the role went to Fonda.

What the film missed because of its period script was the challenge of raising twenty children under any set of circumstances. At the risk of sounding simplistic, the task is virtually impossible for any human being or pair of humans to succeed at, by simple virtue of the numbers. Raising a child to the status of well-adjusted adult is a Herculean accomplishment for anyone. But twenty? There are simply not enough hours in the day or ears to hear or eyes to see what twenty children are up to and in need of at any given moment. The leadership of any family will dramatically influence the experience of the children, for better or for worse and the eighteen kids in the new North-Beardsley family were left at a significant disadvantage in the "parents" department. This was another detail the film missed. But then, Lucy was making a situation comedy. Her goal was to turn an unbelievable set of family circumstances into a believable comedy script. She succeeded in doing that and the public swallowed the fictional story hook, line and sinker.

At school, the assumption in the student body was that the North-Beardsley family merger was a great success, we were very rich, and so we all became celebrities. This was also the belief in the broader community of Carmel, and for that matter, across the country. Nothing could have been further from the truth! I was constantly asked by smiling kids at school and in the neighborhood what it was like living with so many brothers and sisters. Seeing the looks of anticipation on their faces, how could I tell them that becoming a Beardsley was a demeaning, often horrific nightmare?

I was walking near the ballpark one day and a little girl commented to me, "It must be wonderful to have such a big family! And to have all the attention you get from the movie!"

I just stared at her and then moved away mumbling something incoherent like "Yeah, sure."

How could I tell her, or anyone else for that matter, that my mother had made the biggest mistake of my life? That the man she married was a tyrant, that living in his household was like living in a war zone, and that I was never sure when the walking land mine named "Frank" would go off or who the casualties would be.

Someone once said that children's minds are like wet concrete— everything that lands there leaves a permanent impression. A lot of negative tendencies developed in my attitudes and persona as a result of living in the "get tough or die" environment of the Beardsley home. The emotional energy and psychological conditioning that my siblings and I received was a continual barrage of insults, name-calling and abusive taunts. It was common for Frank to get my attention by addressing me as "Hey stupid" or "Idiot". The currents running through the family were so negative that I lost most of my sense of self-worth and self-confidence in the first few years. I began to display a tendency toward being sullen, sarcastic and withdrawn.

When I was in first and second grade in Oak Harbor, Washington, I attended the Department of Defense Grade School which was provided for the military families who lived on or near the Navy base. One of my teachers at that time later came to visit us in Carmel. When she got to the house, she asked to see me. I had withdrawn so much that she was shocked by my diffident behavior and reserved, frightened demeanor.

"Do you remember me?" she asked.

"No," I replied.

"Well, I was your first grade school teacher. I remember you because you were the smartest pupil in my class."

I looked at her suspiciously. "That's not true," I answered." I'm stupid. My new dad tells me how stupid I am all the time."

The teacher's comment conflicted with my increasingly poor self-image. I couldn't begin to believe that she might be telling the truth. As much as I enjoyed hearing her saying nice things about me, and wanted to believe her, she was only one person. Her positive opinion of me was obliterated by the constantly negative messages I was getting from someone much closer to me than her. It seemed obvious whose opinion was more likely to be true.

Even if I had been intelligent just a few years before, my intellectual abilities had certainly suffered serious decline. I had come to believe that my step-father was right, that I was a stupid person who would never amount to anything.

North children adoption into the Beardsley family

Courthouse, Monterey, California – 1963

6

LIVING IN HELL

When I re-read *Who Gets the Drumstick?* in preparation for writing this story, I was amazed by the difference between my mother's description of combining two large families and my experience of it. I suspect that if you asked each of the siblings what their perspective of their experience was, you would get as many different stories. One thread would weave through them all, though. That thread is the degree to which our mother learned to use every device she could to protect us from Frank, for a time.

My luck at the new school wasn't much better than at home. The nuns who ran Junipero Serra School in the 1960s were a dour lot. It was a typical Catholic parochial school, heavy on religion, heavy on discipline, and short on practicing the humanitarian standards of gentleness and kindness that were espoused by the nuns. The principal was Sister Mary Michael, whose idea of religious education, for example, included her annual Good Friday recitation of the crucifixion of Jesus of Nazareth.

With a furrowed brow and a fanatical gleam in her eyes, she wildly waived her arms around as she described in vivid detail the blood spurting from Jesus as the Roman soldiers pounded nails into his hands and feet and thrust a spear into his side. She set a good example for her students, bowing her head every time she said his holy name; but she spared no details, encouraging the children each year to feel the pain of those wounds. I remember wanting her to shut up with that gory recital. I wanted to believe that it didn't have anything to do with me. But since I was already guilty of Original Sin, which only Holy Baptism and regular practice of the Sacraments could free me from, I would nevertheless leave the classroom feeling depressed and guilty that my sins put poor Jesus through that kind of misery, which of course, was the whole point! What good is it being a Catholic if you aren't depressed about being responsible for Jesus' crucifixion at least once every year?

Just in case we hadn't displayed the correct expressions of horror, Sister Mary Michael also invited representatives from the John Birch Society to lecture the students on the dangers of Communism, while showing slides of executed North Africans with their severed heads lying at their feet and their severed penises hanging out of their mouths. I knew this was not part of the normal curriculum; but in the early 1960s, especially in Catholic schools, children did not dare question the teachers. Reporting this kind of perverse digression from the normal school work would have only brought censure from both teachers and parents, what with Communists lurking in every closet.

Parochial school teachers had a bit of an edge over their public school counterparts when it came to enforcing classroom discipline. The good sisters would raise welts on misbehaving children's hands with a 3-edged brass ruler that was wielded like an instrument of war.

On one memorable day, Sister Mary Michael split Michael Hallahan's hand wide open for talking in class. I could have sworn that she was related to Frank Beardsley. Only one nun in the five years I attended that school showed any sign of fondness for the children she was teaching or any love for the world around her. Her name was Sister Marie Angelica and she taught music. She was an oasis of smiles among the barrenness of this religious desert. She played guitar and sang for her fifth grade class and brought cookies from the Convent. Sister Marie Angelica demanded respect from the children, but gave it back to them in return.

When I was in 7th grade, one of the few lay teachers at the school, Mrs. Baker, asked me to erase the blackboard. It was a simple request, and as I was an altar boy and a Beardsley as well, there was no danger in assigning me this task. Or was there? I turned around halfway through my job and saw her facing the class with her back towards me. It was an opportunity to stand out—to be the funny guy in class—so I grabbed it! I stuck my thumbs in my ears, waggled my fingers, and stuck my tongue out at Mrs. Baker's back. The class erupted in laughter! But in a split second, their laughter turned into a collective gasp. I followed their gaze as they turned their heads toward the classroom doorway—where Sister Mary Michael stood, arms folded across her chest, head tilted downward and a grim stare pointing in my direction. She had caught me in the act and had seen the whole thing! All the nuns in school had a clicker, which is a piece of wood that snaps like a clothes pin. They would click it to get our attention, and Sister Mary Michael clicked it at me that day. I knew I was in deep holy water as she and Mrs. Baker took me out into the hallway.

Mrs. Baker looked at me with a shocked and disappointed expression, her jaw dropping, asking me, "Tommy! How could you! You're one of the good boys!"

I replied, "Oh, but I am Mrs. Baker! I am one of the good boys! I'm sure it was the devil that made me do it!"

I caught a knowing glance between Sister Mary Michael and Mrs. Baker, as they crossed themselves. As I was one of the good boys, this could be the only explanation.

It was, of course, their solemn duty to save my soul, so Sister Mary Michael looked at me with her most serious countenance and commanded, "Tommy, I want to see you at the confessional in church at 9:00 a.m. this Saturday. You are going to tell Father what you did and confess this sin!"

I was relieved and at the same time incredulous that she actually believed my line about the devil and let me go without additional punishment.

Life at Junipero Serra School wasn't all conflict and pain. Flocks of pigeons swarmed around the courtyards the school shared with the old Basilica, where my mother and Frank had been married.

Having hunted rabbits and pheasants with my dad, my predatory instincts were still alive and well and looking for an outlet. There were also six to eight-inch goldfish in the central fountain in the courtyard. I had my eyes on the fish and the birds whenever I crossed the courtyard, often wondering how I was going to catch them.

One day, I saw the parish priest walking from the school to the rectory and went up to him to ask for permission to hunt the pigeons on the Church grounds. "Father, can I hunt the pigeons?" I inquired.

He looked down at me and smiled, fumbling with the beads that were wrapped around his waist and hung down to the ground outside his black robes. He must have been distracted and not imagining that I might have the wherewithal to actually "hunt" the birds.

He said, "Why sure, little fella! If you can catch them, you can hunt them. Now run along and chase the pigeons."

Whereupon I went home, borrowed my neighbor's pellet gun, and returned to the church, loaded for pigeon. Luckily for me the church facade, being made of stucco, was under regular, if not constant repair. The hallway eves that opened out onto the courtyard had scaffolding rising fifteen feet or so to the ceilings, where the pigeons roosted above the arched entryways. I climbed the scaffolding, pointed the pellet gun point-blank at a pigeon, and, right through the eye, bang! I shot it dead. The sound of the gunshot echoing down the hall sounded like a ball peen hammer striking on metal, and brought the janitor running from the maintenance closet around the corner. I was reloading to shoot another pigeon when he appeared below me and asked, "What the hell are you doing up there!?"

My concentration interrupted, I looked down at him and calmly replied, "Hunting pigeons. Father said I could."

The janitor squinted up at me and thought about it for a moment. "Father wouldn't let you shoot the birds!" he exclaimed.

"Yes he did! You go ask him!" I insisted.

The janitor turned around, shaking his head, and headed off in the direction of the rectory. I took aim, pulled the trigger of the pellet gun and killed another pigeon. I may have been the only person to fire a rifle in the church courtyard since the time of the Padres. Looking down at Phil and Gerry, who had come with me, I said to them, "Catch, we've got enough!" Tossing the two birds down to them, I climbed down the scaffolding and we proceeded to the beach a mile away, where we dug a fire pit, roasted our pigeons in the coals and ate them. Mmm! Tastes just like chicken! All right—a little gamey, but close.

A Little League baseball field adjoined the school's campus on part of the old mission's property, which was half a block from our house. I was a natural athlete, so I was able to play in the Junior Little League; I subsequently earned a spot on a Little League team, playing utility outfielder and first base. To my disappointment, in the four years of my playing baseball, Mom and Frank did not attend a single game. I asked Mom if she would come to the all-star game I played in. She said she was too busy. I felt ashamed when I saw the neighborhood moms working behind the concession counter, and the dads coaching the teams. Where were my parents? I knew that Frank was not fit to coach children in baseball. I also understood that running a big household took a lot of effort on their part, but not one game? The younger kids in our family came and watched, but not the parents.

Frank got the bright idea of introducing Nick and me to the game of golf. I tried to beg off, explaining that I already knew how to play. His insistence resulted in another typically disastrous experience I had with that man. I suppose one might say that he was at least trying, which he was; but by this time, we wanted nothing to do with him.

Nick and I went along with Frank and Mom to watch them play at a local course. Thank God it was just the four of us. On the first tee, Frank sliced the ball badly, went into a towering rage, threw his driver as far into the air as he could, swearing vile incantations at the club all the way up into the air and back down to the ground. I was amazed that a golf club could fly so high! With all of his swearing, though, this was a scene for mature audiences only. Nick and I were embarrassed by Frank's inexcusably loutish behavior and by our mom's profound and intense feelings of disappointment and shame. It was obvious to the three of us that bringing us along to see how the game of golf was played was a terrible error in judgment. I have no idea what was going on in Frank's mind. At that moment, it seemed that a tsunami of rage was consuming him so completely that perhaps he forgot we were there, preventing him from caring about the effects that his behavior might be having upon his wife and stepsons. I will never know.

Mom turned to us and with her cheeks turning scarlet said, "Why don't you boys go home." We were glad to be out of there. But once again, I felt anger at Frank for putting Mom through that kind of embarrassment. I had hoped that single stroke of Frank's club might be the end of our golf experience with him. We weren't so lucky. On several occasions afterwards, he took us to the driving range at the military golf course at Fort Ord and made us shag golf balls for him. We picked up his golf balls as he berated us for not moving faster.

What could have been an enviable childhood in a beautiful community with so many resources at my disposal was severely damaged by the influence of Frank Beardsley in the mix. But I was soon to learn that his barbaric influence was more widespread than I'd thought, not just affecting my siblings and me.

Many of my memories of the earlier years in the Frank Beardsley home were lost in pain and confusion and swallowed up in the domestic jumble that my siblings and I had been thrown into. The early sixties was a time of sporadic media coverage. Occasionally, pictures appeared in the newspapers of the twenty-two of us sitting around the family dinner table giving the impression of a quality of family harmony that I could only wish for. Being in the dining room or any room with Frank Beardsley was like sitting next to a road-side bomb, an incendiary device that could go off at any time. Time after time my aunts and uncles tried to point out to my mother the danger she was exposing her children to. Mom would protest, though, insisting that bringing some degree of love and security into the lives of the Beardsley children was more important. Our Uncle Bob was particularly vocal and often came to our defense, but Mom would have none of it. Although the pain we were in was obvious to our relatives around the family, Mom seemed to have her own script about how this domestic challenge was going to play out. She was fond of reminding me when I shared some of my harebrained schemes with her, that, "the road to hell is paved with good intentions." She didn't seem to realize this applied to her, as she laid stone after stone every day in the Beardsley home, guiding us to our own personal hell – and hers.

The only times we could relax at all was when Frank was gone. When he was missing, we all sighed with relief, knowing that at least for a while we were safe from his abuse. When he returned, that anxious quality we felt always returned with him. The word was passed among the kids that "Dad was home". The tone was a warning. None of us could predict who his next victim would be.

Mom had been running interference for us kids for several years, when she began to tire of being our savior. It wasn't that she didn't want to help us anymore. I think she was just plain tired and conflicted beyond her control. It seemed that her emotional shock absorbers were broken. The last straw may have been an incident with a keepsake transistor radio.

On one of his tours of duty, my dad, Dick North, had bought her a beautifully decorated transistor radio from Japan. It was made from bright red and ivory colored plastic, with scenes from a Buddhist temple carved into it. Like so many Japanese creations, it was a work of art, shaped like a globe, with round frequency control dials at the top. The handle arced over it and the radio balanced perfectly when carried. One day while the washing and ironing of clothes was going on in the utility room, Mom's radio was perched on top of a standing freezer nearby. One of the younger kids came in to fetch something from that freezer, and as she opened the door, the radio fell like Humpty Dumpty, smashing on the concrete floor into a dozen irreparable pieces. I was watching TV at the time and was drawn to the sound of the crash. Mom looked over from the laundry nearby and shrieked in disbelief. She was devastated and began to cry hysterically. One of the older girls who was ironing clothes next to the freezer, shrugged it off.

"What's the big deal?" she rationalized, "It's just a stupid old radio anyway!"

Mom screamed at her, "It's not just a stupid radio! It's *my* radio!"

She continued to sob as she gathered the pieces of the keepsake into her apron pockets.

As the girls stooped to help her, she screamed, "Get away! Leave me alone!"

To Mom, the radio was the last treasure she had retained from the man she had been so completely in love with. Memories of Dick North were something Frank did not want in his house, so when they married, he insisted that Mom sell most of her other items; the gun collection, the oriental jewelry boxes, the art work; all gone. When Dad had been on tours of duty in the Far East, he filmed many of the sites he visited. He'd send home his developed reels of film, and Mom would call all of us children into the house to watch movies of Daddy. Gathered in the garage, seated on little folding chairs, we covered the windows with blankets, turned out the lights and turned on the 8 mm. projector, which whirred away while we watched the silent, black and white images parade across the screen. We'd see statues of the Buddha and exotic temples, junk ships in the harbors, kimono-clad women on the streets, and then, as he handed the camera to a buddy and moved into the picture, we'd all shout, "There's Daddy!."

Completely consumed by jealousy, Frank had insisted that Mom get rid of the reels of film. In an act I can only imagine carried with it enormous anguish, she burned them.

I remember watching my mother as she came to grips with the fact that the transistor radio was gone. Her memories of her life before martyrdom were being swept into the dustpan with the pieces of the radio. Since her marriage to Frank four years before, she had been worn down to a point where her resistance to stress was waning. Her inability to manage the ongoing crises was telling on her. Once again, she moved farther within herself. Once again, I felt that helpless feeling sweep over me, unable to do anything about an impossible situation.

It was around this time that Mom finally quit watching out for us and left us to our own devices. She began acting like she was on auto-pilot, there, but not really there at all. For the boys, that was okay. Nick and I had learned to just stay away from Frank as much as we could. But the girls had their gender working against them. Frank would line them up in the family room in the early morning for calisthenics; only they were in their underwear and bras. I remember going by the partially open door and, seeing the girls lined up, thinking, "This just isn't right."

Mom did nothing to stop it. Soon, it was as if Mom began feeding her daughters to Frank to keep him away from her. I know that is an unthinkable idea, but it's what she did. When Collien, Janette and Jeanie approached her and asked why she wasn't stopping Frank from abusing them, she refused to acknowledge his crimes against them at all. She accused the girls of calumny and told them not to speak so of their father.

Frank had a sick sense of entitlement, which he believed gave him the right to impose himself sexually on the women in his family. Although I was not aware of it at the time, as they reached puberty, my sisters became objects of his unrestrained lust. Frank's attitude toward the girls was that they were chattel. They were not human beings with their own perspectives, wishes and destinies, but his property to do with as he saw fit. That they had feelings of their own did not seem to occur to him. If it did, he didn't care.

In her book, *Screen of Silence: The Public Lie,* my sister Collien relates an event that happened to her when she was thirteen years old. Our mother had been asked by then California Governor, Ronald Reagan, to join a committee on the 'Status of Women.' She considered it to be quite an honor, and traveled to Sacramento from time to time for meetings.

Frank encouraged her to go, which gave him uninterrupted access to the young girls in the house. As Collien relates the story, she was summoned by one of the younger girls to Frank's room. She arrived obediently at his door and knocked. He was sitting on a lounge chair in his boxer shorts and said, "Come in and close the door."

She did what she was told. As Collien stood before him, he stood up and moved closer to her. "Take your clothes off," he said and began to remove her shirt.

"I can do it,' she said, not wanting him to touch her. She thought he was intending to shame her in the mirror, as he had done to the other girls who were overweight.

"Look in the mirror," he said. "You're built like your mother, very sexy and desirable."

He rubbed his hand over his round stomach and began to fiddle with the elastic waist band of his shorts. There was a long bulge in the boxers. He pulled down his boxer shorts and stepped out of them. "God the Father has given me the responsibility of teaching you." He began to talk about God and men and women, Adam and Eve. It was a jumble of words sprinkled with "God the Fathers."

Collien clung desperately to the expectation that he would shame her for something and send her out. He slowly moved toward her and she backed up till the backs of her knees bumped into the big bed. She sat down on the bed as he loomed over her. He was still talking about God and teaching and father's duties, as he pushed her shoulders down on the mattress. She felt numb with fear and confusion. Her legs, bent over the edge of the bed felt heavy. The silky satin bedspread was slippery as she tried to slide up the bed away from that wall of flesh who was mumbling about God and duty, while inching relentlessly closer and down on her.

Collien's stomach felt as though there was a hole in it, a hole she would like to have crawled into and disappeared. Her heart was numb and her eyes were filled only with the swollen penis that moved up closer to her pelvis. Terrified, in a desperate attempt to survive, she rolled to the right, slid off the bed and scrambled to the door. She was sure he would grab her in fury. Frank's thick hand reached out to seize her arm, but missed.

"I have homework to do," she blurted out, as she quickly grabbed her clothes off the floor and ran for the door. As she ran down the hallway, she pulled on her shirt, trembling with fear and anxiety about what had just occurred.

Expecting that he would chase her or send for her again, Collien escaped out into the night. She walked and ran to the ocean a mile away and sat on the beach, listening to the breakers as they pounded the shore. She sat there under the stars, her arms wrapped around her knees, wanting nothing more than to dissolve, to become invisible, to melt into oblivion.

Frank didn't confine his sexual perversions to the girls. He also approached me with a dark intent, which, thank God, I was able to thwart.

One day, I was looking for my mother. I peeked in the open door of their room and quietly called out, "Mom?"

Frank came around the corner completely naked. He had his hand on his penis. I observed right away that he was uncircumcised.

"Where's Mom?"

"She's not here. Have you ever seen one of these?" He pulled the foreskin of his penis back, started stroking himself and began to get an erection.

"Some of the guys at school have foreskins. I've seen them in the locker room. I gotta go."

"Just wait a minute there!" he stopped me in my tracks. "I was standing outside your bedroom door a few nights ago and I could swear your brother was having you measure his thing for him."

I looked astonished at Frank. He had been spying again, as was his habit. Nick and I had been in conversation as he had been putting on his bathrobe, but there had been no discussion or intent of a sexual nature. He was on his way to take a shower and had simply put on his robe while I sat nearby on the lower bunk bed.

I replied, "No, that's not what happened at all", as Frank continued to stroke himself. I repeated, "I gotta go."

I ran away with a terrible sense of foreboding. I knew he was inviting me to do something I wanted no part of and it made me sick to my stomach.

Unfortunately for my sister Janette, she was particularly attractive. She had a pretty face, large breasts and a shapely body that caught the notice of men of all ages. These same features made her a target in the Beardsley household.

One evening, Janette, teamed up with another of the girls, was assigned to the task of washing the evening dishes. Considering the number of people involved, this was always a formidable job. Frank came into the kitchen, drunk as usual. As he walked by the other girl, who was carrying an armload of dirty dishes, the phone rang. Frank looked at her and in a slur, ordered, "Answer the phone."

Janette turned from the sink of hot, soapy water, grabbed a towel to dry her arms and hands and said, "She has her hands full. I'll get it."

To any normal observer, this might seem a reasonable thing to do. But nothing went quite right in the Beardsley home when Frank was involved. He yelled at Janette, "Get back to the sink!"

Maybe Janette should have known by now that she shouldn't have expected a rational, adult interaction with Frank, but she tried anyway. "Why don't you answer the phone yourself?"

Interpreting this as insubordination, Frank instantly went into control mode and raised his hand to slap her. Janette turned around and ran to the stairwell that led to the downstairs library. Frank stood at the door of the kitchen and bellowed at her, "You come back here! I am talking to you! Come back here and take your punishment!"

Mom, who had been in the living room, came into the hallway between the kitchen and the stairwell to the downstairs just in time to intercept Frank as he pursued Janette. "Frank!" she interjected, trying to stop him. He pushed her out of the way and started down the stairs.

Janette had reached the landing and headed for the sliding glass door. I was standing right there and opened the door to let her out. I had heard the commotion and knew where this was going. Having seen him chase down and beat most of us in our turn, I was sure he would follow her. He wanted to exert as much control over her as he could. Janette ran for the street. I stayed in the doorway and grabbed the door and the door jam, blocking Frank's way to ensure my sister's escape. I was only 12 at the time, but I was tall for my age and thought I made a decent barrier. Frank didn't think so at all. He grabbed me by the back of my neck and with a flick of his arm, threw me across the room about twelve feet. My head hit a brick wall that was the base for the upstairs fireplace and I slid about five feet down to the floor and landed in a heap. I was dazed, but otherwise not physically injured; and for a moment, I lay there on the floor staring back across the room at Frank, who was leaning out the door where I had been standing, screaming at Janette to come back, swearing into the night. I was astonished at how easy that had been for Frank to do. The way he had tossed me aside, I felt like I had been a rag, weighing little or nothing. It was the first time I realized how much of his fighter's strength he had retained, even into his 50s. Not wanting to chase Janette, he slammed the door, knocking it off its track. He then stormed back upstairs and disappeared from sight. As I stood up, Collien and I exchanged knowing glances and went outside to find Janette.

She was sitting at the bottom of the driveway to the house crying. We made our best effort to console her but she kept asking, "Why is he like that? Why is he like that?

We didn't even try to answer. I suggested that if we were going to stop this kind of madness, we should go see the priests at the Mission up the street and seek their help. It crossed my mind to go to the police, but I knew that would not work. The police would come to the house, Frank would deny any accusations, and when the police left, he would kill us.

The three of us marched up to the church rectory, where the priests lived, and knocked on the door. I had been an altar boy for three years and knew all of the priests. I recognized Father Dudoné when he answered the door. I told him of Frank's violence, his screaming and the beatings we endured. I appealed to the priest from both an immediate crisis perspective and from the more general "What do we do about this madman?" perspective.

Father Dudoné glared down at me for a moment and said, "Tommy, you are committing the sin of calumny. You should not speak ill of your father."

Incredulous, I said back to him, 'But he's not my father!"

The priest looked at me condescendingly and said, "But of course he is. Now you go back home and apologize to your father and ask for his forgiveness." He looked at me down his long beaked nose, adding, "I want to see you on Saturday morning in the confessional, young man." I stared at him in disbelief. He had just gained equal status with Sister Mary Michael. Was there no one who would help us?

We felt completely defeated. We had no idea what to do. On the way home we discussed how we might deal with our impossible situation. Once more, the only solution we could think of was to tell Mom and hope that she could take care of Frank as she had so often done. We were wrong there, too.

The next day, when I came home from school, Mom was at her habitual station, the ironing board at the distant end of the family room. She seemed to somehow find ironing therapeutic. As I walked through the room, I said, "Hi Mom."

She replied in an ominous tone, "Tommy, come here."

I knew I was in trouble, but not sure why. I walked over and stood across the ironing board from her.

She was pressing a shirt sleeve over and over again. Looking up momentarily with steel in her eyes, she said, "You listen to me young man, and you listen good. If you ever tell anyone what goes on in this household, so help me God, it'll be the last thing you do! Do you understand me?!"

My mind didn't go far before it focused on the evening before at the church, which I hadn't had a chance to discuss with her. "But Mom," I started, but she cut me off. "Don't 'But Mom' me! I have never been as embarrassed as when Father Dudoné called me this morning. I have a responsibility to uphold the image of this family, and by God I'm going to do so! Don't you ever do that again! Now get out of my sight!"

The public image of the Beardsley family had become Mom's most important priority. She would protect the image of our God-fearing, traditional Catholic family at any cost. Mom wanted the world to accept the fantasy promoted by "Yours, Mine and Ours." She needed to believe in the success of the merged family, so that she could justify the treacherous path she had taken us on.

North children – 1960

7

A NATURAL ESCAPE

The local beaches and rocky shores along Carmel Bay were an environment I understood and felt at home in, providing a respite that was life-saving. At the ocean I could breathe and relax, and was also able to exercise the instincts I'd developed on the shores of Penn Cove on Whidbey Island in Washington. Like the ocean habitats of up north, this California shoreline had bounty to offer. In the early sixties, abalone was plentiful on the rocks of Carmel Point. Fred Crummey, an older friend of mine who knew the shoreline well, showed my friends and me how to harvest and bring this succulent delicacy home to eat. Fred was in his twenties, and enjoyed helping kids learn about the wilderness. He and his wife, Karen, a beautiful woman whom many of my neighborhood buddies had fantasies about, showed us how to clean, pound and cook abalone. It's got a delicate, unique taste that's not as chewy as calamari, and not as sweet as a scallop, but mouth-watering and delicious. If you've ever tasted conch from Florida or the Caribbean, you know what abalone tastes like. We also caught red rock crabs at low tide, some of them six inches across the back. They had huge pincers that could crush a finger, but those pincers were full of sweet meat. At home, we'd boil them and dip each forkful in melted margarine. Mm-mm good!

Walking across the beach one day with several crabs in my bucket, I passed a group of four adults in their sixties who had built a fire with driftwood. The men had been fishing off the rocks and had caught several large rock cod, which were now roasting over the coals in a square wire-mesh rack. As I walked by, admiring the beautiful fishing rods the men had propped up against a big log, one of them asked what I had in the bucket. Proud of my catch, I showed him my rock crabs. He was impressed and asked me my name.

I told him, "Tommy Beardsley".

He asked if I was one of the Beardsley children.

I replied, lowering my head, "Yes, I am."

"I'll tell you what we'll do," he said, "Let's cook those crabs right here in the fire. You share your crabs with us and we'll share our fish with you. We've got bread, salads and sodas, so we'll all have plenty to eat. What do you say?"

As hungry as I was, it sounded good to me!

He dug a small pit in the sand next to his fire, pushing some of the coals into the pit with a stick. He then put seaweed over the coals, and laid the four crabs on the bed of seaweed, covering them with more seaweed. Very soon, steam began to come out of the seaweed. In about twenty minutes, he removed the crabs, cooked and ready to eat. I had been filling up on fish, garlic bread and salad, so I wasn't too concerned about the crab. The older people were thrilled with them, so I declined when they offered me some. The man's name was Mr. Schaffer, and over time I became very attached to him. He always wore blue jeans, a plaid long sleeve shirt, and a plain brown baseball cap with a rather long bill to shade his face from the sun. His skin was tanned and weather-lined, and his blue eyes sparkled with a knowing that made me want to spend time around him and learn how to fish. He was lean and well-muscled. I remember thinking that if I looked as good at sixty-something as he did I would be thankful for it. Mrs. Schaffer always sat on a blanket on the beach next to the rocks at Carmel Point, with a big wide brimmed straw hat for shade. She kept herself busy with a book or knitting, while her husband fished.

Mr. Schaffer caught fish like no one I have ever seen before or since. He fished with a long rod and reel that must have been ten feet long. He tied two Bull Durham tobacco bags filled with sand to the line about two feet apart. Between them he'd have two big shiny hooks, each about two inches long, covered by three inches of squid.

The first time I watched him cast, he smiled and winked as he said, "Stand way to my side or behind me, or you may go for a ride with my bait!"

So, I moved out of range of the hooks as he set up his cast. With a graceful motion he slowly and carefully lifted the heavy weights and baited hooks off the rocks. He'd peer over his shoulder and make sure they weren't tangled, lifting them over his head in such a way that when he cast, the line arced up and away out into the sky. The weights and baited hooks would fly high and then come down with a splash, way out in the deeper water. Sitting along side him there on the rocky shoreline, I watched him pull in fish after fish. Over a period of several hours, he hauled in big brown and green ling cod, cabazon, blue rock cod and greenlings, which he called a sea trout. At the end of the day, Mr. Shaffer went home with between five and ten big fish on his stringer, each weighing between five and twenty pounds.

Once in a while, I would show him the little eels I'd caught in the low tide zone. He'd smile and tell me I could keep them if they were the size of his wrist; otherwise, they were too small to eat. He had a big wrist. I looked at my little eels, none more than six or eight inches long, and wondered how to catch the big ones.

I was soon to find out from "Betty," another person who fished off the rocks. As we talked, I asked her what her last name was, so I could call her "Mrs."

She said, "Just call me Betty".

She looked older than Mr. Shaffer, and always wore the same jeans and plaid shirt and tennis shoes, just like he did. She wrapped her curly grey hair in a bandana tied in the front like the poster I had seen of a factory girl standing next to a WWII airplane. Betty wore thick lens glasses in big black frames. I wondered how she managed to climb around on the rocks, treacherous as they were, with such poor eyesight. But Betty managed quite well.

Betty fished with a hand line that looked like a clothesline to me. White and about an eighth of an inch thick, it looked like it was a hundred yards long. She coiled it at her feet and it never seemed to tangle. Just like Mr. Schaffer, Betty tied a tobacco bag filled with sand on the end of her line, with several hooks baited with squid strung along the first three feet or so of the rope. Her hooks were hanging from leaders that were much weaker than her line. She explained to me that if one got caught on a rock or the kelp, she would pull hard on the line, the leader would break off, and she'd lose just the one hook, not the whole hook, line and sinker. She held her baited line in one hand and swung it around her head in a circle several times like a sling, then let it fly far out into the water. It paid out through the other hand, almost to the end. She couldn't cast as far as Mr. Shaffer, but she was good.

I watched her pull in a huge eel one day and asked her if she'd teach me how to catch them. She put her eel, which was much bigger around than Mr. Shaffer's wrist, in a pillow case, tied a string around the open end of the bag and then put it in a tide pool. Betty told me that she used the hand line mostly for bigger fish farther out in the water, but the best way to catch eels was by using her poke pole.

"Your what?" I asked.

She repeated herself, her poke pole. Betty used a long handle from a push broom that had about three feet of heavy twine on the end, not unlike the hand line she used for fishing. On the end of the line were a small weight and a short leader and hook, again baited with squid. She walked carefully to the edge of the rocks and dropped the short line in between two boulders where it sank into a dark pool under the rocks. She held the end of the broomstick in the water. Within minutes, her broomstick began to twitch at the far end. Betty lifted the pole out of the water with some difficulty. On the end of the fishing line was a long, fat grey eel. I watched, transfixed. Forget his wrist; this eel was as big around as Mr. Shaffer's arm! Thinking about how Mr. Shaffer fished and how Betty fished, I decided that it was less expensive and just as productive to fish like Betty did. With my next pop bottle refund money, I bought the clothesline, hooks and weights, and went down to the rocks where Betty often fished, dragging along my new friend Chris. Chris's family was from Palo Alto and rented a house next door to my home every year. He was my age and I enjoyed playing with him for quite a few summers afterward.

After tying the lines, hooks and weights as I had seen Betty do, I told Chris to hold the clothesline in his hands and let it pay out as I threw it. I held the line in my grip and swung it around my head as Betty had done. At the right moment, I let it go. The weight and hooks at the end of the line flew high and far. I was thrilled! Then, I saw the end of the line following the rest of it, and turned to Chris, who was watching, too.

I yelled at him, "Why didn't you hang onto the line?!"

He looked dumbfounded. "Was I supposed to?"

We came back on another day with a new hand line, and, with Betty's guidance, managed over the course of the summer to catch a few fish.

My neighbor up the street had a bamboo hedge which stimulated my imagination with a "fishing idea." The weekend after the miscommunication with Chris, I was walking by the neighbor's house and noticed a pile of very long bamboo poles the man had culled from his hedge. Seeing that they were easily ten or twelve feet long, I asked him if I could have a few. He said sure. I gathered three or four of them in my arms, took them home and stripped the branches off of them. The bamboo was strong, flexible and light. Thinking about Betty's broom handle, I imagined that I could control the direction and depth of the bait if I used a coat hanger instead of just clothesline. I took a hanger, cut off the hook, and straightened it out with pliers into an eighteen-inch long piece of stiff wire. I found some electrical tape in the tool shed and wrapped the tape around the hanger, fastening it to the end of the bamboo so that about 15 inches of hanger extended beyond the pole. With the pliers I twisted the stiff wire of the hanger and made an eye at the end of it and tied my hook to the eye. With only six inches of leader, I figured I could thread that bait right into a fish's mouth!

I took my modified version of Betty's poke pole down to her rock and looked over the edge into the depths of the sea. It was like peeking into a room which I was forbidden to enter.

Taking the fat end of my poke pole firmly in my hands, I slid the baited end into the deep dark pool under the boulders. The pole kept disappearing into the darkness. It was ten feet long and I was holding onto the end of it. Since the pool was so deep, it was hard to see what was going on down where the bait was, under the shadows of the kelp and rocks. But quicker than I'd imagined possible, I had a bite! A big bite! While the fish thrashed about and pulled my pole from side to side, I steadied myself and pulled the pole out. On my hook was a huge cabezon. This monster reminded me of a catfish without the whiskers, but with a grey-green head as big as a volleyball. It seemed as big as any that Mr. Shaffer had caught. I was so excited that, of course, I wanted to tell someone. I had seen Mr. Shaffer fishing in his usual spot, just as I had arrived on the rocks so I went over to show him my fish.

Knowing that he had a handheld fish scale in his tackle box, I asked him to weigh it for me. After hefting my fish into the air and reading the scale, Mr. Schaffer told me I had an eight-pound cabezon and I should be proud.

When I brought my fish home, my mother was surprised. I had watched Betty fillet her fish at the rocks; so on a cutting board out on the back patio, I imitated her procedures. There was nothing to it. In no time that cabezon was ready to cook and eat. With my "newly invented" bamboo poke-pole, I began catching cabezon, rock cod and huge eels on almost every outing.

Mom soon gave me my dad's old fishing equipment, which I thought Frank had forced her to get rid of. My dad had been an avid fly fisherman before he died, had tied his own flies and did some deep sea fishing as well. Mom had kept the tackle boxes and fishing poles away from Frank, thinking her sons might want them someday. I was ecstatic!

However, more often than not, the hooks I had cast from my rod and reel became caught on the kelp or were wedged between rocks on the bottom and stayed there when my line broke. Considering this, I developed a results based strategy. When I got my cast right and was waiting for a fish to come along and bite my bait, I'd set the pole down on the rocks and pick up my poke pole, wandering off in search of deep holes and crevices that might hide a fish or two. This turned out to be an effective approach. I caught many more fish with the poke pole than I did with the rod and reel.

I seemed to have better luck at fishing than Nick did. When we came home from the shore with a stringer of fish over our shoulder one day, Frank asked us who caught what.

Invariably, I had caught most or all of the fish, and, especially important to size-oriented male thinking, the big one.

Frank turned on Nick and frowning, bellowed, "What's the matter with you?! Can't you catch a fish like your brother?"

I hated him for it. What made the situation worse was that Frank genuinely liked me, but at Nick's expense. Frank was so twisted that he couldn't give a simple compliment. He had to make a cause for celebration into a miserable rebuke. Internally, I was tearing myself apart. I craved the praise, as most children do; but I wanted Frank to shut up and leave Nick alone. I had often thought that if I could kill him I would and I wanted to kill him at that moment. I felt guilty for not standing up for Nick, reviling myself for my cowardice in not speaking up. I hung my head, turned, and walked away, distracting myself with the thought that I'd better clean the fish.

In the 1960s, the Carmel River's wildlife was abundant and steelhead trout that migrated to their spawning grounds after the winter rains filled the river. For the uninitiated, a steelhead is a rainbow trout that swims out into the ocean as a fingerling about six to nine inches long, and then comes back about four years later. An adult steelhead can be two to three feet long and can weigh in excess of twenty pounds! They migrate to their spawning grounds in the rivers of the Pacific states of California, Oregon and Washington. At that time, most of the western rivers had steelhead runs. The run in the Carmel River was healthy and supported many thousands of fish.

For the outdoorsmen in Carmel, the steelhead run was an exciting annual event. More of a stream than a river by national standards, the Carmel River is only about 30 miles long, including its source tributaries in the Los Padres National Forest. During the steelhead runs, fishermen of all ages lined the banks of the river from its mouth at the Carmel River Beach to above the Highway One Bridge – about a mile from our home – for a form of angling known today as "Combat Fishing." Anxious anglers, often elbow to elbow, would cast their lures and baits, hoping theirs were the most enticing to the migrating fish. Most often, the fishermen cooperated with each other. But sometimes tempers flared and fights broke out among the drunken "sportsmen." Either way, it was exciting to watch the big fish being hooked, played and landed.

My cousin, Mike Brown, who was my mother's nephew, had given me a most unusual looking fishing rod as a gift. It was white fiberglass, about six feet long, with the reel encased in a hard black plastic bulb at the base of the rod. Unlike any fishing rod I had ever seen, it was well balanced and would cast a long way. Mike told me that he had fished all up and down the coast of Oregon and Washington and caught very few fish. He said he hoped that I would have better luck than he did. And better luck I did have!

Around the time that I was about nine years old, I took three or four of my younger brothers and sisters fishing with me, with my new pole. I knew they would have fun fishing (what child doesn't?), thinking that if I didn't teach them, no one would. We went down to the Little League Park, where, having pulled a clump of long grass from outside the baseball field's perimeter, we collected fat earthworms that hung from the dirt.

I made fishing poles for them with a cottonwood branch taken from a tree by the river, and a length of monofilament line, a couple of small lead weights and a hook, which we baited with one of the worms. When the rains let up and the Carmel River's level dropped to a manageable depth, about six to twelve inches, the channel spread out, leaving a broad, quiet, shallow streambed. To the sides of the main flow of the river were deeper eddies and clear, blue-green pools, one to four feet deep, where the trout would congregate. The kids and I would position ourselves, cans of worms hanging from the belts of our cutoff jeans, upstream from the pools and let the worm on the hook float down over the edge of the sandy channel into the pool. The trout were waiting for just such a morsel to drop into their reach... and wham! Fish on! It was not uncommon to go home with a creel of ten to twenty fish, which turned into fried trout, eggs and fried trout and fried trout sandwiches smothered in butter and mayonnaise— as good as it gets when you're a hungry kid!

Over the years we fished and hunted along the river banks with a joyous sense of adventure. We saw pheasants, quail, wild ducks and geese, hawks and eagles, deer, wild boar, mountain lions, bobcats and badgers. Since we were just children, most of our victims were animals that we could hunt with BB and pellet guns. I had lobbied my mother to allow me to buy a BB gun with my paper route money. She interceded with Frank for me, explaining that my dad was a hunter and I simply wanted to emulate him. In one of his better moments, Frank actually said yes. After a couple of years of demonstrating good gunmanship (which means I hadn't put anyone's eye out), Frank and my mom relaxed about the BB gun around the house. Per common sense and their orders, I kept it unloaded and put away when not in use.

In the summer of my thirteenth year, I planned a five-day backpacking adventure for Nick and our neighborhood friend Ray, that spanned almost the entire length of the Carmel River. I figured we could hike from the Los Padres Dam, twenty-five miles up the Carmel Valley, down to our house. Five days of adventure! Ray, who was fifteen and lived a few blocks away, had a .22 caliber rifle and a .22 caliber pellet rifle that we could take with us for hunting. My notion was that the three of us would live off the land and take little in our backpacks other than our sleeping bags, some butter, salt and pepper, fishing tackle and a few cooking utensils. We didn't encumber ourselves with fishing poles, but planned to tie our fishing lines to swatches of cottonwood branches. We'd drink water from the river, catch fish, frogs and crawdads to eat, and supplement meals with birds, rabbits and whatever we could shoot.

Perhaps she felt relief at having two fewer children in the house for a week, but once again, my mother interceded with Frank and we received permission to go. One of my step-brothers drove us to the drop-off point below the dam and the camping adventure began.

I remember watching the fly fishermen ply the stream below the dam. We knew that every fisherman likes to brag about his catch, and we talked with them as they showed us their stringers and creels, with 10 to 15-inch rainbow trout glistening blue, pink and green in the sunshine. I couldn't wait to start fishing myself.

Having hiked our first five miles along the boulder-strewn river, we stopped for the night. I could see a large pool downstream from our campsite. It was ten or 15 feet deep, about 25 feet across, and shaded by cottonwood trees. I climbed stealthily onto the top of one of the large rocks defining the pool and peeked down into the depths where I saw several trout, much like the fly fishermen had caught, in the clear water below me. I went back to Nick and Ray, excited about the prospects.

"Let's catch dinner!" I shouted.

We broke off and stripped some nearby cottonwood branches, tied our monofilament fishing line to each branch's end, and went into the meadow by the river to catch grasshoppers. We baited our hooks with grasshoppers, put a small lead sinker two feet above the hook, hid behind the boulder, held the poles over the pool, and dropped the grasshoppers into the gentle current of the stream.

Our jury-rigged tackle turned out to be nearly perfect and permitted the bait to sink slowly into the waters of the pool. I imagined that I would get a strike right away but after 15 minutes nothing had happened. I could see my grasshopper on the bottom of the pool with disinterested looking fish milling about above it; so I decided to try something else. I lifted the tip of the pole, and as the grasshopper came off the bottom, a 16-inch rainbow trout grabbed it in an instant! Nick caught one the same size shortly thereafter. Fifteen minutes later, they were frying in a generous layer of butter on the bottom of our pan. Those trout provided one of the greatest meals of my life, and we ate every last morsel.

On the second day of our journey down the river, I was collecting firewood for the breakfast meal and came across a three-foot-long rattlesnake. It had obviously been in a fight with some raptor because several inch-long slices were apparent at several points on its back where the bird's talons had ripped into it. But the rattler had survived.

The snake was crossing the trail as I was retuning to camp with the rifle and wood. I had heard that rattlesnake is a delicacy in some parts of the world, so I shot it through its head. Nick and Ray had caught some red-legged frogs in a pool. These are now on the list of endangered species, but nobody thought about such things four decades ago. Both the rattlesnake and the frogs tasted, well, just like chicken! That afternoon, we hiked the river with our cook pot, collecting crawdads and arrived at our next campsite with our pot full of about 150 of them. We boiled them and ate them for dinner with a little salt. Mm-mm! We were eating well, and as far as I could tell, the adventure was playing out just as planned!

On the third day, we arrived at the San Clemente Reservoir. The river flowed into it, spreading out and disappearing into the lake. The trail also disappeared, leaving us wondering how we were going to get to the other side, which was a mile away. We decided to cut across the forest and find our way to the dam. Climbing and crossing several ridges and canyons between them, we chose a dry wash and followed it in the direction of the reservoir. We had to climb down a thirty-foot cliff, which, in the wet season, must have been a waterfall. Ray went first, followed by Nick. I handed the backpacks and rifles down to them at each successive ledge we came to on our way down.

Ray climbed down to the last ledge, about five feet above the bottom of the dry waterfall. As he let himself down from his hand and footholds, he froze.

He said quietly, "Tom, give me a gun."

I said, "Why do you want a gun?"

He repeated himself, only this time with clenched teeth, "God damn it, Tom, give me a gun! There's a rattlesnake a foot from my face!"

The rattler was coiled, tail a-quiver. Ray slowly backed away to the edge of the ledge as I handed him the loaded .22. He raised the rifle to his shoulder, took careful aim and shot the snake through the head. After cutting off the snake's head, Ray put the body in a plastic bag and then in a backpack, saving it for dinner, later that evening, all the while admonishing me for not responding sooner.

As we reached the end of the dry creek bed, we were confronted with the reservoir, and an island about fifty feet off the rocky shoreline upon which we stood. The island was about a hundred yards long and covered with trees down to the water line. We couldn't see any other dimension of the island so we had no idea what was on the other side. Suddenly we heard a car door slam and voices talking to one another in greeting. Somewhere on the other side of the island was help.

We began to shout, "Hello! Can you hear us?!"

One of the voices responded, "Yes, where are you?!"

We yelled to "the voice" that we had come down from Los Padres Dam and needed to get across the reservoir. Then we heard the sound of an outboard motor starting. Within a couple of minutes, an aluminum skiff rounded the corner of the island, with a smiling young man wearing a blue shirt with "Cal-Am Water Company" stenciled above the shirt pocket. He kindly gave us a ride across the water. As we came around the island, I could see several white buildings behind a pick-up truck. The dirt road leading to the cluster of buildings wound down an oak and madrone-covered hill to the San Clemente Dam. We thanked the workman for the ride and resumed our hike, setting up camp by the river bank a mile below the dam.

With only 15 months in age between us, Nick and I had, over the years, our fair share of sibling rivalry seething just beneath our skins. I resented his close, favored relationship with our mother, and I suspect that he may have resented my greater height and athleticism. We were both in that time of life when hormones, particularly testosterone, are running rampant through the blood, and it was about to manifest in a startling way.

On the fourth morning, when I woke up, Ray had already gone hunting to shoot some breakfast. With my sharp-tongued sarcasm, I had been harassing Nick about his sexual development, virility, or lack thereof. I said something particularly unkind to him and I remember hearing him say, "You'll never say that again."

Suddenly, I heard the sound of a gunshot and felt a sting in my chest, like a bee sting. It was a complete surprise, because I was looking down at the sleeping bag and hadn't seen him point the pellet gun at me.

I suppose if he had used the .22, somebody else might be telling this story but, nevertheless, the pellet gun had been loaded and pumped 15 times, in case we had a chance to fire at small game. He fired it from point blank range, so it had plenty of velocity. I looked at my shirt, saw a hole at the level of my chest near the sternum, and realized that my brother had just shot me! I was completely dumfounded and looked up at him incredulously. He had turned ghostly white, as the implications of his actions began to sink in.

The experience was bewildering. This was not what happened when John Wayne shot someone. In the movies, a person who is shot is always thrown back several feet and lying dead on the ground. Perhaps they exclaimed, "I've been shot!" or something like it, if it was in the script.

But there I was, kneeling in the sunshine that filtered down through the leaves on the trees above us, listening to the babbling of the stream and the chirping of song birds around us, looking at the hole that had suddenly appeared in my t-shirt. I remember thinking that being shot with a gun was possibly not so bad a way to die. At least it was not as painful as I had previously imagined. I looked at Nick again and finally remembered my line from the movies. "You shot me!" I said in earnest.

Then Nick departed completely from any cowboy movie we had ever seen, because he put the gun down and began to cry. My first impulse was to try to make him feel better. "It can't be that bad, Nick," I said reassuringly. "At least it doesn't hurt."

Ray had not been far from camp and wanted to find out who had fired the gun and at what. As he came around a big sycamore tree, he jokingly asked if something had been killed for breakfast and was it cooked yet? When he saw Nick crying, Ray asked, "What happened?"

"Nick shot me." I replied flatly.

Looking at the small, perfectly shaped, round hole in my chest, just to the right of where my heart would be, Ray turned to Nick and shouted "Knock it off! We've got to figure out what to do!"

My body at last began to acknowledge the foreign object that had entered my chest and I was suddenly struck by debilitating pain that sent me into shock, immobilizing me in excruciating agony.

Fortunately, there was very little blood, because the bullet had missed my blood vessels and buried itself in bone. With the drama of the movies still rolling through my head, I quietly became disappointed in the one drop of blood that rolled down my abdomen. I figured that if I might die from being shot, I should at least see a lot of blood.

The riverbank we had pitched camp on was just below the road that led to the dam, a mile or so up the hill from us. Ray headed back up to the dam at a run to find help. The road probably didn't see five or six cars in a week; but it just so happened that before he ran 100 yards, he came upon a man who had left his car parked only a few hundred yards away. I was still immobilized by the intensifying pain of my wound; so they loaded me on to a sleeping bag, and, using it as a stretcher, hauled me up the embankment to the station wagon. Then the Good Samaritan drove me to the fire station at Carmel Valley Village, where I was transferred to an ambulance. I never learned his name or thought to thank him.

As I lay there on a gurney, a crowd gathered to stare into the windows of the ambulance at me. Two elderly women were talking, as they cupped their hands around their eyes and placed their faces on the window. One said to the other, "I think some young man shot himself."

I protested to myself that they had it wrong, but I was in too much pain to correct them. As I lay there waiting for the ambulance driver to show up, I wondered again whether I was dying. The throbbing pain in my chest suggested that it was a distinct possibility. I felt completely calm inside, without any fear of death, which surprised me. My internal dialogue went something like, "Wow, I wonder if everyone who gets shot feels like I do? What will it be like if I die? I don't really care right now if I die or not. Why is that?"

Since I was a military dependent, I told the ambulance driver to take me to the military hospital at Fort Ord, the local Army Base. Even in my pain, I thought to mention that it would cost my parents less that way. Mom told me later that she blanched and nearly fainted at the news. As she answered the phone that morning, the last thought on her mind was that it might be the Monterey Country Sheriff on the other end. "Mrs. Beardsley," he said with a note of caution in his voice, "This is Officer Smith. Your son, Thomas, has been shot and is on his way by ambulance to Fort Ord Hospital."

The doctors eventually decided to leave the bullet in my chest. Before the x-rays were developed, the doctor who performed the exploratory surgery by slicing open the bullet wound, couldn't find the bullet and asked me where I thought it might be. I described it as having traveled at a downward angle because I had been bent over, rolling up my sleeping bag when the bullet hit me. With that in mind, he made a second incision below the entry wound, conducted another exploratory surgery and found nothing but more bone; but this time there was a hole in it. X-rays showed that the slug had stopped just shy of my right lung, bulging out of the inside of the sternum but trapped by the mushrooming of the bullet. Trying to remove the bullet would have been far more dangerous than leaving it alone, for he risked puncturing my lung and damaging the pleura that lined my chest cavity. In addition, getting to the site of the slug would have been more traumatizing to my body than the wound itself. It sits there to this day.

Because the accident involved a gunshot wound, a police report had to be filed. Before we had left the campsite, Ray, Nick and I had concocted a story that the gun had been leaning against a tree when Nick had knocked it over and it had discharged, accidentally hitting me.

Of course, the three of us ended up telling slightly different versions of this story. The adults, including the two sheriffs who had come to interview us, didn't believe us for a moment, but they never pressed the point and simply chose to let it be. I don't know if that was ignorance or wisdom on their part. They seemed to have concluded that there was something we weren't telling them, but if we were satisfied with our version(s), they apparently weren't interested in sending someone to jail. Foremost in my mind was what Frank might do to Nick. While it was true that Nick had almost killed me, I was sure that Frank would kill him if he knew the truth.

Four days later I was allowed to go home, and had a gauze bandage wrapped around my chest in proper John Wayne fashion. But before leaving the hospital, I developed a hematoma (blood clot) that had split the stitches and bled quite a bit. Upon replacing the bandages, I was pleased that there was finally a large area of blood visible to everyone. Now, this was more like it! Ol' John would have been proud. My brothers and sisters were, of course, impressed with the size of the bandage and the blood stains, which improved my sense of self-importance proportionately.

As the station wagon drove up to the house, I saw the windows of the house filled with children's faces. I was still in pain from the surgeries, and the hematoma that had been re-stitched. Sympathetic, concerned looks were everywhere as I was helped out of the car, bare-chested, revealing my bloodstained, wrap-around bandage. As I came in the front door, Nick was standing with the other kids, and Frank was nearby.

Someone asked, "How did it happen, Tommy?"

Frank mumbled, "I know how it happened!" and began to lunge at Nick, fists clenched while grimacing with his jaw tight.

Mom shouted, "Frank!" and grabbed him by the arm to restrain him.

She moved up close and through a grimace of her own, told him, "If you can't control yourself, then stay away from the boy!"

Frank stayed away from both Nick and me during the rest of my recuperation. He had no idea how to handle the situation without becoming violent. From time to time for the next couple of years, Frank asked me, "Come on Tommy, what really happened on that camping trip?"

I responded by narrowing my eyes at him and replying, "What we told the sheriff is what happened."

Tom – Age 15

8

THE TWENTY-FIVE CENT SOLUTION

In spite of having been shot in the chest at the age of thirteen, fond memories of days in the woods hunting with my father had instilled in me a desire to further develop my skills. As I grew older, I wanted to recapture those exciting times and establish new ones. When I was 16, I went to my mom and told her that I wanted to buy a hunting rifle so I could hunt deer and wild boar in the mountainous forests not far from our home. True to form, she worked her magic with Frank on my behalf.

I'm not exactly sure how much "magic" she had to work though. It continued to bother me that, in spite of all the terrorizing and negativity he subjected me to, Frank actually preferred me to many of my brothers and sisters. It would have been so much easier if I could have shared the burden of his hatred with Nick. But I seemed to be the counterpoint to that animosity. I had managed over the years to anger him less than many of the other children, mostly by staying out of his way, I think, and learning early on not to talk back to him. My hatred of the man grew as I watched him go after Nick or one of the other siblings, wondering, at the same time why they didn't just make more of an effort to stay out of his way.

During my second year in high school, I had been working in the evenings at a restaurant, washing dishes and bussing tables, and had saved enough money to purchase a hunting rifle, a

30-30 Winchester Model 94. This was one of the older models, made before 1964. It had features which made it a sturdy, reliable brush gun, well-suited to the local chaparral terrain where wild boar and deer live. To my way of thinking, though, it seemed logical to have a pistol to compliment the rifle. Since I was too young to purchase a handgun myself, one day I went to a gun show with an older friend of a neighbor and had him purchase for me a 357-Magnum pistol. It was a Ruger Blackhawk, with a long, seven-inch barrel. With white bone handles and a beautifully worked leather holster, it was the perfect balance to the rifle, and I fell in love with it. Now, I felt ready to go hunting, with the 30-30 in my arms and my .357 on my hip.

It wasn't long after my purchase of the firearms that I realized the solution to the violence in the Beardsley household might be at hand. I had watched Mom suffer for too long and I was feeling desperate about the dark hell of sexual abuse Frank was putting my sisters through. A discomforting realization suddenly came to me, that I had in my drawer the means of forever ending the nightmare that all of us — the girls, especially — were living in.

A single bullet through Frank's forehead would instantly end my troubles and the family's troubles, I thought. It would only cost me 25 cents for the bullet, too. I would sit on the edge of my bed, night after night, staring at my .357 magnum pistol. I realized perfectly well the consequences that would follow upon my action. The law would punish me for the crime of patricide, and sentence me to prison for a long time, but in my hate-filled and feverish thinking, no consequence from the act could outweigh the deliverance that killing Frank would accomplish. I imagined stopping the violence with one final crescendo. I imagined seeing smiles on the faces of my brothers and sisters. They would sing the song from the Wizard of OZ,"Ding dong the witch is dead!"

So, I continued staring at the gun, trying to solve the dilemma raging through my heart. Taking out Frank would be a public service. The man was garbage. I could be an agent in an act of waste removal that would make the world a better place. Going to prison and being persecuted by a vengeful society would be nothing other than a noble sacrifice that I would gladly endure for my family. My twisted logic instilled within me a determination to kill Frank Beardsley, and then face the consequences.

At the time, my bedroom was on the basement level of our three-story house. One night, when I felt that everyone must have gone to bed, I finally loaded the gun and walked to the base of the stairway. However, after standing there a few moments, I convinced myself that this wasn't a good idea after all. I turned around, walked back to my room, unloaded the gun, put the locking device back on it and went to bed. I was always careful about the locking device, which fit around the trigger and prevented anyone from getting shot accidentally.

Half an hour later I loaded the gun again. This time I climbed the stairwell to the second level before realizing, once again, how overwhelming the consequences of my act would be. Once again, I unloaded the gun and went back to bed; but not to sleep. A short time later, I repeated the process for the third time, and this time climbed to the third floor, walked down the hallway to the doorway of Frank and Mom's bedroom, and stood outside, staring at their door. Ruger Blackhawks are single-action revolvers. This means that the hammer must be pulled all the way back before the gun can be fired. I cocked the gun with a click that was clearly audible.

Hearing the noise, Frank called out "Who's there?"

This was the moment of truth; either I was going to kill him or forever give up the fantasy of doing so.

My hand was on the door handle, when suddenly I had a vision of what was to follow:

I walked into the room with the gun held behind my back, just like I had seen Mr. Muzzal do when he approached the cow before he shot her in the ear.

Frank sat up in bed and scowled at me before yelling, "What do you want?!"

My mother, her head still on the pillow, looked sleepily at me and with fatigued disinterest asked, "What is it Tommy?"

I looked at them both and with tears in my eyes said, "I'm sorry Mom."

I quickly brought the gun around and pointed it at Frank's head. I fired one shot. The bullet went through Frank's forehead and cracked the wall behind him. The look of angry astonishment on his face went quickly to dismay and then to sadness, all in one moment. His head was knocked back and then forward as the velocity of the bullet whipped through it.

I stood there looking at Frank, slumped dead among the bloody bed sheets, dark red fluid pouring out of his shattered head. My mom bolted upright, screaming in horror and reviling me for having committed such a ghastly and despicable deed.

Her face contorted with hatred as she wrung the sheets in despair. I stood silently... momentarily confused. The knowledge suddenly overtook me that my mother wouldn't thank me for ending the family's pain, but would forever hate me for interrupting her martyrdom, and in the process, expose the truth about our family. I was ruining her plan to save Frank's children from him and saving him from himself.

I had also killed Henry Fonda. I would have to be deranged to kill Henry Fonda, and would be reviled as the murderer of a man whom, thanks to his great role in the movie, the public had come to perceive in an idyllic and even heroic fashion. No one in the family would step forward and tell the truth. No one would tell the sheriff or the judge or the jailer that I had kept my brothers from being beaten or that I had prevented the ongoing molestation of my sisters. I put the gun down on the floor and crumpled into a heap, crying uncontrollably for the life I knew I would never live... for the happiness I might have found someday, but would never experience. I was going to jail for the rest of my life.

When the shot rang through the house, all the other kids came running. Someone called the sheriff's office. When the officers arrived, I was taken to juvenile hall where I was incarcerated until I was eighteen, and then I was sent to prison.

Snapping out of my reverie, I looked down at my violently shaking hand on the doorknob, still holding the cocked gun behind my back. I began to cry. Tears streamed down my chin onto my shirt. I sniffed to hold back the mucous starting to come out of my nose. There was no way I would be able to endure my mother's censure. Prison was one thing, but my mother's hateful reaction would have been intolerable. That was the end of my murderous plan. I went back downstairs, unloaded the gun, locked it again and put it away, leaving the situation to resolve itself without my terminal, 25-cent solution.

After the passage of years, I am, of course, relieved at having averted an act that would certainly have ruined, or at least altered, my life forever. I am also glad that Frank had not ever beaten my mother, although on several occasions I had seen him come close. Had he done so, I most certainly would have killed him. For a time,

I wondered if passing up the opportunity of sending that man to whatever hell awaited him was the better choice. I would have freed our family, especially my sisters and mom from the unspeakable things they would yet experience. It would have ended the reign of terror. No more beatings, sexual abuse, or screaming sessions. No more fear of meeting him coming around the corner in the hallway. Might it have been worth the price of giving up the normal and productive life that I have been able to live by putting that gun away? I've decided that it's pointless to wonder, since I chose not to create that alternate reality.

I'm certainly aware that the act would have been an evil one. Ultimately, there is no good that comes out of evil. Only evil comes of evil, no matter how much good might seem to result from it. At the time, I believed Frank richly deserved death, and I could have given it to him. But, as a famous wizard once observed, "Other people who die deserve life. If we can't bestow life upon those who deserve to live, we must keep our hands back from giving death to those who deserve to die." (Obe Wan Kenobe)

Ye Olde Donut House, Monterey, California

9

THE DONUT SHOP

Frank Beardsley had retired from the Navy in 1964 and purchased a franchise for a business called Ye Olde Donut House. After many fits and starts, which included the bankruptcy of the original franchisor, he got it up and running and all the children, when they reached ten to twelve years of age, began to work in the donut shop. The business of making and selling donuts was difficult work. I began working there when I was 11 years old, and over the next dozen or so years, the Beardsley's Ye Olde Donut House cranked out millions of donuts at the rate of 500 dozen donuts a day, 365 days a year. I worked many weekends and all summer long. We all sacrificed for each other, especially to keep Frank out of it, to whatever extent possible. At the donut shop, like everywhere else he went, he was a demanding taskmaster with a powder keg temper, truly a disaster looking for a place to happen.

The process of making the tasty treats we sold in the shop was anything but simple, and at certain stages, potentially dangerous. The donuts were made in a machine about eighteen feet long, separated into three sections. The humidifier section was only for raised (as opposed to cake) donuts. It consisted of an aluminum frame about a foot wide, six feet long and about six and a half feet tall. The dough, once mixed in twenty to thirty pound batches, had to sit for 15-20 minutes to rise.

The donut maker then scooped up a wad of the sticky white dough and stuffed it into a funnel shaped receptacle that swung back and forth in a ninety-degree arc, depositing a round, measured amount of dough, that was sucked down by a hydraulic plunger onto a tray held in place by what looked like a bicycle chain. The tray then immediately disappeared into the humidifier. This automated, all-metal contraption looked like something out of a mad professor's laboratory. As the donuts proceeded slowly through the humidifier, two to a tray, they were warmed and moistened by a temperature-controlled environment inside the Plexiglas windows of the machine, causing them to rise. Coming out the other end about three times their original size, they were blown by a stream of air off their trays into "section two" of the machine, the cooker. The cooker was a six-foot long, one-foot wide container of grease with heating elements at the bottom to keep it hot, and a conveyor system to move donuts along while they were frying. They bubbled at the edges when they hit the grease and then were lifted and floated along, cooking one side of them. In the middle of the cooker, they would glide onto a flipper which turned them over so the other side would cook. By the time they arrived at the lifting conveyor, which brought them out of the grease and deposited them onto the drying conveyor, the raised donuts were a perfect golden color with a white ring around the middle where they had floated just above the grease. Once on the drying conveyor, the donuts were given time to drip dry before being flicked under the glazing tube, which poured glaze over the hot donuts, giving them that wonderfully sweet, sticky flavor and soft texture they were famous for.

That is, this would be the glorious result if the donut maker kept the two-gallon water bottle filled with warm water to provide the perfect range of humidity and if the funnel-shaped receptacle was kept filled with enough dough to contribute to the vacuum that allowed the hydraulic plunger to suck the dough onto the tray in a size that wasn't too big — which happened if there was too much dough in the receptacle — or too small if there wasn't enough dough in the receptacle. Oh yeah, and a few other conditions were essential for the raised, glazed donuts to come out the way I described them. For example, the hydraulic plunger had to be kept lubricated with a kind of watery batter, which had to be the right consistency or the donuts wouldn't come out onto the tray at all; and the grease reservoir had to be kept full of hydrogenated vegetable oil and the oil had to be the right temperature to cook the donuts correctly; and the blower had to be working and pointing in the right direction to blow the donuts off their trays when they hit the grease; and the grease had to be deep enough so that the donuts didn't stick to the tray and jam the machine, as the tray was carried back under the humidifier; but the grease had to be not too deep so that when the donuts hit the flipper, they floated over the flipper, instead of turning over to cook the other side, so that the first side cooked too much and the second side didn't cook at all… and as I hope you can imagine by now, it was common for many of these complications to happen all at once. And with teenagers in charge much of the time, the making of donuts often played out as if it was taken from the script of a famous "I Love Lucy" episode called The Candy Factory. That classic TV episode was absurd and hilarious, and it worked so well that millions of people,decades later,still recall with laughter how quickly Lucy became forced to gobble up candy from a conveyor belt, simply because she got behind in performing the candy packaging task her supervisor had just demonstrated.

The making of donuts relied on meticulous attention to the many details of the process, and, like Lucy, we often screwed it up. When everything was going wrong with the donut making machine, it was not uncommon for the donut maker to panic and forget to start the next batch. Then the timing of the batches would be thrown off, and time gaps would ensue between batches which made the deliveries late, and Frank livid.

At the end of the candy factory episode, Lucy gets fired; if only we had been that fortunate!

The cost of the wasted, uncooked, overcooked, and unsold donuts was a profit killer. However, Frank figured out a way to fix that. An empty one hundred-pound flour sack was kept near the donut machine, and all the damaged, dropped or uneatable donuts went into the sack. Every couple of days when the sack was full, they were thrown into the big Hobart mixer with chocolate base, walnuts and sugar. Mix it all up and…voila! Brownies! With a coating of chocolate frosting, they actually looked edible. As long as the buyer didn't ask why they weighed so much or why the bag became greasy-wet so quickly, the sale was on. We sold a lot of brownies. Some customers came back for more. Others brought them back, dropped them on the counter, and walked out with a disgusted look on their faces. I cringed when the bag hit the glass counter, fearing it would break.

For a man who had no patience at all and whose only response to increased stress levels was rage, the donut shop was not the place for Frank. One afternoon, he showed up at the shop as we were cleaning up. He was in one of his typically foul moods and began complaining that we were late in the cleanup. Yelling at the girls, he pointed out dirt on the floors and smudges on the counters that needed attention. He sent more than one of them home in tears.

Shortly after that incident, Mom decided to keep him busy managing the other family business, Morrow's Candy and Nut House. Now isn't that a delicious irony? "Morose" Candy and Nut House would have been a better name. But no matter, he couldn't turn a profit there, however much he tried. We children didn't get much in the way of quality food at home, so having us around his candy and nuts was a great way to go broke. I was reminded of Gary Larsen's Far Side cartoon, the one in which the bakery shopkeeper is doing the books and can't figure out why he's losing money. Behind him stands an extremely obese kid sweeping the floor. That was us.

Not that we were all obese; some of us were, but we ate candy and nuts like there was no tomorrow. The rule was that we could nibble here and there, but what we did to Frank's inventory gave a whole new meaning to the expression, "Like a kid in a candy store."

I had a preference for the nuts, which were roasted onsite; the giant cashews were my favorite. I could, and did, put as much butter and salt on them as I wanted! Then, there were the macadamia nuts. They were so expensive, we were forbidden to eat this particular item. Uh-huh, right! And mind you, I didn't leave the candy alone either, not by any stretch. I went straight for the Rocky Road, chocolate peanut clusters, cashew clusters, almond clusters, macadamia nut clusters, in both light and dark chocolate, of course. Yes, I also regularly dipped into the "hard" stuff, the brittles (all of the same nuts in caramelized sheets of toffee). And I can't leave out the truffles or the caramels or the sugar coated gummy drops. Jeez, I'm lucky I have any teeth in my head! For Frank, the candy and nut business was an exercise in frustration. For us, it was a free-for-all. We weren't paid in cash but we extracted our wages, nonetheless.

With Frank out of the way, Mom took it upon herself to make the businesses work. She marshaled the available "forces" and assigned jobs to the ten of us who, in our teen years, could help operate the donut machine, cash register and the assembly counters, where a simple raised or cake donut became a chocolate, coconut or candied sprinkled donut. As soon as any of us boys turned 16 and had a driver's license, we were recruited to deliver donuts to the various high schools, military bases, gas stations, and convenience stores. It was considered a plum job at the shop, because: a) it was an opportunity to drive, and b) there was no Frank to deal with on the delivery route. During the summer, my shift was from 12 midnight to 12 noon the next day. During that time, I ate a dozen donuts and drank a quart or more of coffee a day. As good as a donut tastes, there is nothing in it that can be called "good for the body," white sugar, white flour, and indigestible grease…
Mmm—Yuk!

On one such night, I was loading a 50-pound block of grease into the reservoir, when I noticed that the pump wasn't working and that the fan belt was still. Sometimes, all it needed was a kick and it would start up again. So, I kicked it— nothing. I booted it again— nothing. I reached down and grabbed the fan belt with both hands and gave it a tug, to see if I could get it moving again. Suddenly, it roared back to life! But before I could get my hands out of the path of the belt, they were whipped around between the belt and the wheel and all ten of my fingers were squeezed between the two! It happened so fast I couldn't stop them! The pressure popped my fingers right out from under their nails and the ends of them literally exploded! I stood up, raised my hands in front of my face and watched as blood dripped from my eight longest digits. I went into shock, mortified by what I was seeing.

I called to my sister, Jeanie, to watch the machine while I got a ride home from one of the older kids. When I got into the house,

I ran upstairs, dripping blood to my elbows and knocked on my mother's bedroom door.

Frank answered the door, took one look at my hands, and shouted, "What are you doing!? Don't bleed in here! Go outside and bleed!"

I stared incredulously into Frank's hardened face as Mom pushed by him, took one look at me and marched me to the bathroom for bandages. Once my fingers were bandaged, she said, "Now go back to work. You'll make the deliveries late."

My heart sank to my grease and sugar crusted shoes. While I recognized that she was correct about the deliveries, I was crushed, to say the least, that my welfare meant so little to her. I realized that I was simply a means to an end; not her son, but a "worker." Mom's concern was to get the donuts made, not to take care of an injured child.

I think Mom had a tough time deciding where to draw the line with me, especially in terms of controlling my curiosity and excitement about life. I had an unending drive to experience as much adventure in the world as I could, which didn't fit into her plans at all. When I was twelve years old, I asked my mother if I could learn to scuba dive. For years I had been watching the television show, "Sea Hunt", starring Lloyd Bridges. From the first episode, I was hooked, and thought it was the coolest, most exciting thing imaginable. I wanted to be "Mike Nelson" more than anything. Mom, knowing that I had quit my paper route to work at the donut shop and was therefore without a source of money, thought she would cleverly side-step my request. She agreed that I could learn to scuba dive when I could pay for the lessons and equipment by myself. Working at the donut shop without compensation made the likelihood of my paying my way slim to none.

One afternoon, manning the sales counter and listening to the local AM radio station KMBY, I heard the DJ announce the next airing of their contest, "Can You Name The Songs?" The station had been running this contest for months. They'd play about two seconds from five different songs and if the designated caller could name all five songs, he or she would win a prize. Working long hours at the donut shop gave my brothers and sisters and me many opportunities to guess at the songs. Most of the station's listeners had, by this time, identified four of the five songs, but still hadn't named that last one. The station's DJ seemed to tire of the game. That one day, though, was the last day of the contest, and as I listened, the DJ said the winner of the contest would win $50, and that he would be taking the fiftieth caller. I listened to the montage, identifying the first four songs that everyone had already identified. Then came the mystery song, "I Got You, Babe" by Sonny and Cher. This time, the radio played several seconds of it, so they could ensure a winner. I was so excited that I kept calling the radio station. "You are the fourth caller, you are the twenty-third caller, you are the thirty-fourth caller, you are the fiftieth caller, please stay on the line."

I was just about jumping out of my skin! I could see myself in that wetsuit already! Mike Nelson, move over, here I come!

The disc jockey came on the line and asked, "What's your name, 50th caller?"

"Tom Beardsley" was my reply.

"Are you one of the Beardsley's from the big family in Carmel?"

"Yeah." was all I said.

"Well, what's it like with all those brothers and sisters?" the DJ asked.

"Oh, it's all right," I lied, not wanting to discuss it.

He must have noticed the reticence in my voice, so he changed the subject and asked, "Tom, do you know how the game is played?"

"Yeah."

"OK, then, you know that I'm going to play a few notes from five different songs and if you can identify them, you win fifty dollars! Tom—are you ready?"

"Yeah."

"OK, here we go!" Snippets of the five songs came over the radio in rapid succession. The DJ came back on. "OK Tom, what are the five songs?"

"Well, the one that no one could guess is 'I Got You Babe' by Sonny and Cher" I announced proudly.

"Very good! Now just name the other four songs and fifty dollars is yours!"

I named three of the songs in rapid succession, but then I stumbled. There was a Beatles song in the mix—and, and, I couldn't remember the title of the song!

I pleaded with the DJ, "Oh, you know! That Beatles song!"

He replied, "Yeah, I do know, but do you?"

Just at that moment, one of the donut shop's regular customers came in the front door.

I asked him, "Gary, Quick! What's the name of that Beatles song on the KMBY montage game?"

"A Hard Day's Night" was his reply.

I relayed the title through the mouthpiece of the telephone and in the back of the donut shop the radio blared out, "Hey! Hey! We've got another winner on K-M-B-Y, NUMBER ONE!" The DJ sounded relieved when he said, "Wow, Tom, that was close! For a moment there, I thought you weren't going to name that last song, but you did! So what are you going to do with all that money?"

"I'm going to take scuba lessons," I replied matter-of-factly.

I was so ecstatic at having actually won something, that I turned to Gary, who was waiting to pay for his donuts and coffee, and said, "On the house! Thanks for coming in when you did!"

At the end of the work day, I went home and explained to Mom that I had won fifty dollars on a radio game show and asked, "Can I please schedule my scuba lessons."

She took one look at me, rolled her eyes, and in an exasperated tone, said. "I only said you could take scuba lessons because I knew you couldn't come up with the money!"

I pleaded, "You promised!"

She still had that exasperated look on her face as she stared at me, lowering and shaking her head, and muttering, "I'll talk to your father."

Whenever she had said, "I'll talk to your father," my first thought was always, "You can't! He's dead!" I never once thought of Frank as my father, and it irritated me to hear him referred to in that way. Bringing him into the conversation brought me right down to earth.

I knew I was a goner. But, by that time I had been bringing fish home for the dinner table for a long time and through some unexpected miracle they agreed that a promise is a promise, and yes, I could take scuba lessons.

Frank and Mom felt it was only fair to include Nick. They also paid for Nick's lessons, but I still had to pay for my own lessons, which wasn't fair. However, all I wanted to do was dive, and if they wanted to pay for Nick to come along, that was fine with me.

The lessons were $40, leaving me $10 for equipment which I knew wouldn't go very far. Being the determined and resourceful young fellows that we had become, when Nick and I were not working at the donut shop, or the candy and nut shop, we'd started washing dishes and working in the pantries of local restaurants to make enough money to buy the required gear. So, during that summer of 1967, at the age of 13, I became a certified scuba diver. Frank and Mom thought this idea was looking better all the time once Nick and I began spear-fishing and bringing home larger stringers of fish for the table. And with time, we were bringing in even larger stringers and even bigger fish! Once we graduated from fishing to spear fishing in Carmel Bay, where the kelp beds were home to a wider variety of rock cod, as well as halibut and other fish, we could feed the whole family with one outing, and sometimes with one fish!

On one of our first dives, I hadn't gone far from shore at the rock-covered, southern end of Carmel Beach. The water was as calm as a lake in summertime and as clear as a swimming pool. I was free diving about fifty feet from shore in water about ten feet deep when I saw a ledge that hung out from a reef. I took several deep breaths, bent my torso downward and my feet up in the air, and dove to the bottom, my spear-gun in my right hand held out in front of me and my underwater flashlight in my left. I shined my flashlight under the ledge and saw that it was a small cave entrance, about five feet wide and three feet high. Moving my fins slightly, I edged closer and directed the beam of light into the enclosed space of the cave. I was startled as a very large fish's head came into view right inside the hole. It was a huge ling cod, an excellent food fish. It's long, brown and yellow-gray body extended for what seemed a very long way beyond its head. Large, fierce brown eyes sat behind a wide mouth filled with razor-sharp, needle-like teeth. I pointed my spear gun at the fish's head and fired. My heart was pounding as I headed for the surface and the precious air I was desperate for. Once I'd reached the surface, I saw that the line that connected my spear to the spear gun was taut. I took a couple of quick breaths and headed back down, concerned that the big fish might free itself from the spear and swim away. When I reached the bottom again, I saw that the fish was spinning wildly in circles just inside the cave. I grabbed the spear and pushed it to make sure it went all the way through the fish. It had been a good shot, through the gill plate and out the other side. This fish was not getting off the spear. I pulled the spear out of the cave with the hefty ling cod coming along with it. I slid my gloved hand under its lower jaw and kicked to the surface.

Bobbing vertically in the water, I took my first calm look at my prize. The fish dangled by my side and extended from my shoulder down past my knee. I didn't know how much it weighed, but I knew it was over twenty pounds. It was so big that it was awkward to drag around with me from the stringer which was clipped to my weight-belt. I decided to take it to shore. Once there, I showed my fish to Nick and my friends, amidst wide-eyed, wide-mouthed expressions of "WOW!" and "How much do you think it weighs?!" This was a question I was curious about myself. When we got home, the bathroom scale said the fish weighed twenty-four pounds. It was four and a half feet long and, later that night, fed the whole family with plenty left over.

It strikes me as wondrous how seemingly innocuous events can have such huge consequences. By my winning the radio contest and fifty dollars, the course of not just my life, but my brother's life was changed forever. Nick went with me to take scuba lessons, became a certified scuba diver and immediately after high school, went into the Navy and became a Navy Seal for the following twenty-eight years. He was one of the youngest Navy Seals to serve in Viet Nam, eventually assigned to Seal Team One.

In my mind, he was *the* Navy Seal and may very well have been just that. From what I understood, as the fuse man on the team, he was the first guy in and the last guy out of the hot zone. His career spanned almost every military crisis from Viet Nam in the sixties to the current war on terror.

Would Nick have become a scuba diver and then a Navy Seal on his own? Perhaps, but the events of that day at the donut shop ensured that he at least leaned in that direction.

Tom – Age 16

10

THE SUMMER OF LOVE

The summer of '67 was the Summer of Love in California and across America. Living in Carmel, originally an art enclave during the late 1800s, and still home to dozens of artists and art galleries, gave me a stained-glass window perspective on the cultural revolution of the 60s. Carmel was a stopover for hippies on their way to Big Sur, a stretch of the California coastline characterized by dramatic redwood forests and cliffside ocean vistas threaded by Highway One. Its scenic beauty and rugged forested terrain fed the imaginations of young people wanting to get away from "society" and get back to the land. They flocked to Big Sur by the thousands.

Seeing these young adults and teenagers in their colorful tie-dye shirts and bellbottom pants, "John Lennon glasses" and long, free-flowing hair was a wonder to me. It seemed that everyone out there was having a very different existence than I was having. At the time, I had made the transition between Catholic grammar school and public Carmel High School. In 1967, Carmel High was a local vector point for this revolutionary new way of thinking and behaving. I met students who wore those same colorful clothes and who exemplified all that was "hippie." It was a new and exciting set of possibilities to me, a young man who had been stultified in the ultra-conservative, militaristic Beardsley home.

Looking back, I recall wanting to fit in with kids my age, but found it difficult to do so. I resented anyone who seemed happy or seemed to be having fun. I was in constant emotional turmoil, finding myself snapping at siblings, friends or strangers, and then regretting it afterward. At times, I had difficulty focusing on or caring about school work, which isn't so uncommon among young people, but I was almost schizophrenic about it. I would come up with a great score on a test or write a paper that attracted compliments from the teacher, and then I'd not turn in school work for weeks, unconcerned about the consequences. One year, I was cast in the lead role in a Shakespearean play, and gave a respectable rendition of the comic character Falstaff in *The Merry Wives of Windsor*. When told that I had acted well, I could not bring myself to believe it or accept the compliments I received. I wouldn't allow myself to feel good about the "A" grade I received for that quarter's work. For the next quarter's play, I was asked to take on the lead role, but I refused, to everyone's consternation and disbelief. It didn't dawn on the teacher or my classmates that I was in emotional trouble. I cut class for the entire quarter, receiving an "F." Sullen, often surly, I attracted negative attention from the school bullies and shrank from their challenges to fight. It occurred to me that if I wanted to stand my ground, I could learn boxing skills from Frank; but I wanted nothing to do with him. Besides, I suspected that he would use the opportunity to inflict pain and not deliver on the training. The probability of that was fairly high, so I decided there would be little point in taking the chance.

When I watched these hippie kids, I was drawn to their seemingly care-free spirit. I imagined that if I were one of them, I'd feel differently. I might even be happy. I began to think that perhaps I could be liberated from the constricting bonds of the nightmare I was living in our house of horrors. Yes, I wanted to be free like the hippies.

This was also the age at which I began to take a serious interest in girls. In fact, I could think of little else. I had crushes on five girls in six months during my freshman year. My biggest problem was self-confidence. I had none. I was so defensive that I couldn't talk with girls without sarcasm slipping out of my mouth. There are young men who are well adjusted at that age, but I was not among them. I was a boiling tea kettle of hormones whistling down the hallways of Carmel High School, my hands in my pockets, trying to keep my excitement pressed along my leg to hide my embarrassment.

When I was fifteen, I became fatally infatuated with Chris, a girl who was more than I could have dreamed of. She was blonde, about five-foot four and curvaceous. Her smile could have opened the vault at Fort Knox. She seemed comfortable in her own skin, something I was painfully far from. Also fifteen, she was already a woman to my clumsy, late to mature boy. Kind and considerate, she didn't dissuade me from my attempts to speak with her. After some time, I asked if I could visit her at her home, which was fifteen miles from my own. To my surprise, she said yes. One Saturday I was blessed to not be working at either the donut shop or the Hatch Cover (a steak house where I was bussing tables). Motivated by an ever-rising testosterone level, I gathered my courage and hitchhiked out to her home. Upon arriving at her door, I found that she wasn't home. Her parents were very nice to me, though, telling me that she was babysitting down the street, giving me the address, and suggesting I go visit her there. Miraculous! I was shocked that they were so open and encouraging to me. In the world I came from, there was only one thing that could result from a boy and a girl together in an unsupervised home for hours on end, and that was a sin. I walked down to the address they gave me and knocked on the front door. Chris opened the door. Dressed in pale slacks and a simple white blouse, she smiled at me and invited me in—another miracle. My first thought was, "God! I have excellent taste in women!"

After some pleasant conversation, I began kissing her and she gave me the third miracle of the day by kissing me back. I took her ample breasts in my hands and was sure I was in heaven. As her body pressed against mine, my heart was pumping furiously, sending blood racing through my veins as though I were running a marathon. Reaching around her back and under her blouse, I took the clasp of her bra in my hand. She pressed closer to me and a surge of elation swept through me. She actually wanted me to keep going! I fumbled with the clasp but couldn't get it opened. Not knowing what to do, I panicked; and in the next second, all my insecurities and self-doubt came rushing forward. It never occurred to me to ask her for help.

I began thinking about all of the things that could go wrong if we had sex. She could get pregnant, or the parents of the nine-month-old sleeping baby in the other room could walk in. Or, God forbid, I wouldn't know what to do, which I didn't! I bailed.

I took her by the shoulders and held her at arm's length. Conjuring up the best look of startled remembrance I could muster, my mouth uttered, "I just remembered, I have to be at work in twenty minutes."

Then I stood up from the couch.

She looked at me in puzzlement. "Well, are you sure?" she disappointedly replied.

"Yeah, I gotta' go."

And I was gone, leaving behind my miraculous moment.

Back at school, Chris wouldn't talk to me. I had failed to deliver her from that burden called "virginity," and she soon found another guy who was more capable than I. Oddly, when I heard about it, it seemed only fair and I was happy for her. After a time, she spoke with me again; but by then she had acquired a nineteen-year-old boyfriend, and I took the role of "nice friend," but not "boyfriend."

My failure as a first-time lover crushed my already damaged ego and became a tipping point. I began dwelling on it day and night. Having had lots of practice in feeling bad, I became obsessed with Chris. My friends told me to get over her, but I took that as a reason to feel even worse. Wallowing in self pity, I convinced myself that if I couldn't have Chris, who clearly didn't care about me, then I didn't have to care what other people felt, especially the girls. Any girl I dated would have to take care of her own feelings. I had my own to take care of. I decided I was self-sufficient and needed no one. My slogan became, "I am a rock, I am an island" after the popular Simon and Garfunkel song. It sounded perfect to me, because as the ending lyrics of the song proclaimed, "And a rock feels no pain— and an island never cries."

I continued reeling from my fiasco with Chris, but after many months of feeling sorry for myself and pining in misery, it dawned on me that neither would get me laid. Looking around me and seeing that there were endless possibilities among the many girls I knew, I began to explore those possibilities, dating more, and searching for who would be my first conquest.

In spite of a grueling work schedule at the donut shop, whenever I could, I continued diving and spear fishing with a growing group of divers my age. My best friends, Harry Goulding and Ralph Martini, were also divers and Harry knew some kids from Palo Alto who came down on weekends to visit and dive with us. During the summers, they would stay for weeks at a time. Harry's mother, Alice, owned a giant Tudor house on over an acre of land in Carmel, which became our unofficial-official hang-out. Harry's younger sister, Kelly, was fourteen, going on twenty. She was pretty, intelligent, athletic and seemed to know exactly how to use her sexuality to control the boys. Her friends congregated at Alice's too. So there we were, ten teenage boys and about the same number of girls, hanging out at Alice's, with Alice getting high on all the sexual tension in the air. All summer long we ate donuts, dove day and night, speared fish and cooked feasts at Alice's. All the while, we enjoyed drinking beer bought by older friends, and sharing our free-spirited adventures on the coast.

One day, while driving down Coast Highway 1 in a jeep owned by one of the kids, we clearly had too many people in the vehicle. There were four in the back and four in the front. There should have been four in the car period. I thought it was great, because I had Gretchen on my lap and Liz sitting next to me on a bucket seat made for one. The three of us were jammed into that one-passenger seat so that Doug, the driver, could use the stick shift. Lest you think that something awful was going to happen... relax. Doug was a good driver and I was helping, holding Liz close to me with my left arm, so she wouldn't get in Doug's way as he shifted gears. I began using the opportunity to slide my left hand under her left arm and around her left breast. I could feel her heart rate increase. Her face flushed, but she didn't let on that anything was amiss. It occurred to me that in my position, I could do double-duty. On my lap, Gretchen sat with her right arm around my neck for support.

I could smell the sweet perfume and lotion on her skin. It sent my imagination to faraway, exotic places. I reached around and slid my right hand under her sweater and fondled her right breast.

I could feel her heart rate increase, too, and a flush rose up her neck to her face. With each hand occupied with a different girl, each of whom thought she was the sole object of my attentions, I believed I was being very clever. I had no idea what I would do when we got back to Alice's; but for the moment I was high on the possibilities.

Back at the house, I invited Liz up to Harry's bedroom. Lying down on Harry's bed, I kissed her full and willing lips. We made out for a while, but when I reached down to remove her pants, she said she was not ready to have sex. She quickly stood up and left the room. Rats! I missed again. It seemed that I had chosen the wrong girl! Oh, well, there would be other girls and other opportunities.

Although I was still a virgin at 15, life was taking on a more sensual aura for me. I had taken a dishwashing job at the Hatch Cover, one of the most popular restaurants in Carmel. The first night I reported for work, I was supposed to enter through the service entrance; but I wanted to see what the dining room looked like when it was busy. The atmosphere of the place was overwhelming with smells, sounds and sights that set my nerve endings on fire. I came in through the front door, and immediately my nostrils were assaulted with the aroma of the cigarette and cigar smoke hanging in the air, steaks sizzling on the grill, and perfume from the ladies waiting in the lobby area. The sounds of live rock music coming from the bar mixed in with the laughter of the patrons. The lights were dimmed, giving the entire restaurant an air of sophistication I hadn't previously experienced, but wanted desperately to infuse into myself. The Hatch Cover was electric with interesting, energetic young people, many of whom were attractive women.

As I had been used to not being paid for my work, just being in their presence was compensation enough for me. The prospect of actually getting a paycheck was like a bonus.

Washing dishes wasn't a difficult job. Compared to the donut shop, it was easy. And the food, my god! The Hatch Cover had a limited menu, consisting of various high quality steaks, lamb, lobster and grilled chicken dishes. A well-stocked salad bar and limited wine menu made it a "reservations only" destination most nights of the week.

As I took the dishes that the busboys placed in the window and emptied them into the garbage can, I was amazed at the food people left on their plates. I set up doggie bags on the shelf above and behind my head and swept the half or uneaten steaks, not into the garbage can, but into those bags. At the end of the night, I spirited them away like Aladdin from the magic cave. I ate and ate and ate meat like I had never been able to eat before— twelve ounce teriyaki sirloins, filet mignon, rack of lamb— and every morsel was mouth-wateringly delicious. I had absolutely no concern that someone else had eaten part of the meat, and neither did my brothers and sisters, with whom I shared the bounty. No more concern over slivers of pot roast. We were eating like the rich people, or at least people who were fortunate enough to go to a restaurant and order a steak.

It didn't take long to notice that when the cooks cut the steaks from large 30-pound blocks into smaller individual portions, they were sloppy about their work. They wasted meat like they didn't care. Seeing the opportunity to bring fresh high quality meat home to the family, I waited until the cooks were done cutting and scavenged the usable portions of beef from the tallow barrel and took them home. When I'd get them home, Mom made beer stew for the kids; and although she seldom said anything in the way of thanks, I knew she was grateful.

The owner of the restaurant was a young entrepreneur named Michael Tancredi. He was the most unusual man I had ever met, in that he was warm, engaging, sincere and direct. His whole demeanor radiated confidence, honesty and a whimsical sense of humor. I met him a few days into my new job. I was taking a brief break, and happened to be leaning against the ice cream freezer with my arms and legs crossed. He must have read my body language, and, amused, he stopped in front of me and, cocking his head my way, motioned to Eddie, the restaurant manager.

Michael smiled and asked, "Who do we have here?"

Eddie introduced me as the new dishwasher adding, "He's one of those rich Beardsley kids."

Michael gave me a firm handshake, and still smiling, said, "Welcome to the Hatch Cover. Now get back to work."

The restaurant was a haven for me. I worked hard and as often as I could. When a busboy position opened up, I asked Eddie if I could have the job.

He looked at me up and down with contempt, and said, "C'mon, rich kid, I want to give the job to someone who really needs it. With the movie and the bread commercials… you sure don't need the money!"

I was incredulous and pleaded, "Eddie, The movie didn't make any money for my family. When I'm not working here, I'm either in school or helping out at the donut shop, where I don't get paid at all! I need this job! Please let me be a busboy!"

Eddie's expression went from contempt to surprise. He shrugged and said, "O.K., you're a busboy. Now find me a dishwasher."

Eddie's willingness to listen was one of the best things an adult had done for me yet. It allowed me into the dining room, where the real money was. In 1969, forty or fifty dollars was a lot to earn in a night for a fifteen-year-old on a part-time basis. Besides, I had fun working with the waiters, the waitresses, and the whole crew. There was a rhythm and a flow to the dining room experience which I plugged right into.

Once in the dining room, I was working more directly with Michael. He was proud of his restaurant, and at only twenty-five years old, he was one of, if not the youngest, restaurateur around. He had a charming demeanor and an articulate communication style. Michael stood at a lanky six-foot five, and moved like a lion, slowly and with intention. He loved the role of host and worked the crowd like an entertainer. As I watched him move among the tables, I noticed patrons looking his way, hoping he would stop by their table for a visit. But he was not to be trifled with.

One evening, he was checking the salad bar to be sure it was stocked and spotless. A woman had just filled her salad plate and was moving past the dressings, dipping her finger into each one and tasting as she went. As she got to the blue cheese dressing, Michael reached over, pushed on her elbow and shoved her hand deep into the blue cheese dressing in the crock pot.

"Be sure you get a good taste," he contemptuously admonished the shocked woman. I doubt she ever did that again.

Michael was revered by the employees. He seemed to genuinely care about people. He inspired everyone around him and me, in particular. As a diver, I often regaled him with stories of diving adventures I had experienced.

Quite soon, he went out and took scuba lessons, and in short order, we became diving buddies, which we remained for the next 25 years. His presence in my life was like a light shining into a dark place. His positive and philosophical perspective brought me the first hint of encouraging male presence I had known since my Uncle Bob had been banned from the Beardsley house by Frank.

Not long after taking lessons, Michael invited me to join him and his scuba instructor friend, Ken, on a three-day dive trip to the Channel Islands off of the Santa Barbara coast. Ken was a highway patrolman and taught scuba part-time. I agreed to go, as I had the most island diving experience among the three of us and knew some of the good dive spots. By swapping shifts at the donut shop and working overtime to make some weekends available, I had been able to travel to the islands on large charter dive boats on several occasions as a member of a dive club I had joined the year before.

Ken owned an eighteen-foot inboard motorboat that seemed to me to be a bit small for crossing the Santa Barbara Channel, which was eleven miles across at its narrowest. The channel was famous for its sudden winds and squalls which seemed to come out of nowhere, making it a dangerous waterway for such a small boat. But in spite of my concerns, I was willing to ride in just about anything that would motor me across to the islands and the spectacular diving there. I was also excited to be going on an adventure with these two older men. Some positive male energy in my life was way overdue.

We launched Ken's boat at the Ventura harbor and headed across the channel. Once on the water, Ken surprised me and went through a transformation from Ken the safety-minded scuba instructor and law-abiding highway patrolman to Ken the wild man, crazy-ass boat driver.

The surface of the ocean was so calm, you could have water-skied on it; so Ken opened up the throttle on the boat, while simultaneously reaching under the dashboard and pulling out a fifth of Jack Daniels. Ken was as tall as Michael, but much broader, and the boat was small. In spite of this, he suddenly stood up at the steering wheel, took a big swig of whisky, and let out a wild war whoop. With one hand on the wheel and the other pumping the bottle of Jack into the air, we raced across the channel toward Anacapa Island, as Michael and I looked cautiously amused at one another and hunkered down in our seats.

Anacapa is the smallest of the four Northern Channel Islands, but also the closest and most accessible. Its excellent underwater terrain was perfect for game hunters like the three of us. While palm kelp covers some of the shallow reefs that surround the island, the deeper reefs support a huge variety of plant and fish species. Caves abound at all depths, and kelp beds provide the underwater forests that are the basis for the food chain.

I guided Ken and Michael to dive sites where I'd caught lobsters, abalone and rock scallops on previous dive trips. But this was summer; so lobsters, which are only legal to take during the fall and winter, were off-limits. We caught quite a few scallops and abalone that first day. On our last dive of the day, I returned to the boat to find that Ken had speared three small lobsters. I was shocked! He was not only a wild man, he was a law-breaker! It was one thing that lobsters were out of season; but he was using a spear-gun, which is prohibited, as well. I said nothing, not wanting to upset the excitement in the atmosphere.

Ken was so excited by our great diving on the first day that he repeated his antics with the whiskey, standing up almost all the way back to the mainland. He was drunk by the time we reached the harbor.

At night, we went to a public campground and found a vacant barbeque pit on which to prepare our feast. Michael had brought thick New York steaks from the Hatch Cover, and for dinner, we barbecued them along with lobster and scallops. We ate ourselves silly and had a grand time. With more food than we could possibly eat, we invited campers from surrounding campsites to join us, telling stories and laughing till late in the night.

On the last day, we focused on filling out our limits to take home. We were allowed five abalone each, and ten scallops. I needed three more abalone to complete my limit, and the other guys needed a couple as well, so I was designated as the "finder of limits" for the day. I put on my scuba tank, jumped off the boat and kicked in toward the shore of Anacapa Island. As I began scanning a rocky wall for the abalone I needed, I felt someone tap me on my right shoulder. Kicking with my powerful scuba diving fins, I had swum quite a ways from the boat, so I knew neither Michael nor Ken were nearby. I was sure there were no other divers in the area, so I was perplexed by the sensation. Of course, I reflexively looked over my right shoulder for the source, but there was no one in my field of vision. I thought it peculiar, and wondered if the many dives I had done over the previous days was having some odd effect on me. I shook it off and went back to looking for abalone.

Then the tap came again, but this time on the left shoulder. Now I was concerned. I quickly looked over my shoulder and saw no one. The tap on my shoulder had been firm and urgent, and I knew I was not imagining it. Suddenly, I realized what I was dealing with. Anacapa Island is frequented by scores of weekend divers, but it is also home to colonies of harbor seals. Stories of human-seal interactions were common among divers, so it wasn't too much of a stretch to imagine that I was being played with by just such a harbor seal.

I asked myself, "If I was a harbor seal, where would I go next, after tapping a diver on both shoulders?"

I figured that the seal would be right over my head, where I couldn't see it. In a flash, I jerked my head up and found myself nose to nose with the seal. It had been playing with me and had been just about to tap me on the top of my head! I had caught it in the act and it knew the jig was up. Without moving at all, with its nose about four inches from mine, it broke into a huge grin! I was astonished at its perfectly human reaction, so I smiled back at it. It was as if the seal was saying, "Okay, you got me!" It moved a few feet away and hung around for a few moments, then disappeared. I collected the abalone I had been searching for and returned to the boat. That encounter with the harbor seal was one of the great diving experiences of my life.

Tom, writing at Carmel Beach

11

DOWN THE RABBIT HOLE

Carmel High School was a drug mecca. The unofficial drug use statistics in California at the time ranked Berkeley, Carmel, and Palo Alto High as the top three schools in student body drug use, in that order. Through my freshman and sophomore years, I had avoided the drug scene, thinking that taking drugs was wrong. But damn, the people I observed who were taking drugs sure looked like they were having fun. At the few high school parties I attended, I was intrigued by the smell of marijuana and listened to the cool people laugh and joke about things I couldn't even imagine. Not to mention that the girls who smoked pot were behaving in a very sexy manner. My resistance was weakening.

The cook at the Hatch Cover was a long haired rock-and-roller named Jim who tucked his waist-length ash blond hair under a wig while he worked the grill. When Jim wasn't grilling steaks, chicken and lobsters for the patrons, he dealt drugs. Any drug a person wanted, Jim had it or could get it, except heroin; that was the boundary he wouldn't cross.

I finally succumbed to the offers of free marijuana when I was 16. Free? Yeah, right. I had heard the jokes about how the first time is always free, but that you eventually pay another price not advertised. But that couldn't apply to me, could it?

I found smoking pot an excellent way to escape my Frank Beardsley-induced misery. What the hell. From what I had been told by more and more friends, it was fun to get high; smoking pot made one feel free. Pot didn't have the chemicals that tobacco had, and didn't burn my throat or make me cough like cigarettes did. My first high was amazing. I became instantly paranoid – absolutely sure that everyone on the street could tell I was stoned and was staring at me! Jim explained that no one knew I was stoned, and more to the point, no one cared. I sat in the backseat of his Ford Comet looking around through a new set of eyes. Once I realized that the police really weren't going to come and arrest me as soon as I took a puff on a joint, I began to relax.

Jim and his friends didn't just smoke a joint. They smoked until they couldn't smoke anymore...until their eyes narrowed almost shut...until it was time to go to work. Go to work...

"Oh, my god!" I yelled. "I have to go to work like this! Everyone will know! What am I going to do?!"

Jim smiled through the slits of his eyes and explained, "Just relax and be cool, man. You'll be fine. No one knows; no one cares. As long as you keep your cool, you'll actually work better. In fact, you'll have more fun."

He was a good teacher, and, in a way, he was right. I went into a kind of zone, a stoned zone in which I felt relaxed and free of the inhibitions I had felt in my non-intoxicated life. Never mind the fact that a significant percentage of on-the-job accidents are drug-related. Never mind that I was accumulating toxic chemicals in my blood and muscle tissues that would later in life have negative consequences. Never mind that the state of mind I was chemically creating was a complete delusion. The real attraction was that, when I smoked pot, I found I was able to not care anymore about my low self-esteem or my bouts of depression or my broken heart. My home life was hell, I had been a disaster as a first-time lover, I couldn't seem to get laid, and my ego was crushed. When I was stoned, I didn't care about these negatives anymore. It was as though I could create for myself an entirely new persona and be just who I wanted to be at the moment — confident, happy, self-assured and even funny. Never mind that I was on a road that, in my case, led to drug addiction.

One night at a party at Jim's house, I snorted coke for the first time. We were smoking a lot of pot and snorting what seemed to be endless lines of coke. I needed to go to the bathroom and relieve myself. When I stood up from the couch, the room started to spin all around me. I leaned against the wall to steady myself. Jim gave me directions to the bathroom. I went into Jim's bedroom closet instead. I found myself swimming, floundering in clothes in a dark room. I got vertigo, the whirlies. I threw up— all over Jim's clothes. Then I passed out. In the morning I woke up on the floor under the kitchen table. I didn't know how I got to the kitchen from Jim's closet, but I remembered throwing up all over his clothes. I felt terrible. My mouth tasted like,well, you don't want to know what my mouth tasted like. I felt badly about the mess. I apologized to Jim, who said it was no big deal. He shared with me that early in his drug days he had puked in the back seat of his friend's Rolls Royce Silver Shadow, all over the leather, all over the carpet."Don't worry about it," he said. So I didn't worry. But I did start buying cocaine from him. I bought cocaine before going off to see Steve Marriott and Small Faces at the San Jose Civic Center. I bought cocaine before going to see Rod Stewart at the Fillmore and more cocaine for the Who at the Cow Palace. I went to more and more concerts, I did more and more coke, and I smoked more and more pot. I was a mess. I was living two lives; the straight one, miserable, and the stoned one, delusional.

I moved out of the Beardsley house as soon as I graduated from high school. For obvious reasons, I wanted to leave as soon as possible, and in order to lighten their kid-load at home, my intention was supported by Mom and Frank. To my delight, Mom informed me that if I went to college, even junior college, I would receive five hundred dollars a month from my father's social security benefits. That, in addition to what I made from my restaurant work, would support me in the rental of a room somewhere. As luck would have it, one of the cocktail waitresses at the Hatch Cover was going on a trip to Europe for a year. She agreed to rent me her home at a rate below the market. I was getting a whole house for the price of a room.

Because I had been a good enough kid helping with the family businesses and had regularly provided food for the family from my diving and from the Hatch Cover, Mom and Frank co-signed a car loan for me so that I could buy a brand new Volkswagen bus. It was a simple "Kombi" model; no frills, plain white, no accessories, but it became my wheels of freedom.

During my first summer on my own, at the age of seventeen, I continued to work at the donut shop from 12 midnight till 12 noon, sleep for a few hours, then head to the Hatch Cover to work from 5 p.m. until 10 p.m., grab a couple of hours of sleep, then do it all over again.

If I had the right sisters working the donut shift with me, we would smoke pot in the storage room of the shop between batches of donuts. We kept a can of air freshener handy to hide the smell.

I was in the back room one summer night lighting up the second or third joint, when two cops on a graveyard shift came in the shop's front door. As soon as they closed the door behind them, one of them took a sniff and poked his partner in the ribs. The other nodded in a knowing manner. One of my sisters looked out the door of the storage room and said, "Hey, there are two cops out there! I'm not going out there!"

I understood her concern, volunteering to handle it. I walked up to the counter, stoned out of my mind, smiling all the way. I greeted the officers with, "Hi guys, what can I get for you?"

They each ordered a coffee and a couple of hot glazed donuts right off the conveyor. I bagged their purchases and as they moved to put money on the counter, I held my hand up and said, "No charge officers. Thanks for just being around."

They grinned, nodded with an unspoken acknowledgement and left. I took a deep breath, let it out slowly, and went to load the next batch of dough.

Having graduated from smoking dope to snorting coke, I figured I had clearly demonstrated to myself that I was invincible. Why not experiment with a broader range of recreational drugs? A few of my fellow students from Monterey Peninsula College, where I was now taking classes, told me they had scored some windowpane LSD and wanted to go to Big Sur and "trip", so, would I drive? Yessirree!

We piled into my VW bus and went down to Pfeiffer Beach, one of the many picturesque beaches on the Big Sur coast. We stopped on the way to pick up Steve, a high school friend who was managing the convenience store at the Ventana Hotel, a couple of miles from Pfeiffer. Sitting in the employee lounge where Steve worked, the six of us each did a quarter of a pane of the acid. We were neophytes and had no idea what to expect, so we were a bit timid about taking a whole tab each, right away. Fifteen minutes later, we weren't feeling anything, so we did another quarter; then another and then another. We were just starting to come on to the acid when we jumped into the bus and drove down the winding, bumpy road a couple of miles to the beach. Getting out of the bus, we were laughing and joking as the effects of the LSD intensified. The path from the parking lot to the beach at Pfeiffer leads through a small thicket of willow and cotton wood saplings, across a small creek. Walking through the thicket and then the sedges and beach grasses, we came upon the sand. After taking only a few steps, it suddenly felt like wet cement around my feet. Opening out onto the beach, we walked past the small lagoon formed by the creek as it reaches the ocean. A giant rock formation sits on the waterline three hundred feet in front of the entrance to the beach. Made of sandstone and composite rock, it rises a hundred feet above the sand. Two hundred feet wide, it has a forty-foot high arch that rises in the center of the rock formation, allowing the surf to come crashing through, accentuating the dramatic presence of the monolith.

Standing in a small group, we suddenly became oddly somber, staring around us at the grandeur of the environment. As if on cue, the six of us spread out, saying nothing to one another. Some of the guys climbed the central rock formation. I walked northward along the waterline, alone.

Staring at the cypress and pine trees covering the hills that rose from the beach, then at the rocks and sand, and raising my gaze to the sky, I felt insignificant, almost non-existent. The waves pounded the shore, each one of them a peal of laughter, mocking me. I was nothing. In ten thousand years they would still be pounding the shore, and I might as well not ever have existed. The trees felt the same way. So did the sand and the rocks. I was nothing to the earth, and even less to the universe. Disconnected from everything, the aloneness I felt was crushing me. I stopped, looking at the sky, seeing beyond the shades of blue to the blackness of the void, sensing a divine indifference to my presence.

This was my first acid trip. It was unlike anything I had read or heard about or imagined. My hallucinations were not yet visual but tactile, and it seemed, existential. I felt stuck in the sand with every step. My aloneness served to reinforce my sense of isolation from all the people I could see frolicking on the beach.

I went back the way I had come and climbed the big rock with the arch. There were well- worn footholds in the steep face of the sandstone, testifying to the thousands of feet that had climbed there before me; but still, I had to pay attention to my balance to keep from falling to the rocks below. As I reached the top, I looked out to sea. The sun was setting, turning the sky and its reflection on the water to shades of copper, gold, red and yellow. A freighter was passing from south to north, unusually close to shore, maybe two miles out. Directly in my line of sight to the freighter, a huge herd of hundreds of sea lions was working its way south, leaping out of the water, barking and breaking the water into thousands of prisms through which the sunset glimmered for a moment and disappeared. My friend, Tommy, sat on a ledge about twenty feet below the rock I stood on, staring out to sea. I hadn't made a noise as I approached, but he turned around, looked me in the eye and our minds locked in wonder at what we were seeing. We said nothing as we descended to the beach and made our way back to my bus.

On the drive back up Sycamore Canyon road to Highway One, Jeff, who was sitting in the back of the bus complained, "Wow man, the road is really bumpy. I think you've got a flat tire."

With my mind thrown open by the drug, I was sensitive to any and all suggestion. I glommed onto that idea and within a few seconds, every one of the six of us was convinced that all four tires were flat. "What am I gonna' do, man!" I worried out loud.

A couple of the guys thought my anxiety was funny and started to play on it.

"Yeah, man, I think the tires fell off, man."

Suddenly, in my mind, there were parts flying off the car in every direction. My anxiety level went up like a cartoon thermometer and burst.

My friend, Tommy, noticed my discomfort and said, "Just keep driving man, your doing O.K., just keep driving."

Not knowing what else to do, I kept driving, hoping to get back to the gas station at the hotel. As we arrived at the station, the attendant greeted Steve, as my passengers jumped out of the bus, laughing and heading to the store for food. He was an old grey bearded fellow with long hair down his back in a ponytail. I grabbed him and, barely able to contain my panic, told him my car was falling apart and could he fix it for me. He looked at the bus, stepped up to it and rocked it back and forth a few times and checked the tires. Then he came back and stood in front of me and took me by the shoulders.

He looked me in the eyes and said, "Listen to me. The only thing falling apart here is you. What did you take?"

I thought a moment, "Uh, four quarter-tabs of windowpane."

Rolling his eyes, he smiled and said, "Give me your car keys."

He told me to take a deep breath and relax, that the car was fine. He rounded up the six of us and told us to go to the bunk house (which was the employee lounge) and stay there until we came down. We agreed. The guys laughed all the way. I was still worried about my Volkswagen bus falling apart, wondering if it would hold together long enough to get us home.

In the bunkhouse, we shared our experiences on the beach. None of us had felt we had seen the colors or hallucinations we had expected. In my case, the universe laughed at my insignificance and my car fell apart all around me as I was driving it, but I wasn't hallucinating. Uh, huh.

About 6 to 8 hours after I had swallowed the windowpane, I started coming down. I felt like the wrong electric current was racing through my nervous system, a very uncomfortable electric current that caused my whole body to vibrate in a mild state of electrocution. I couldn't stop shaking. I could function, but it was like being too cold and too hot at the same time. I dropped the rest of the guys off at their respective cars and homes. They must have been feeling it, too. They sat in silence as the tape deck played Jimi Hendricks singing, "There must be some kind of way out of here…." They said nothing as they went on their separate ways. I continued to do drugs just about every day. For the next five years, my life took on a pattern of work, school at the local Junior College, more work, scuba and skin diving, multiple girlfriends, casual sex, parties, more work and drugs of one kind or another in a steady stream. Then, I started to crack.

After four days of non-stop partying, I woke up feeling terrible after spending the night in Jim's spare bedroom. I could not remember feeling so low. I was angry, depressed and sullen, all at once. I went to the bathroom and before doing anything else, I took out a small dime bag of coke and started to chop it and line it up. I looked up into the bathroom mirror and wondered how I could look so bad. I was pale as a ghost with black circles under my bloodshot eyes.

As I cut up the coke, I asked myself, "Why am I snorting coke in the bathroom by myself at 6:30 a.m.?"

"Am I going to a concert?"

"No."

"Am I going to a party?"

"No."

"Then why am I doing up coke?"

"So I don't have to feel bad… that's why."

The questioning continued, "And what do we call it when we do coke so we don't have to feel bad?"

"Addiction" was the word that came to mind.

Wow, I thought. I'm getting addicted to cocaine.

In a split second, I took a look at that possible reality path and saw my life as a coke addict. I saw myself unable to hold a job… lying, cheating and stealing to get money for coke. I didn't like what I imagined. Realizing that it was clearly a downward spiral that I wanted no part of, I turned around and emptied the small envelope of coke into the toilet and flushed it. That was the last of the hard drugs for me. Had I not made that choice, it might have been my life that had gone down the toilet instead of the white powder.

The next few weeks were hell, but I knew I had brought it on myself and had it coming. I was depressed most of the time. Bouts of paranoia plagued me in public places. I was in line at the grocery store when, suddenly, all noise stopped. Looking around, I saw that everyone in the store had stopped and was staring at me. In my mind, I was naked to the world, and all my sins, all my transgressions were visible to everyone everywhere. They were all judging me, condemning me, and only with an extreme effort of willpower was I able to keep from screaming and collapsing to the floor with my hands over my head. Once I had made it home and had a chance to relax, it became clear to me that I was going through withdrawals and would have to be careful until my system was cleared of drugs.

Soon after, I took my bus to renew the registration at the local California Department of Motor Vehicles office. I had become adept at rolling joints with one hand, while steering the car with the other. In my mind, smoking pot was not doing drugs; cocaine and LSD were drugs, but not marijuana. I smoked my way to the DMV and, while pulling in to the parking lot, I cut right in front of a police car coming toward me as I made my left turn. The car was white and had disappeared in the sunlight behind it.

As I cut in front of him, I heard tires squealing on the pavement and looked up to see his car slam to a halt. I had to think fast. I pulled into the first stall I could find that was between two other cars, so the cop couldn't park next to me and look into my bus. I jumped out of the car just as the cop, lights flashing, pulled up behind me.

He got out of the squad car, eyes ablaze. I approached him and asked, "Are you all right?"

Not expecting my concern for his welfare, he was thrown off guard. "What?" he asked, confused by my demeanor.

"I am so sorry!" I apologized. "I lost you in the sunlight, but that's no excuse. I was wrong. I deserve a ticket. Write me up."

He stared at me, not knowing what to do. Fortunately, I kept myself downwind of him so he couldn't smell the pot that must have reeked from my breath and clothes.

He looked at me squarely and said, "Well, if I give you a ticket, you'll just go into the DMV there and pay it off, so... just be more careful next time!"

"Thank you for being so understanding, sir." I replied.

After he drove off, I went to the car to get the registration envelope and as I opened the car door, smoke billowed out. It occurred to me right then and there that I had really been screwing up a lot lately. I wondered, at least for a moment, how many close calls or breaks like this I might have left before my luck ran out.

In the meantime, Michael, my boss, was worried about me, too. He sat me down one evening at the Hatch Cover and asked me if I was okay. I responded that I was. He said that I had better start working like I was okay, or he would have to fire me. Looking into his eyes, I saw his concern and sadness and I knew he was serious. My friend, my dive buddy, my mentor, was going to fire me.

Harry and Kelly Goulding's father, Dr. Robert Goulding, was a psychiatrist with a thriving practice in the nearby town of Watsonville. He was famous in the nascent Humanistic Psychology movement that was flourishing in the 1960s and '70s. His business, the Western Institute for Group and Family Therapy (WIGFT), sat on several acres on a prominent hilltop 200 feet above the Pajaro Valley, looking out over vast agricultural land and the blue Pacific Ocean five miles distant. It was an inspiring view and a perfect site for WIGFT, or "Wigfoot" as it became known. Dr. Goulding's institute was a "happening" place, with intellectually stimulating conversation buzzing throughout the atmosphere. I found the energy of the place to be electrifying, and listened closely to conversations that seemed way over my head. Dr. Goulding, or "Bob" as he preferred to be called, taught the newest variations on Gestalt therapy, which he called "Re-Decision Therapy" and ran workshops for psychologists, students and trainees. One Saturday, Harry and I were visiting his dad's place when I heard voices coming from beyond the wall closest to me. There was one voice in particular that was crying out in emotional anguish. Instantly I felt the need to go in there and be that person. I wanted to cry out like that and relieve some of the subterranean pressure that boiled inside of me.

I waited patiently for Bob to finish a conversation, and when he turned in my direction I timidly asked him, "Bob, I couldn't help but hear the voices in the next room. What are they doing in there?"

Bob smiled and put his hand on my shoulder, as we walked down the hall toward the lunch room. He explained that his trainees were practicing group therapy methods on people who were in need of psychological help. These "guinea pigs" were given a wonderful meal and a day of guided introspection in a safe environment. In return, they gave the trainees someone to help.

Plaintively, I asked, "Could I be a guinea pig?"

Focusing intently, Bob looked at my eyes as though he were looking deep within me. I felt his attention probing my psyche, asking why I would want to seek psychological help at such a young age.

Then he smiled and said, "I think we could arrange that. You come around next Saturday and we'll get you in a group."

I thanked him, shook his hand, and went off with Harry to meet new people, hoping it might be the young female type.

The following Saturday, I arrived at WIGFT early to make sure I didn't miss out on anything that might happen before the group therapy session. The place was already busy at 8 a.m., with people gathering around a buffet of breakfast items that looked like they came from a five-star restaurant. I stared at the fruit trays, assorted pastries, bagels with smoked salmon, cream cheese and capers, eggs Benedict, waffles and pancakes, all looking mouth-watering to me. I was thrilled to be sitting down with serious, thoughtful looking people, listening to them using words and phrases like "Gestalt," "Re-Decision Therapy," and "Transactional Analysis." These conversations primed my fertile mind to want more of.... whatever it was they were talking about.

After breakfast, I went into the group therapy room and looked around. There were ten folding chairs arranged in a circle in the middle of the converted living room. A floor to ceiling brick fireplace painted white bisected the east wall of the room, with curtained, sliding glass doors that opened out onto the sprawling lawn to one side of the fireplace. Couches framed by large hourglass shaped ceramic lamps on end tables sat against the east wall of the room, perhaps thirty feet away. Large, impressionist paintings adorned the walls. It looked just like a normal living room, except for those ten chairs.

I sat on a couch, waiting, enjoying the view of the Pajaro valley out the far window, as people started filing in. I stood up and joined the group as greetings were exchanged. I was glad that most of the people seemed as nervous as I was. There were eight "guinea pigs" like me and two therapists; a young man who looked to be in his thirties and a young woman who may have been in her twenties. They were both dressed casually, as were the rest of us. They smiled at each of us in our turn, and seemed to be trying to calm us with their eyes and the tone in their voices, nodding their heads reassuringly. We had, after all, agreed to go where we were not necessarily comfortable going… inside ourselves. After we sat down and everyone was introduced around the circle, we were given a simple orientation.

The young male therapist-trainee suggested, "Just close your eyes now and relax. Be present with yourself." He continued, "Think back to when you were six or seven years old, and just allow yourself to be that age again and let come up whatever feelings might arise." He explained in a soft, slightly hypnotic voice, "You are safe here. There are no wrong feelings; just allow them to come out and be present with them."

As soon as I took a deep breath and allowed myself to settle down, I felt an overwhelming sadness welling up from deep inside, engulfing me. Suddenly and without warning, I began to cry uncontrollably. I was surprised, not knowing where this feeling came from and tried to choke it off, embarrassed at my outburst; but I was heaving with sobs I couldn't control. At the same time, I was curious and excited at this spontaneous outpouring. I was the only one in the group to express anything at all, so all eyes were on me.

The therapist drew attention to me by calling my name and in a compassionate voice asked, "What is happening for the six-year-old Tommy you've made contact with?"

I raised my bowed head and looked up from staring at my hands buried in my lap and explained, "When I was six years old, my dad was killed in a military jet crash."

The young man smiled again at me and nodded.

He said, "Tom, is there something, anything, that you want to say to your dad?"

I felt like everyone was staring at me…which, of course, they were.

In spite of my self-consciousness, I gave in to the emotions pouring out of me, my face contorting in grief, as I blurted out in the voice of a six year old, "DAD…WHY DID YOU HAVE TO DIE!?"

Breaking down again, I lowered my head and, burying my face in my hands, cried for the relationship with my dad that I had not known, shedding fourteen years of pent-up grief and pain down the front of my sweatshirt, soaking it. After what seemed like a few minutes, tear ducts emptied, I took a deep breath and raised my head from my chest, looking around the circle. I was embarrassed not knowing what had happened, not knowing any of these people, not knowing how I was supposed to feel or what to do next. The faces I looked into were faces of compassion and understanding. They smiled at me and nodded their acceptance and support of what I had just done.

The male therapist asked me to close my eyes again and focus inward for just a moment.

He said, "You've done good work, Tom. Now, just relax and be aware of your breath. Watch the air going in and out of your nose."

I listened, eyes closed, as he explained, "We humans can, for years, carry emotions locked up within us. In some cases, this subconscious, emotional energy can cause arrested development or even make us ill."

We continued around the circle, everyone taking a turn at expressing their feelings; but when lunch time came, I had been the only one to experience any kind of breakthrough. On the way home later that afternoon, I marveled at what I had experienced, wondering what else was locked deep within me. Feeling like a "broken" human being, I knew there was much to explore and to repair. But I also felt relieved and no longer feared looking inside. If I wanted help, I knew I could get it.

About this same time, I had heard through the grapevine that Chris, whom I had kept a fire burning for, had broken up with her boyfriend. She worked at a veterinarian's office and, as luck would have it, I had just adopted a four-year-old Irish setter whose name was Dylan. Dylan had made the unforgivable error of lifting his leg on a wall socket and shorting out the electrical system of the house his owners were renting. The landlord wasn't amused and Dylan had to find a new home. I agreed to be that new home. Of course, with the news that Chris worked at a vet's office, Dylan needed a physical exam right away! So, off to the vet we went, and by the end of the visit, Dylan had a clean bill of health and I had a date.

Chris was on the rebound and needed a friendly shoulder to lean on. I was given the opportunity to re-live and re-write the disaster of my failed attempt at a relationship with her. We became lovers on that first date. Within a few months, I moved in with Chris and lived with her for the next two years. She had been renting an apartment with a girlfriend, and when I summarily moved in, she understood and moved out. Dylan, who was not allowed in the apartment, went back to his original owners.

Since graduating from high school at the age of 17, I had spent four years trying to distance myself from all the things that reminded me of my connection to Frank Beardsley, which was hard to do when we shared a last name. It was well known around Central California; but when someone at the grocery store saw my name on a check I wrote and said, "Oh, are you from that big family they made the movie about? It must be so great for you!" I would cringe, feeling trapped by the deception that was my family. Fed up, I decided to change my name back to North. I asked my mother if we could meet alone, perhaps for lunch. She said she couldn't have lunch, but she had some errands to run and told me I could meet her at the Monterey Post Office.

I was waiting when she arrived and immediately said, "Hi Mom, I've thought a lot about this, and I'm going to change my name back to North." I explained, "The whole family combination thing was your idea. It hasn't worked out, and none of the North children feel like Beardsley's. We're Norths; I am a North, and I want my name back."

She looked at me with her hands on her hips and fire in her narrowing eyes. In a severe, threatening tone, she yelled; "Now, you listen to me, Mr. high-and-mighty! I have been trying to bring these two families together for eleven years! If you so much as try to undo what I am doing, then you are no longer my son! I disown you! Is that clear?!"

She was purple in the face by the time she finished. I had no idea she'd react that way. I blinked and wondered how I could have meant so little to her; to threaten disownment so vehemently. It didn't matter. I immediately backed down. She meant a lot to me and I wasn't prepared to sever that tie. I had known precious little of her affection and attention through the years and I wasn't ready to give up what minor connection I believed I had.

I responded by saying, "Well, if you feel that strongly, then I guess I won't do it. I won't change my name."

She looked at me sternly and replied, "Good. Now is there anything else you want? I have a lot of things to do."

Stunned, I slowly shook my head "no."

"Good," she stated with finality. And without so much as a "good-bye," she was gone.

I stood there for a few moments, startled at how misguided I had been about how she would react. It was many years later that I learned how little I really did mean to my mother. I was told by her sister Kay that Mom always spoke disapprovingly of me. She was Catholic through and through, and I had rejected Catholicism at the age of thirteen. I was the uncontrollable child, the one who always went his own, unrepentant way. Mom resented my behavior and my rejection of her grand scheme and with so many other children around, it was easy to emotionally cut me off. As a result of the emotional drubbing I had just taken, I resolved to keep the Beardsley name for the time being. But I had created a chasm between my mother and me that never narrowed, never went away. Much to my chagrin, the estrangement I had often felt worsened from that moment on.

All this time, I had continued to work at both the Hatch Cover and the donut shop and had managed to earn 30 transferable units from the local junior college and I even made the honor roll. It is a testament to the resiliency of youth that I could do all this, in addition to getting addicted to drugs, kicking the habit and taking on a third job working at a local scuba diving shop. I had been diving at just about every opportunity I could find and figured becoming a scuba instructor would be a good next step in my efforts to become Mike Nelson; or at least like Mike Nelson.

Ed and Bob Lederer were overweight, middle-aged brothers who answered the siren call of entrepreneurship and opened Aquarius Dive Shop in Monterey. I was one of their first customers and it was there that I would get my tanks filled and buy the occasional piece of equipment. I bought most of my stuff at garage sales, but the little things like o-rings and snorkel holders aren't found there. During the summer of 1974, I told Ed I wanted to be a scuba instructor and he hired me on the spot. Somewhere along the way, the job description changed because I spent a lot of time mopping floors, filling tanks and very little time assisting in the teaching of scuba classes. During the class time I did participate in, I wondered which of the overweight middle-aged doctors, lawyers or contractors was going to have a heart attack and die during class. After about a year of this, I was helping balance the books with Ed and realized that he was making about five thousand dollars a year, net. My enthusiasm for the business side of scuba died right there.

Not long after, I was approached by Mom and asked to take over the running of the donut production line on a permanent basis. She told me I would earn the same wage I was making at the Hatch Cover. I was next in line for a waiter's job which was where the big money was; but Mom led me to believe that if I didn't agree to work at the donut shop, she would have to do the work herself. I felt bad for her and agreed. I had been making about eight hundred dollars a month at the Hatch Cover, so I expected to be paid that amount for the work. Very quickly I found out she and Frank lied. I should have known better. I felt like Charlie Brown trying to kick the football, when Lucy says she promises she won't pull it away. Good grief!

After three months of being paid with donuts, coffee, and promises, I asked the new manager at the Hatch Cover if I could have my old job back. He told me I would have to start again at the bottom of the busboy pecking order. I swallowed my pride and took the job. I told my mother I would work at the donut shop until they could find a replacement. Wrong move again; she simply couldn't find a suitable replacement. Imagine that!

By this time, I was 21 and had been feeling physically horrible all of the time. The doctor who gave me a physical looked at me after the results of the examination were in and said, "I'm finding it hard to put the results of your physical in perspective. "What have you been doing to yourself?" he asked, incredulously. "You have the body of an out-of-shape forty- year-old. You've got two hernias and an ulcer!"

Sheepishly, I replied, "Well, I guess… I'm eating my own cooking! Every shift at the donut shop, I drink a half-gallon of coffee and eat a dozen donuts."

That diet and the heavy manual labor had taken its toll. I was a mess.

"Well then, you should quit," the doctor counseled me.

"Will you write me a prescription?" I asked.

"Absolutely!" he said with disgust in his voice. The prescription he gave me was the permission I needed to sever myself from the indentured servitude I felt toward my mother.

Planning my departure from the family business raised the question of what I would do next. I had known since grade school that college was somewhere in my future. Riding in a car with her one day, I had told Mom that I wanted to get a degree in business.

She tried to dissuade me, saying "You don't need to go to college, Tommy. Just keep working. If things go right, you can take over the donut shop someday. Besides, you aren't cut out for college."

I stared out through the windshield, knowing and believing she was wrong. I thought, perhaps she's telling me this because she wants to make sure she doesn't have to pay for my education. Or maybe she just wants to keep me working at the donut shop. But the worst thought was the most hurtful. Maybe she really thinks I'm stupid. Regardless, I'm going to college and no one's going to stop me.

I knew that some of my young male relatives had gone to Alaska to work for Auntie's husband in his fishing canneries, and figured I could work for him, too, and save money for school.

Leaving the donut shop was the first in a series of events that helped me make a break from the twisted ties I had to my family. Shortly before I quit, Frank approached me and told me I would have to take on two more days a week. I had been working only four days a week there, so that I could work weekends and a couple of evenings at the Hatch Cover, where I actually made money. I quickly did the math in my head and realized Frank's demand would cut into my other work, costing me valuable income.

I looked at him with determination, something that was hard for me and told him, "I can't do that."

He looked at me with his usual scowl and said, "Well, you don't have a choice. I'm telling you, you're going to work, and that's that!"

I looked him square in the eye and said, "No. I'm not going to. Do it yourself!"

He looked back at me and turning beet red with rage (something I had seen all too often) blurted out, "You have to! I am the father and you are the son! The son has to do what the father tells him to do! Now, do as I say!"

I could have avoided the confrontation by giving him his way, but I was determined to stand my ground. I wasn't sure if he was going to try to beat me; but in spite of my two hernias and ulcer, I considered myself a reasonably strong young man and thought maybe I could hold my own if he wanted to fight. Actually, up to that point in my life, I had never been in a fight. I had bluffed my way through a couple of confrontations in high school, but I wanted nothing to do with fighting, given the steady diet of violence I couldn't escape at the Beardsley home. I had occasionally worked out with Nick, who had been on the wrestling team in high school, and at that moment, I thought I might be able to draw on what I had learned from him.

I also realized, though, that those skills might not be much use against a man who had been trained as a boxer; but they were all I had. I was ready to stand my ground. Frank clenched his jaw and started to raise his fists. I looked at him calmly and said, "No. Do it yourself. I quit. Not only will I not work your extra two days, but I quit. I'm going to Alaska to work for Uncle on his fishing boats. Then I'm going to college."

I turned and walked away from him, ignoring his furious shouts for me to "turn around and come back this instant!" Previous to this moment, I had not known such certainty and resolve in Frank's presence. I knew that I had made the right decision. I felt free and ready to walk into my future. I had defeated Frank as one adult to another, and left him in the middle of his temper tantrum.

Mom and the eight of us, nine months after my dad died
San Leandro, California –1961

12

THE PATHMAKER

About a year before I left for Alaska, I was sitting around smoking pot with four of my friends. As we were solving all the problems of the world we focused on the extraordinary experience we were having together. We were relaxed, we felt expansive, laughter came easily and great ideas for world peace flowed freely from one to another of us. We marveled that we were able to get high by chemically stimulating neural connections in our brains. I suggested that if we could get high chemically, this proved that neural connections can, in fact, be stimulated. If this shift could take place chemically, then why couldn't it be stimulated in other ways? It seemed to me that there must be some non-chemical way to achieve this shift in awareness. In the bravado of the moment we agreed that the pot we were smoking involved a chemical overload that was no doubt doing damage. But, was it worse than alcohol? We didn't care. Or did we? Sure, we were enjoying ourselves, but how could we get the high without destroying brain cells or invoking side effects we were unsure of? I realized and had been thrilled that drugs provide an escape to an alternate reality, but there are side effects to every drug, some of which are unhealthy. Realizing this had helped me to kick using the harder drugs, but marijuana was different; or so I thought.

I was a desperately unhappy person living an emotionally abysmal existence. Marijuana helped me to feel better, to forget, however briefly, the lie that my life had become. Smoking pot may have been a recreational pursuit for my friends, but for me it was therapeutic. Intuitively, I knew that I couldn't cope in this manner forever, but at the time, I didn't feel like I had a lot of affordable options. Thankfully, I didn't have to wait long before one came along.

In January of 1975, one of my good friends, Tom Snyder, came to my house and told me that he had discovered a way to stimulate the shift in consciousness without using chemicals.

"I just learned how to do it today at the center for Transcendental Meditation," he said. "It's amazing!"

"Then you are in a potentially dangerous spot, my friend," I replied, "because you are standing between me and the door! I'm heading down there right now!"

The Transcendental Meditation (TM) center was across from the Post Office in Monterey that led "spiritual seekers" through a seven-step, three-day process that began with an introductory lecture. I drove my bus to downtown Monterey and walked into the small office suite they occupied. The entrance was through a Dutch door. The glass paned top was open. On the door, hanging under a pushpin from a string was a white cardboard sign that said, "Shhh, someone is meditating." I walked in and seeing several pairs of shoes on the floor just inside the room, I took mine off and set them with the others. I sat down in the small lobby and looked around. There were posters on the walls with multi-colored graphs that looked very scientific. They had phrases on them like Increased Brain Wave Coherence, and Lower Blood Pressure. I hadn't a clue what that meant, but it seemed encouraging. The aroma of sandalwood incense came from the next room. I sat there for a few minutes taking in the feel of the place. I felt excited, as if a new chapter in my life was about to begin.

The door to the other room opened and out walked a young man in his mid to late twenties dressed in a business suit. I introduced myself and learned that his name was Dan and he had been a classmate of my older step brothers and sisters at the local Catholic high school. He gave me some brochures and asked me to come back for an introductory lecture the next evening. The lecture was a sales pitch, telling me all the benefits I would receive from practicing TM. The next step was a preparatory lecture which explained the mechanics of thought as it relates to the experience of meditation. I was told I would be given a "mantra" and would be instructed to repeat it internally, but to never say it out loud. I thought this was charming, although perhaps a little strange. I asked why we don't say the mantra out loud. Kathy, the TM instructor giving the lecture, answered, "In the same way we don't plant a seed and then dig it up every day to see how much it has grown, we let the vibration of the mantra establish itself in our physiology and in our psychology. We want the mantra to allow us to dive deep into our own being. We want it to penetrate, deep into the inner-sphere. We can't do that if we are saying it out loud into the atmosphere. That would be sending the vibration in the wrong direction." That made sense to me, and I was intrigued by how deep and wise she was. She seemed so dignified and respectful, so together.

The next day I returned for my "initiation." I was nervous, but also excited. I hoped that this might be the start of something new and important in my life. When I went into the initiation room, I could smell the sandalwood incense. On a small table covered by a white tablecloth was a picture of a bearded dark-skinned Indian man in robes sitting cross-legged and smiling gently. In that simple smile was a message for me. It said, "Everything will be all right." My nervousness began to subside.

The first time I meditated I found my spirit suddenly growing lighter, and I felt less emotionally bound up—as though a weight had been lifted from my shoulders. This experience, however brief, made an impact on me in that I felt an expansion that was at the same time physical and profoundly spiritual. It was similar to, but unlike the consciousness expansion I had known through drug use. However, this time I was sober and straight. After that first meditation, I resolved to follow the guidance I was given and never say the mantra out loud.

Having suffered so many traumas as a child, I had become cynical, sarcastic and unwilling or unable to sincerely compliment another person. And yet, after my first TM experience, it was as though that barrier disappeared and I could give a compliment to another person when appropriate. I went over to the Beardsley family home that evening and my sister Jeanie looked like she was going out on a date. She had on a dress and make-up and was looking particularly attractive. I found myself complimenting her on her looks and telling her how lucky this young man was that she was dating. She was surprised, as a compliment was a rare thing in the Beardsley household. (I was not the only one short on compliments.) I was surprised to hear the encouraging words come out of my mouth. I went home to Chris and found myself able to sincerely express my feelings to her in a way that I had not been able to articulate until that evening. I shocked myself with my directness. I told her, "I love you!" She looked at me in surprise and said, "Something is different about you. What is it?" I told her about meditation. She smiled and said, "Well, it certainly seems to be bringing the best out in you." But she avoided responding to my declarations of love.

Needless to say I was intrigued and wanted to learn more about this new experience of TM. I looked forward to the next day, when I would go back to learn more about what was actually taking place inside my head during meditation." I was pleased to attend the follow-up class because I got to meditate again. "No effort or judgment; just be with the mantra," Kathy calmly told me. The high of meditation was much better than the high of smoking pot; I never smoked again… well, almost never.

I have always been a subscriber to that very American value that if a little is good, more is better. I asked Kathy, my TM teacher if I could meditate more than twenty minutes. She said, "Only under controlled circumstances. Meditation is not child's play. While it may have aspects that you find entertaining, it is not an entertainment. It is a serious spiritual exercise. Don't treat it lightly." I asked her what those controlled circumstances were. She said there were meditation retreats available where I could meditate for twenty minutes, more than twice a day. I said, "Sign me up!"

Two weeks later, I was at the Asilomar Conference Grounds in Pacific Grove, attending my first meditation retreat. I was taught how to do a specific set of yoga postures, which I could do for 15-20- minutes, followed by five minutes of alternate nostril breathing. I found myself calming down as I did this yogic breathing. After trying this for five minutes, with eyes closed, I was instructed to begin my mantra. Wow! I dropped right out of my body. I didn't know where I went, but I was gone. It seemed like a couple of minutes had passed when I came out of it, but it had been twenty minutes. This was cool!

The Retreat lasted only two days, but even so, I felt a new set of possibilities opening up inside of me. The knots of tension in my abdomen seemed to be not quite so tight. Observing my growing sense of internal calm, I wanted to be in that peaceful state forever. Filled with hope that I could straighten my life out, I asked how I could do more meditation. Kathy said there was a fully-accredited university in Fairfield, Iowa, where students break from their studies as part of the curriculum and are allowed to meditate several times a day for a month. A month! This just had to be for me; I could study business and meditate. I resolved at that moment to attend Maharishi International University (MIU), now called Maharishi University of Management (MUM). The one prerequisite was a course called the "Science of Creative Intelligence." The what? Kathy explained that what she called SCI was the philosophical basis for the experience of meditation. Without the knowledge of SCI, the experience of meditation is like eating a strawberry without knowing what it was. "Having the knowledge enriches the experience," she said. Fine with me, I thought. Just get me to where I can meditate more.

Having made this decision, I wasn't sure how I was going to announce my plans to Chris. We had been living together, making it up as we went along for well over a year. My idea was going to be a radical change in direction. She was intrigued by my new, more positive slant on life, and had made arrangements to learn to meditate also. After a few weeks of practicing TM and then attending a Residence Course together, I suggested to her that we get married and go to MIU and become students. Before the words had left my mouth I could tell by the look on her face that this was not going to happen. She confirmed it with a single "No." Her response was no surprise to me.

I knew all along that she did not return my passionate feelings for her, so it was painful, but no great shock. I was grateful for the time I had spent with her and the closure it had given me, but it was time for both of us to get on with our lives, albeit in different directions.

Having continued with the daily experience of meditation, I regularly went to share my discovery with my younger brothers and sisters who were still living at home. I tried to put into words what I had experienced. "It was like…well, it was like…um, it was like…" I couldn't explain it. In spite of my poor communication skills at the time, my family members said there was something different about me. I seemed happy and more relaxed to them. Mom and Frank wanted to know how this had happened. I arranged to have an introductory lecture given at the Beardsley home. Frank invited the parish priest from the Carmel Mission to attend because he was afraid that TM was a religion. The TM teacher was Dan again, who, as mentioned earlier, had attended a local catholic high school with some of the older Beardsley offspring. Dan understood the issues surrounding TM and religion. He handled the priest's and everyone else's questions with a calm dignity and satisfied them that meditation is a stress management technique, not a threat to any religious beliefs. Eventually ten members of my family learned to practice TM, including Frank and Mom. Most of them expressed some sense of improvement in their lives, except Frank, who complained that he shouldn't have had to pay to learn.

I reminded Mom of my plans to go to college to earn a degree in business.

She looked at me for a moment and said matter-of-factly, "Tommy, you don't need a college education. It's just not necessary."

I couldn't believe my ears and just stared at her, thinking, but not saying, there you go again, trying to undermine me.

I was used to her rejections, her put-downs, her pulling the rug from out from under my feet, but it didn't make it hurt any less. I wondered how she could say such a thing to me. The skin on my face tingled as I squinted at her trying to understand why she constantly tried to frustrate my efforts to improve myself. I thought that perhaps she didn't want me going to college because she hadn't. There are people who feel slighted if their children have a better life than they do. Maybe my mom was one of them.

Regardless, her disapproval convinced me more than ever that I was doing the right thing by going to MIU. I told Frank that I wanted to go to MIU. He looked at me seriously and with his hand on my shoulder said, "Let me give you some advice, Tommy. When you get into the business world, there won't be time for this meditation stuff. You can't take twenty minutes out of your day when you are working. You have to be realistic about this. And anyway, why would you want to go to a meditation school? Go get a real education."

I don't know why I expected to find support among my family, so I quit talking to them about my plans, which left me almost no one to talk to except myself. I knew I wanted to be a person of substance in the world, someone who mattered. However, looking inside, all I saw was grief, pain, anger, abuse and the darkness that came from it. None of what I saw within myself was good and I knew that without a dramatic change in direction, I would become just another lost soul, wandering the planet, blaming everyone else for my problems. I clung to the hope that TM and maybe MIU (as opposed to some other college) could help me start to heal—because in my own sense of reality, I was a seriously broken soul.

I didn't know it then, but I had enlisted many of the forces of nature to be my guardians. The rivers and the forests, the ocean and the beaches had been my place of refuge, my protectors when I needed a break from the insanity of my domestic environment. They were the places where little Tommy could breathe and stay spiritually alive.

What was about to become my next adventure became a quantum leap on my journey as it magnified the healing power of nature on the wild and pristine waters of Alaska.

Tom, Seattle, Washington – 1975

13

ALASKAN ADVENTURE
PART 1

The only thing that stood between me and my college education was money. I had been making enough at two of my three jobs to support myself, but I had little savings. With an uncle in Seattle who owned a huge fishing operation in Alaska, I decided to ask him for a summer job on one of his salmon fishing boats. But before asking him, I knew I'd need to get myself prepared for the job.

In order to gain the skills necessary for working on a large fishing boat, I volunteered to work on the first charter dive boat in Monterey, where I worked weekend mornings as divemaster. *The El Tigre* was a converted fishing boat about 35 feet long and at least forty years old, harkening back to the heyday of the Monterey sardine fishery. Her propeller drive shaft was bent, causing her to pull to port, unless the person manning the wheel kept her on course by steering to starboard all the time, which became exhausting. Another issue relevant to my preparation for a job in Alaska was that I had always had a tendency to be seasick, but I decided I'd just have to tough it out. How bad could it be? I found out it could be miserable. Dramamine, the seasick pill of the day, made me drowsy to the point of falling asleep, so I stopped taking it. That left me "toughing it out." I can only imagine the conversations that took place between the customers and the owners of the vessel as they described the divemaster (me) as having spent more time heaving over the rail than filling tanks and crewing the boat. But I was working without pay, so I never heard a complaint.

Red, the skipper of the *El Tigre,* was also a holdover from the bygone sardine days. A grizzled, seventy-something-old sailor with a perpetual three-day beard on his lined and weathered face, he wore a tattered blue captain's hat and a pea coat at all times. Scandinavian in appearance, he had grown up in Nebraska and didn't see the ocean until WWII when he had joined the army and was shipped to Europe to fight the Nazis. Somewhere along the way, he fell in love with the sea and resolved to become a sea captain. After the war, he had been in the Merchant Marine for a time before settling in Monterey as a fishing boat crewman. Unfortunately, his other love affair had been with the bottle, which had kept him as a crewman most of his life.

Red came with the boat. He had been the skipper of the *El Tigre* before it was purchased by the Monterey Bay Company, an outfit owned by a couple of Monterey real estate developers who had a romantic notion of operating the first charter dive boat in Monterey. Red barely spoke, other than to quietly give an order or request something. When I met him in the tiny galley of the boat, a young woman about my age sat beside him. She was slender, perhaps about five-foot five and very pretty with dark eyes and black hair that hovered around her shoulders. The owners of the boat introduced me as the new deck hand and divemaster, which shocked the young woman, who had apparently been Red's deck hand and had some kind of dependency relationship with him which I never understood. Red shrugged at her. I was willing to work weekends for free, an arrangement which she could not compete with. However, I hadn't been told that I was displacing her and costing her a job; so I felt bad. But I needed the experience and kept my mouth shut, as the boat owners explained to Red and the young woman, whose name I cannot recall, how the dive boat would be operated. It would be a two-man crew: one on the deck, filling scuba tanks and assisting the divers, and one in the wheelhouse, operating the boat. Red would help me out on the deck when the boat was anchored.

After the owners left, the young woman began to cry and held fast to Red's arm. He gently explained to her that the scuba tanks were heavy and, besides, she wasn't scuba- certified. With a despairing look, she insisted she could learn. Red gingerly replied that she couldn't gain the experience needed for the job fast enough, adding that I was already an assistant scuba instructor and divemaster. Red went out to smoke a cigarette and I was left standing there, alone, with the suffering young woman. I genuinely felt sorry for her and apologized for taking her job.

"If it hadn't been me, it would have been someone else with scuba experience. I'm sorry."

She looked at me sadly and replied, "I wish I had been able to meet you under other circumstances. I'm sorry, too." With that, she stood up and left the little galley of the *El Tigre*, climbing up the two steps to the main deck and stepped off the boat. I never saw her again.

Over the next four months, I developed my sea-legs enough to earn the job in Alaska. My uncle agreed to give me and my brother Phil, who had recently turned 18, a 'lowest-man-on-the-totem-pole' deck-hand position. Chris and Phil's girlfriend, Laura, drove us to the San Jose airport for our flight to Seattle, where we were met by Uncle and Auntie.

Auntie was my mother's second eldest sister. She had always been supportive and loving to her many nieces and nephews. With only one daughter, Auntie had helped her extended family generously over the years. She had tried to talk my mother out of marrying Frank, for she wasn't fooled by his superficial attempts at charm. She had seen what he was, and did what she could, as had many of my mother's family; but to no avail. What she could do was be there for the kids, something she has excelled at through the years.

Uncle had been an Army Air Corps rescue boat captain in the Philippines during WWII. His assignment had been to rescue downed pilots who had landed at sea. He had spent the four years of the war cruising the many islands of the Philippines, contacting the native chiefs and maintaining a support network among them. When the war was over, he helped rebuild the Philippines' fishing industry. Uncle was fearless, notoriously mischievous, and even at a young age, had a nose for a good deal. A story is told by Auntie that when Uncle was in high school in Spokane during the Depression, he was loitering downtown with his buddies when they spotted the police chief and a couple of his men looking suspiciously this way and that, making sure they were not followed as they stopped their squad car and turned into an alley. This aroused Uncle's curiosity, so the boys sneaked up to the corner building and peaked around into the alley. They watched the police chief and his men come out of an old clapboard garage, double check the lock on the door, and drive away. When the police were gone, Uncle posted a lookout and broke a window to get into the garage. He and his buddies found it full of booze. Not just any booze, but cases upon cases of Canadian Scotch whiskey. As this was during the time of prohibition, a pretty penny could be made if the right buyer was found for the Scotch. The boys brought around a pickup truck and spirited away the Scotch, burying it in a remote area of a nearby forest.

Uncle took a couple of bottles to the town brothel and asked how much they would pay for the liquor. Testing his developing negotiating skills, Uncle and his friends made what was to them a small fortune selling their treasure to the madam of the house.

At the end of WWII, while assisting in the rebuilding effort, the opportunity to deal in surplus military equipment presented itself. Uncle had the connections and the savvy, and knew who needed what among the various tribes on the many islands. He made money trading and selling, but it lasted only a short time. As the chaos of the end of the war gave way to a more orderly accounting of equipment and personnel, the deal-making slowed down abruptly.

Before the party was completely over, Uncle made a last ditch effort to broker the sale of an entire freighter full of beer. Unfortunately, the Navy took the freighter out to sea and sank it, beer and all. That would be unthinkable today, of course, but at the end of WWII, government and military surplus equipment was plentiful. The concern was that if all that stuff came back to the U.S. mainland, then the excess supply would drive prices of consumer goods down and depress the economy. However, an idea was planted in Uncle's mind that blossomed many years later.

Uncle had worked in the fishing industry before the war. He knew that Alaska was a place where his military leadership skills could be put to good use. When he went back to civilian life, he began using fish traps to catch large quantities of salmon at the mouths of the rivers that they returned to during their spawning runs. Back in the 1950s, resource management was in its infancy. By the time fish traps had been outlawed by the brand new state of Alaska, he had made enough money from them to buy an old, defunct cannery near the mouth of the Kenai River. He slowly rebuilt and added to it over the years. One of the great salmon rivers of Alaska, the Kenai was famous for its giant king salmon and runs of literally millions of sockeye salmon. Because of their firm flesh and deep red color, sockeyes were prized for canning.

Uncle researched the purchase of surplus Navy vessels left over from the war. He knew that there were dozens of them, floating in 'mothball' fleets in many of the coastal waters of the U.S. and could be had very cheaply. Employing his astute sense of business management and uncanny people skills, by the 1960s, Uncle had built a fishing empire consisting of three canneries, six coastal freighters, which he converted to salmon tender/king crab fishing boats, and over 400 gill-netters which were the 30-foot boats that the salmon were caught from. Uncle innovated the construction of fishing boats out of aluminum. He leased them to fishermen for the salmon season and bought their fish from them, hauled the boats at season's end and did all the maintenance. He became affectionately known as "Uncle" to the fishermen. Uncle treated them well, catered to their needs, and they loved him for it.

Uncle was the first to have the holds of his cargo ships converted to refrigeration. He then had the ability to fill the holds of the ships with sea water, add more salt to create brine—which doesn't freeze—and lower the temperature to 27°F. The fish caught in the far-flung islands and bays of the 34,000 miles of Alaskan coastline could then be transported to the canneries at Kenai and Kodiak for processing. It often took days or weeks to deliver the salmon, but at that low temperature they arrived as fresh as the day they were caught. Many of the other canneries lacked storage facilities, so when the run was on and they had as many salmon as they could process, fishermen were often told to stop fishing. What the fishermen heard was, "Stop earning money." Not Uncle. He told his fishermen to keep fishing, and he would buy as many salmon as they could catch.

Phil and I arrived on a Friday and spent the weekend visiting with Uncle and Auntie, and sailing with them on their 45-foot sailboat. May weather in Seattle is often calm with clear skies, and it was just like that for our visit. We sailed about Puget Sound, listening to Uncle tell us stories of the Alaskan wilderness and the old days of the fishing industry. At 62 years of age, he had seen a lot and was a great story-teller. Auntie sat next to him in the cockpit of the sailboat, working on astrological charts for Phil and me. She had been interested in astrology for years and had developed a degree of skill that even had Uncle paying attention to the guidance she gave him.

During that first visit, I was sunning myself on the foredeck of the boat, just within earshot of Uncle and Auntie. Through my sunglasses, I noticed as Auntie looked up from her charts and stared at me for a moment. She then leaned over to Uncle and said, "This one will be successful at whatever he puts his mind to. If I were you, I'd train him to run the business." Uncle glanced at me, silently looked at back at her for a moment, and nodded, saying nothing.

When it was time to report for work on the ships, Uncle drove Phil and me down to the docks at Lake Union, where his corporate headquarters was located. We walked straight down to where the "dog fleet" was being loaded with cargo bound for the five canneries in Alaska. These converted steel cargo vessels, each about 130 feet long and 35 feet abeam, were painted black along the water line, to about five feet above it. White above that level, the steel ships showed rust spots here and there. The two-story wheelhouse was set in the stern where the crew lived and operated the ship. On top of the wheelhouse were the antennae for the loran, telecom and radar equipment. Below the roof, copper green awnings shielded the picture windows of the bridge from the sun. From there, the captain could see the sea about him and survey the deck, fifteen feet below. Each of the two holds in the center of the deck was covered by 15 by 15 foot steel hatch covers. The holds could carry half a million pounds of salmon between them. The decks swept forward and rose to a raised foc'sle, rising ten feet above the main deck. The bow lockers were housed there. Within them were the refrigeration system and freezers.

As I watched the action on deck, salty-looking, bearded seamen were lowering into the holds pallets loaded with cases of cans and equipment bound for the canneries. There were 2-ton hydraulic cranes with 20-foot arms mounted on each ship, operated by a senior crewman. Down into the holds the cargo was lowered. A few minutes later, voices in the hold would echo, "Bring her up!"

My uncle introduced me to Captain Dave, skipper of the Airedale, the ship I would be crewing on. Dave was a big Norwegian whose face could barely be seen through the bushy blond hair and beard that covered his head, creating a mane around his shoulders that hid his shirt collar. Dave's plaid shirt barely covered his bulging belly, and his blue eyes glared at me from beneath bushy yellow eyebrows, sizing me up. Then he smiled and said, "Welcome aboard. Stow your gear and join the millionaires club in the hold. You can start stacking cans."

I smiled back and replied, "Aye, sir."

Uncle and Dave shared a laugh as I left them to go aboard, wondering what the "millionaire's club" was.

After stowing my gear inside the door of the wheelhouse, I climbed down a ladder that was welded to the inside of the hold, twenty feet to the bottom. Entirely made of steel, every sound echoed off the walls of the hold. Whispers between the several shabbily dressed old men around me could easily be heard. Their sunken cheeks under week-old whiskers suggested something other than millionaires. I introduced myself around as Tom, just as the next pallet of boxes filled the opening above us. I loaded boxes for the next few hours. The boxes were light, as they contained nothing but empty cans that would ultimately be filled with salmon at the canneries.

Eventually, the crewman on deck shouted, "Lunch in the galley!"

Without a word, the "millionaires" stopped what they were doing, and climbed the steel ladder that was welded to the hold, and headed for the galley. I followed them, and learned over a meal of chicken stew and mashed potatoes that the millionaire's club was comprised of local winos who earned $20 and two meals for a day's work loading cargo into the holds. Their sunken cheeks were accentuated by noses covered with deep blue veins and small red capillaries. Whatever gray and white hair they had left on their heads stuck out from beneath dirty blue and brown woolen caps drawn low across their foreheads. The millionaires kept to themselves, every one of them wearing somber expressions that reminded me of Grumpy from Snow White. Their conversation centered on who was coming and going down at the soup kitchen and the shelter. Fat Bob had brought a gun to the shelter and got caught with it. He wasn't allowed to come back anymore. Little Johnny had brought in a bottle of whiskey and he, too, was kicked out.

Over lunch, I met the other members of the crew with whom I would be spending the summer. The first mate, Richard, was a late twenty-something, with thick, dark brown hair down to just below his shoulders. His dark hair and full beard gave him a look that very much resembled a biblical picture of Jesus. The crew called him J.C. He seemed dismissive and cold, however, unlike my imagined sense of his namesake. His attitude may have been the result of my relative status on the crew. After all, I was the new deck hand, the lowest position possible, and he was the first mate.

The engineer who kept the ship in running order was Eric, another blond, bearded Norwegian. Soft-spoken and polite, he seemed to have a respect and consideration for people that was endearing and helped me relax around the others. The senior deckhand was Tommy. He was a big kid, about my age and height, but weighed about thirty pounds more than me. He had a bush of dark curly hair on his head, but none on his round baby face that made him look much younger than his age. He was likable, but didn't seem to have much to say. I would be sharing a stateroom with him. This was his fourth year on the ship and it was his job to show me my way around the deck.

After lunch we took a quick jaunt over to our stateroom. As he showed me my bunk, I was surprised at the relatively large room we shared. About ten by twelve feet, it was more like a bedroom than I had expected. Below two portholes on the outer wall was a desk that was wide enough for two chairs and a row of drawers on each side. Without looking at it, Tommy pulled open the larger bottom drawer and said it would be for my toilet kit and other non-clothing items. There was a closet for the hanging clothes and drawers for the folded ones like underwear and socks. As I stared at the drawer he had opened, he looked down and grinned at me.

"Oh yeah, I forgot about that." We were looking down at nearly five pounds of pot that filled the drawer. "I'll move it. This is still your drawer."

"That's a lot of weed," I commented casually.

"Yeah, a summer's worth: scored it last week. I've been so busy getting the ship ready that I forgot about it."

I smiled at him. I spoke the language and played the game (all too well). He sensed my comfort and we both knew we would get along well together. Tommy's bunk was by the door. Mine was on the opposite wall from Tommy's, against a bulkhead. On the opposite side of the bulkhead was a twelve-thousand horsepower generator. I was to find that the steel wall vibrated like holy hell with the generator right on the other side. The steel frame of my bunk would shake, too. So would my mattress, and so would my bladder several hours into every sleep. However, I didn't find that out until we were underway.

After lunch and for the next three days, we loaded boxes and more boxes and more boxes of cans. My brother Phil was doing the same on the Labrador, another of the dog fleet. *The Iron Head*, the third boat in the Seattle group was loading next to us. With hydraulic cranes whining and whirring, men scurrying and Dave's big voice shouting orders, we were ready to set sail, or rather, motor out to sea, by week's end. I was excited and had been careful to avoid making any stupid or embarrassing blunders.

The food on the Airedale was exceptional. The cook was Dave's girlfriend, who, I was glad to learn, had attended five cooking schools and was a master of international cuisine. She was tall, blonde, slender, had a sweet disposition and on top of all that, she was beautiful.

I fantasized that if Dave was not good to her, I'd be happy to step in and rescue her. In my dreams! She was thirty-something and worldly-wise. I was just a pup.

As we cast off lines from the dock, my pulse raced. *The Airedale* was "built for comfort, not for speed" as they say. At about five knots, the speed limit, we motored out of Lake Union, which narrowed into the Seattle Ship Canal and led to the locks, giant concrete containers, each one like a small dam, that helped ships and boats of all sizes negotiate the decline between the lake and the

Seattle harbor. Once in Puget Sound and around the peninsula, we headed north past Whidbey Island toward the straits of Juan de Fuca and the San Juan Islands.

The weather in the Pacific Northwest is at its best behavior in the summer. A few bright white clouds hung in the sky, but there was no wind and the temperature hovered in the eighties as we motored slowly north toward the inside passage. The salmon season was in full swing. Sport fishing boats dotted the calm waters of Puget Sound. I watched as fishermen reeled in and netted the silvery fish that we were on our way to Alaska to catch, although on an entirely different scale.

Whidbey Island passed on our right, and I stared at my old home, feeling odd, knowing it belonged in a former lifetime I had been disconnected from and could not return to. I was seven years old when I left the island and now, fourteen years had already gone by. We passed on the seaward side of the island, away from Oak Harbor, where I had spent the first years of my childhood, so the terrain wasn't familiar. Still, I couldn't help but wonder, What if my dad had come down with a cold and hadn't flown that day? What if the commander had found him a desk job when Dad had tried to turn his wings in? What kind of life might I have known in those intervening years? I'd still be a North. Funny, isn't it, how one event changes so many lives?

The narrow waters between the many islands that define the western boundary of the Inside Passage and the Canadian mainland that is its eastern boundary are both spectacular and potentially treacherous. The evergreen mountains of Vancouver Island and the sunshine coast of British Columbia squeeze a narrow waterway many hundreds of feet deep but less than a thousand feet wide in places. One of these is the Seymour Narrows. At less than a quarter mile wide, the volume of water that moves through the straight with each change of the tide is enormous. As the tide ebbs and flows, it increases in speed from slack to as much as seventeen knots. *The Airedale* approached the narrows when the tide had been flowing for most of the afternoon, picking up speed against us as we approached. If Dave could get us past this point before the tide reached its maximum speed, he could motor for several more hours before stopping for the night. If not, he would lose valuable time waiting for the tide to change and carry us through the narrows as it rose. At a maximum speed of twelve knots, the Airedale was much slower than the seventeen knot current at its peak. It seemed to Dave that he could make it. Thinking he might just squeeze through before the current became too fast, Dave throttled up to maximum speed. The bow wake rose as the Airedale fought the tide. Sport fishing boats lined the sides of the narrows, lines out, many of them landing salmon. The plucky Airedale chugged along, approaching the narrowest point of the waterway. Suddenly she slowed. Dave was lucky, though. *The Airedale* made it through the Narrows in time, with just a few seconds to spare.

Tommy looked at me and smiled, "If we were heavier and riding lower in the water, Dave wouldn't have tried that." Lacking experience, I had been oblivious to what had just taken place.

Every crew member except the cook stood watch. Tommy and I took the late night watch from midnight to 4 a.m. Looking out the wheelhouse windows, we could see only the lights on passing boats and the distant lights of the few buildings we passed. Given the narrow waterways, all the boat operators seemed to be aware of the increased danger of collision and kept well away from each other. I learned to read the radar and track our position. With my head bowed over the radar screen, I could see the other boats represented as a small or larger blinking dot moving across the screen. The boat's trajectory was tracked as a green line. Watching the other ships and boats passing by, I marveled at how I was participating in one of the great adventures a young man can have: life at sea.

During the day, I watched bald eagles soar above us, swoop out of the sky to grab a fish out of the water, or perch on a tree limb near the edge of land. Tugboats pulling barges of timber were a common sight, as were cruise vessels. The passengers on sailboats watched us motor by and often waved. The crews of the working boats seldom waved, however. They seemed a dour lot, taking for granted or having lost appreciation for the spectacular scenery around them. In contrast, I was feeling like those eagles, stretching my wings, soaring and reveling in my new found freedom.

We were between ports, so the work was light and sporadic. It consisted mostly of grinding rust off of the railings and re-sealing and painting the repaired spots. I enjoyed standing watch with the other crew members, listening to the sounds of Procol Harum play "A Whiter Shade of Pale" on the stereo in the wheelhouse.

The overall workload was made even lighter because Dave had given a ride to a couple of hitchhikers in Seattle. He made them work their way up the inside passage, which they did gladly and with a cheerful attitude. They were headed for Alaska, and planned to get off the ship as soon as they arrived. John and another Erik, both about my age, had camped their way from San Diego to Seattle, stopping for stretches of time in wilderness areas to explore and hunt. In the Trinity Mountains of California, they had shot an elk with the collapsible 30-06 they kept in their backpacks. Having smoked and dried the meat to make jerky, they generously shared it with the crew. It was the best jerky I had ever tasted—salty, peppery, and gamey—and I savored every chewy mouthful.

Our first port of call was Ketchikan. A small fishing and lumber town at the foot of the Tongass Rain Forest, Ketchikan has been Alaska's southernmost and first frontier port for a hundred and fifty years. It has called itself "the salmon capital of the world" for much of that time, and for good reason. The waters to the west of Ketchikan and its surrounding areas are teeming with salmon.

It was late in the evening when we docked. As soon as the ship was secured, Dave gave us permission to go into town. J.C., Tommy, Eric and I headed for the bars. We bade farewell to John and his pal, Erik. As I walked into the smoke-filled entrance of the first bar, I felt a rush of excitement course through me. Except for the juke box next to a small dance floor and the neon Miller's draft beer sign behind the bar, this place looked like we had just walked back in time a hundred years. Moose and deer heads next to ancient wolf hides adorned the walls, with crisscrossed snowshoes next to them, while straw and sawdust covered the wooden plank floor. Off in the corner, past the five tables next to the dance floor, were two pool tables. J.C. ordered a pitcher of beer and four glasses. As we were pouring beers from the pitcher, he toasted Alaska and all its pretty women while nodding toward the dance floor. An old

Native woman had come into the bar and went straight to the juke box. Long grey braids flowed past her weathered and sadness-lined white face, down to her waist. She was a tiny person, not more than five feet tall, entirely covered in a long brown skirt and a blue denim shirt under what looked like a ceremonial white vest covered in beads and shells. Looking hopefully into the domed glass of the juke box, she seemed to find what she was looking for, plunked quarters in the slot and moved gracefully to the middle of the dance floor. She began to dance what looked like a traditional native dance, even before the record queued up. It struck me as odd that, moments later, Procol Harum began to play "A Whiter Shade of Pale." She raised her hands over her head and swayed like a tree in the wind, her movements unrelated to the rhythm of the music. I watched her in amazement and felt a sadness sweep over me. I felt like an intruder; like the entire Anglo world was an intrusion. The collision of these two cultures was etched deeply and permanently in this old woman's face. As she danced, her sadness was masked behind a smile and closed eyelids. Lost in a world or a dimension I would never visit, she seemed, for the moment, apart from the troubles I sensed she had brought in with her.

I turned back to my crew mates and shook my head quizzically, as we smiled at each other and took a long draught from our beers. I kept glancing at the pool tables. J.C. caught my interest and challenged me to a game. He broke, and as he did so, said, "Oh, yeah, loser buys the next pitcher," all the while smiling like a spider to a fly.

But on my first turn, I ran the table. J.C. stared at me, frowning.

I nonchalantly nodded toward our table and said, "Whatever they want to drink."

Tommy and Eric began to laugh at J.C. Eric slapped his knee and bent over in delight.

"You been whooped, brother!" he chortled at J.C.

Tommy looked at me in awe. "Where did you learn to play like that?"

"We had a table in the basement floor of our house when I lived at home. Used to play four to five hours every night I could. You should see my high school report card. It's a disaster."

J.C.'s mood changed as he brought back the second pitcher from the bar. "Well boys, I don't think we're going to pay for much beer this summer," he said, grinning at Tommy and Eric. Eric turned to answer my questioning look.

Smiling wryly, he said, "To keep it friendly, there's an unwritten rule that we play for pitchers of beer. That way no one gets into too much money at the pool table and fights are kept to a minimum. You play like that, and we aren't spending much on the town this year, except for the hard stuff."

My currency on the boat rose that night. It might have been my imagination, but I seemed to notice just a bit more respect in the way I was treated by the crew; well, everyone except Dave, who never went into town with us.

From Ketchikan we motored around the northern end of Prince of Wales Island and out into the Gulf of Alaska. The seas were calm and the crossing uneventful for the seven hundred mile passage that took us five days. Our next port of call was the Kenai Packers Cannery at Kenai.

Kenai felt like a frontier town. Many of its roads were gravel or dirt, its buildings simple and drab. It sits on the north bank of the Kenai River, one of the most productive and famous salmon rivers in the world. All five North American species of Pacific salmon return to the Kenai every summer to spawn. Most sought after among them is the King salmon. Growing occasionally to over five feet long and weighing over 100 pounds, they attract sport fishermen from all over the world. The official world record sport caught King salmon from the Kenai weighed 97 pounds. My brothers, Phil and Gerry collected a 108 pound King from a gill netter in Kalgin Island one year, but that is not an official weight.

Much of the economy of the town is based on serving the commercial fishing industry. Kenai Packers is an important summer employer, with over 100 workers in the cannery and again as many fishermen dependent on selling their catch to Uncle.

The salmon runs are sequential and overlap. As one run is ending, another starts. It's common to have two or more kinds of salmon in the river at the same time. The best fish for canning is the red salmon, as it is a firm, oily and flavorful fish. Silver salmon are also sought after for the same reasons.

The Kenai River is about a hundred yards wide at its mouth. Milky blue in color, the water is fed by glaciers in the Kenai mountain range above Kenai Lake. The waters in the river run swiftly over gravel beds, in which the salmon take a break among the calmer, deep pockets in the gravel on the bottom. As we pulled up to the Kenai, the Airedale was forced to sit at anchor in Cook Inlet just outside the river mouth, waiting for the twenty-seven-foot tide to rise. We prepared the decks for unloading by loosening the huge, two-inch bolts that held the hatch covers in place. At the cannery, the hatch covers would be lifted with the ten-ton cranes and the cargo unloaded onto conveyors that carried the boxes of cans up into the warehouse.

While we worked I watched people in chest-high waders moving along the shore or in the shallow water. Early in the season, locals venture out into the river holding onto long wooden or aluminum poles at the river mouth, arms extended. They're staring at the end of the pole that disappears into the milky blue water, hoping for and expecting to see a wiggle of the pole as a red salmon swims into the small, two-foot long net at the end of the 15-foot pole. I watched the fishermen walking in the shallows of the river mouth to and from the shore as they retrieved the fish they had caught in their dip nets.

When the tide rose, the anchor was raised and the ship began to move upstream. *The Airedale* stayed in the main channel of the river, deep enough to accommodate the ship. Dave kept his eyes on the charts and his depth gauges. With a fifteen-foot draft, it would be a terrible embarrassment to run aground this close to the cannery which was only about a mile upstream.

The arrival of one of the dog fleet causes a stir at the cannery. The workers come out to the catwalk that runs around the building and gawk at the boat and its crew. The women want to see what kind of men there are, and the few men who work in the cannery stare in a state somewhere between envy and jealousy as they dream of working on the boats themselves.

Unloading the thousands of cases of cans and equipment took the better part of a week. Without the millionaires club, the work fell to me, Tommy and a couple of the guys from the cannery. The work was back-breaking, but also part of the adventure I had chosen. The summer days in Alaska are famous for lasting close to midnight. It is well-named "the land of the midnight sun." After Dave had worked us till we were about to drop, we ate a meal of steaks and potatoes, washed it down with creamy milk, and headed into town to bar hop. Tommy produced a big fat joint. He, J.C. and Eric took a hit and passed it to me. It was now June and I hadn't smoked at all since starting to meditate in February. But I wanted to be sociable, and be one of the guys, so I took a toke. I felt instantly guilty.

To compound my feeling, Eric looked at me quizzically and said, "I'm surprised that you'd smoke dope with the meditation you do. Most yogis don't do drugs."

I felt like a traitor to myself and to the new discipline I had started. On the next round of the fatty, I passed.

On the nights when we hit the bars, we didn't actually experience night. As we entered the first bar at 10:30 pm, the sun was still shining like high noon. I was surprised to see out on the dance floor, once again, an old native woman, much the same as I had seen in Ketchikan. I looked at Tommy with a question in my eyes and nodded my head that way. He understood and said, "Yeah, there's one in just about every bar. Go figure." I was then startled when the old woman plunked another quarter in the juke-box and "A Whiter Shade of Pale" began playing. I couldn't help wondering, what is it with this song?

Given my pool table performance in Ketchikan, the pressure was on for me to produce.

Eric was encouraging. "OK, Tom, bring us the beer," he said with a smile.

Tommy and J.C. were more challenging and doubtful. "But can he perform under pressure?" J.C. smirked, as I headed for the pool table.

After running the first four tables, there were two and a half pitchers of beer still to be consumed. The crew couldn't drink fast enough. Tommy grinned at me, "Hey, Tom! Slow down!"

The crew shared a very liquid belly-laugh. On the way back to the boat, I marveled that at 2 a.m., it was light again. We had completely missed whatever darkness had taken place.

Once the cargo was unloaded, the few items to be delivered to *The Airedale's* next destinations were loaded on board. Food supplies were re-stocked after our two-week trip from Seattle, and we cast off for the second leg of my Alaskan odyssey.

Tom aboard the M.V. *Airdale*-Kenai, Alaska – 1975

14

ALASKAN ADVENTURE
PART 2

The *Airedale* stopped overnight at Kodiak Island at the entrance of the Cook Inlet to deliver some equipment to the Alaska Packers Cannery which Uncle owned. Since there wasn't much to do on the ship besides read a book, listen to music, or write a letter, the crew jumped ship and headed into town to find a bar. As we entered our first stop and settled into chairs surrounding a small round table, I glanced over at the dance floor. Fortunately it was empty. The barmaid who came to take our orders was a twenty-something with black shoulder-length hair, about five feet tall and five feet wide. Yes, she was almost perfectly round. As she approached our table, I was looking around the room glancing toward the pool tables, looking for a game. I felt a hand brush against my cheek, and looked that way to see the smiling face of the barmaid not far from mine.

She said, "You have such beautiful eyes," as she blinked her lashes at me.

Tommy and Eric started to laugh, as I struggled to think of a response. She had taken me completely by surprise. I couldn't think of anything to say except, "Thank you."

J.C. wasn't laughing. If I wasn't mistaken, he looked as uncomfortable as I felt at the moment.

In my confusion I looked at Tommy and asked, "What the hell is going on?"

He leaned over to me and whispered, "The last time we were here, she said the same thing to J.C. He went home with her!"

Suddenly I understood; the joke was not on me at all.

After Kodiak, the *Airedale* set a course for Bristol Bay in the Bering Sea. We sailed toward the Aleutian Islands which reach out 1,200 miles, almost to Siberia. Standing the late watch, I looked into the green glow of the radar screen at dozens of small unnamed islands surrounding Unimak, the first Island of the Aleutian Archipelago. It struck me as odd that one of the smaller islands was moving.

I turned to Tommy and asked, "Do islands move?"

He smiled and said, "Not that I know of."

He walked over and peered into the radar screen. An object larger than any of the smaller islands we were weaving through was coming our way. If it was a ship, it was gigantic. Tommy changed the resolution of the screen to make the object larger. We stared at it for a while, realizing we would be passing within a mile of it in a short time. About an hour later we saw it; a Soviet liquid natural gas tanker ship. As it passed, we could see the deck lights illuminating the entire ship. CCCP was glowing out of the shadows of the hull. A giant catamaran, it was bound from some Siberian Soviet port to where, we couldn't even guess. I had never seen a ship so big. It seemed much bigger than an aircraft carrier. LNG tankers are often a thousand feet long, the decks a hundred and fifty feet off the water. The wheelhouse can be another hundred feet higher. By comparison, I was sitting in a wheelhouse thirty feet off the water. We were the proverbial David to this water-borne Goliath.

There is a gap between Unimak Island and Unalaska Island that provides a way to shorten the 1,200-mile trip around the whole Aleutian chain. Even so, it took a week to get to Bristol Bay. At the extreme inside point of Bristol Bay is the fishing village of Naknek on the banks of the Naknek River, home to one of the largest salmon runs in the world. Several large fish canning companies have processing factories here including Peter Pan, Star-Kist, and others.

Uncle made the decision early on not to build a cannery at Naknek. Canned or not, the fish had to be transported by ship to market; so it didn't make sense to keep a large employee base in such a remote area when the fish could be refrigerated and transported to Kenai for processing. It was closer to market and the fish could be processed in a modern canning factory. Instead, he leased a dock on the Naknek waterfront. The ship itself became the buying station.

Three days before, the holds had been filled with salt water, brined and refrigerated in preparation for taking on salmon. Fishermen who contracted to sell their fish to Uncle brought their fifteen- to thirty-foot boats alongside, tied up and had their catch lifted off their boats by crane. Some of the fishermen thought ahead and had lined their holds or skiffs with netting. That made it easier for the crane operator to lower a large scale with a hook dangling from it and have the fisherman slide metal rings attached to the corners of the net over the hook for hoisting the load. Then, up the net went, bulging with salmon, off the boat and over the railing of the ship. The crane operator, usually J.C. or Eric, swung the net full of fish over to another crewman, who recorded the weight of the load on a clipboard from the scale. Once the data was gathered, the fish were lowered into the hold. If the fisherman had been lazy or hadn't thought to line his hold, the crane operator lowered a brailer, a stiff, circular net about four feet across and just as deep. The fisherman had to put dozens of fish into the brailer in ones or twos. It wasted time and was frowned upon by the crew and the captain.

Tommy told me the Airedale had a capacity of over a hundred thousand fish, so we loaded as fast as we could. I was sent down into the hold of the boat to help the fisherman load the brailer. I was shown how to swipe a sharp fish pew, which looked to me like a hay hook, into the fish's head and swing it into the net. Some of the fishermen were either lazy or surly or both, and would pierce the fish's belly with the pew. Bacterial contamination then became a concern. The rule was if you punctured the fish anywhere but near the head, the buyer could refuse the fish. I was in the hold of a boat watching a fisherman with a nasty frown on his face pierce fish after fish in the belly.

I called up to Dave and told him. Dave came down and went through every fish in the brailer and refused about twenty fish. He looked fiercely at the fisherman and said, "I don't care how

low the price is! Be more careful or I'll turn away the whole lot!"
After exchanging a few choice words, most of them four letters, the
fisherman agreed to be more careful.

When the fisherman was done offloading, he would get a check
right away from Dave for his fish. The price had been agreed upon
at the beginning of the season. It was the same price among all the
canneries. The fishermen always grumbled at the price per pound.
This season it was 75 cents, a recent historical low. There was talk
of a strike. In 1975 energy prices were high. The fishermen were
not being paid for the higher gas prices they had to absorb. It was
always a struggle, but this year the tensions ran high.

As fish came off the boats, the fishermen would display the
occasional king salmon. Kings fetched a dollar-fifty a pound,
which the fishermen felt was an insult. They loved selling kings
at two or three dollars a pound. A fifty-pound king was worth a
hundred dollars or more. They would rather have a fifth of Chivas
Regal in trade for a forty or fifty-pound fish than give it to the
cannery at such a low price. With one hand in the gills and the
other grasping just above the tail, I helped hoist such a fish out of
a skiff. As I did so, Dave broke open a case of Chivas at the railing
and handed a bottle down to the boat operator. The fisherman took
off his gloves, shoved them in the pockets of his yellow rain coat
and reached up for the bottle of booze. He unscrewed the cap and
in one gulp, downed a third of the brown liquid.

"Ahhh, goes down like iced tea!" he exclaimed with a smile.

J.C. jumped down from the crane he had been operating and
took the huge salmon from me. This king salmon was not
considered a company fish. The deal had been struck between the
fisherman and the crew. J.C. took the fish, dipped it in the brine
water in the hold to cover it in a thin coating of salt and took it to
the freezer locker where it was hung on a hook. He was back on
the crane in sixty seconds.

When the run was on, loading salmon was non-stop. Dressed in
our rubber boots, dirty jeans and dark green rain jackets, the only
priority was getting as many fish in the hold as we could. For
twelve hours straight we'd work without a break. The cook kept an
eye on us and when a lull would happen, she'd run out with a
platter of sloppy joes and sodas, and we'd chow down on the go.
Any sit down meals were scheduled with the tides, when possible.

Fishermen came in on the incoming tide and left on the outgoing tide. There was no limit to how many fish they could catch, but they could not fish in the rivers or within a certain distance from the river mouth. As a salmon enters a river, fresh water replaces salt ocean water in the fish's gills. This induces a variety of changes in the fish, such as a color change from silver-blue to tints of a duller brownish blue-green. The flesh softens and is not as desirable for canning. The fishermen knew that river-caught fish were supposed to be turned away. Dave kept a close eye on them and turned several loads of fish away. When I asked about it, he said that every year, certain fishermen he was aware of who considered themselves outlaws, were known to fish the river mouths. It was an easier catch as the fish crowded into the narrower space. These guys enjoyed getting away with breaking the law. He had been watching for them and expected them to have mushy dark fish. They arrived as expected and he turned them away. Not all the buyers did.

During a good salmon season, when the run was on, some of the canneries would tell the fishermen to stop fishing, while they processed the fish they had on hand. It took just so long to move a salmon down the conveyor where it was washed, gutted, and had its head and tail removed, all by hand. Women wearing long yellow or white rubber gloves wielding long filet and butcher knives worked tirelessly to process the fish. When the fish backed up, the canneries without refrigeration would signal the buyers on the dock to stop buying. This angered the fishermen, who relied on a summer's catch for as much as eighty percent of their annual income. Telling them to stop fishing was like telling them to pour money right back into the ocean.

Not Uncle, who passed the word to the fishermen that he would buy everything they could bring him. Two days after we had arrived, another of the dog fleet, the Ironhead, showed up and was tied along the dock next to the *Airedale*. Refrigerated and ready to load all the salmon they could catch, Uncle's ships were a reliable and welcome sight to the locals.

Uncle loved the drama of the salmon season. At times he flew up to Naknek in a helicopter to supervise the loading of the salmon from the bridge of the *Airedale* and drink Scotch with the ship captains on the off-hours.

I watched him talk with one of the local fishermen who had sold salmon to one of the other canneries for many years. The fisherman waxed on about how they all loved Uncle because he never told them to stop fishing. Uncle smiled down at the man and told him to spread the word. He wanted all the fish they could catch.

The next morning, I woke to silence. I quickly dressed and went out on deck to see why it was so quiet. The crew, its back to me, was leaning against the railing of the ship looking out toward the river mouth.

The Naknek river runs northwest down from Naknek Lake. Emptying into Bristol Bay, its river mouth appeared to me to be over a mile wide. In the area I could see, the banks on both sides were lined with canneries and their support industries.

This morning, from the east bank to the west the river mouth was blocked by fishing boats, tied one to the other for the entire distance. The strike was on.

I walked over to the rail to join the guys. Tommy told me that no boats were allowed to pass through the blockade. In years past, strike breakers had occasionally been shot at and even killed for trying to get through. It would take days for the fishermen to negotiate a new deal with the canneries, which had a load of fish to process and could use the time anyway.

Only Uncle and the fishermen were unhappy about losing time. But for the crew of the *Airedale*, it was time off. What to do with time off? After the ship was secured and made ready for the next wave of fish, the guys decided to do what rich men from the lower forty-eight paid thousands of dollars to do. They were going fishing!

There were dozens of tributaries feeding into the Naknek. Each of them was a spawning ground for salmon. I didn't have a fishing pole or a license, so I tagged along to watch. The small, tree-lined creeks the guys fished were not more than a few feet wide and a couple of feet deep, with very few salmon in them. No one caught any fish. But we were eaten alive by mosquitoes.

The strike lasted a week and a new price was agreed upon. The fishermen would get a dollar a pound for reds and two dollars for kings. A strike is a rare event, which I felt fortunate to have been able to observe. Seeing the river mouth blockaded by boats and feeling the tension in the air was exciting. Fortunately, no violence erupted, and the strike was over quickly.

In a few days time, the *Airedale* was loaded and we prepared for the return trip to Kenai. Uncle came aboard and visited with me on the deck for a few minutes. As we passed downstream, he pointed at a small peninsula covered in trees and shrubs.

"If I were a younger man, I'd build a cannery right on that point over there," he suggested. Turning his head my way, looking partially over his shoulder, he gave me a serious stare, asking, "What do you think of that?"

I knew I was the younger man he had in mind. Auntie's comment on the deck of the sailboat came back to me. This one will be successful at whatever he puts his mind to. I looked back at Uncle and replied, "Uncle, I want to go to college and get a business degree before I do anything else."

He turned to face me squarely. "You don't need to do that, Tommy. I can start you at a cannery at Kodiak where there's a job for you right now. After a couple of years, when you've learned the business, you move up into a management position. I'm not getting any younger, you know, and I need to groom a successor. That could be you."

I felt the grip of Uncle's charm tightening around my throat. With certainty I replied once more, "I want to go to college more than anything, Uncle. Thanks, but when I've graduated, maybe we could talk again."

Uncle stared at me in silent disappointment. The frown on his face was terminal. Without another word, he stepped around me and went into the wheelhouse on his way to the bridge. Before we left the river, Dave pulled into a cannery dock and Uncle left the ship, having not spoken to me again. I watched him depart, realizing I had just severed any ties I might have had with him.

The journey back to Kenai took a couple of days longer on the return trip. With full holds and sitting low in the water, the Airedale was making perhaps 8-10 knots, instead of its normal 12. It took ten days to get back to Kenai. We arrived on a low tide and had to wait in the deeper waters of Cook Inlet, just outside the river mouth for the tide to rise before going upstream to the cannery. The sun was shining, the sky was blue and there was no wind. The chores were all done and we had about two hours to kill before going upstream. J.C. suggested we play volleyball on the deck, which wasn't a perfect volleyball court by any stretch. The edges of the hatches dropped off about four inches, so the footing was treacherous if attention wasn't paid to the uneven surface. J.C. lowered one of the cranes down across the deck and a net was strung along its length. After about an hour of volleyball, J.C. had a brainstorm. He walked over to the net, and held up one corner of it.

"Do you know what this is?" he asked us in an excited voice.

"Uh, it's a volleyball net, J.C." grumbled Tommy.

"Yes...yes it is. But it's also a gill net!" exclaimed J.C.

A smile crossed Tommy's face. J.C. walked over to the crane controls and, raising the crane arm with the net dangling from it, he swung it out over the river. Lowering the net down into the murky turquoise blue water, the top of the net, still visible above the surface, immediately began to wiggle. Then it wiggled more. After a few more wiggles, J.C. raised the net to expose six or seven big red salmon dangling by their gills from the net. J.C. swung the net over the deck. Tommy quickly clubbed the salmon, dipped them in the brine water and hustled them into the freezer locker in the bow cabin. Down went the net again with the same results. Tommy and J.C. were excited and laughing like kids at Halloween. Every fish caught meant smoked salmon or salmon for sale to friends back in Seattle.

Eric leaned over to me and said, "This is really illegal. We're too close to the river."

Suddenly the crane, hanging over the water again, dipped violently down toward the surface of the river. It came back up and whomped down again, this time going into the water.

"My God, what'd you catch there, a Beluga whale!?" shouted Eric as we crowded closer to the rail.

J.C. raised the net, revealing a giant king salmon rolled up in the net. Its head was too big to go through the gaps in the net, but it had rolled itself up as if in a carpet, in its effort to escape.

Our exclamations and loud shouting of; "Quick! Get it over the deck!" drew Dave's attention from the bridge. The giant salmon was easily five feet long and may have weighed eighty pounds or more. As it unrolled from the net and fell back into the water, an angry bellow swept across the deck.

Dave screamed at J.C. and the rest of us. "God damn it! What the fuck do you think you're doing?! You want to put us all in jail?! How do you know there isn't a game warden up there on the cliff taping you right now?! My God!"

Dave bent over and slapped the railing of the flying bridge and shook his shaggy blond mane in disbelief. J.C. quickly brought the crane back into its stored position. The volleyball game was over.

When we caught the incoming tide and motored up to the cannery, Uncle was waiting for us on the dock. He checked every load of fish to make sure they were still fresh. Once the cover had been removed from the hold, a dip net was lowered into the brine water to retrieve several of the salmon in the hold. Dave took a filet knife and cut open a salmon. Uncle picked it up and looked at its color, both outside and inside the fish. He smelled the intestinal cavity and nodded to Dave in approval. They tested several more fish to Uncle's satisfaction. He then got up and went back up to the bridge with Dave to drink Scotch.

A wide conveyor belt with a large bowl shaped container at one end was assembled to move the fish from the ship to the cannery. With the crane arm fully extended, J.C. dropped a large brailer into the hold where Tommy and I raked fish into it. Lifting the brailer out of the hold he swung it over the deck to the bowl-shaped container. The fish went in at the top of the bowl and flowed out the bottom onto the conveyor and up the hill to the cannery. We worked all day and long into the night in order to empty over a hundred thousand salmon from the ship. It was important to get the job done quickly, because we were due to leave for Prince William Sound as soon as the ship was ready.

The next morning, we had the ship emptied, cleaned and provisioned for the next leg of our journey. Having worked most of the night we were dog tired, but Dave said we couldn't sleep until we got underway. The top priority, he insisted, was that the goods we'd be delivering to the fishermen within the next three weeks had to be loaded. He was as tired as any of the crew, but it was important to him to get this right. Each load of provisions for the fishermen was put on separate pallets marked with the name of their boats. It took some time, but eventually, we finished loading, untied the dock lines, and got some well-deserved shut-eye.

The fishermen in the remote areas lived a lifestyle that brings them as close as one can get to nature in all its glory and all its fury. Isolated by hundreds of miles of ocean and mountain ranges, they spend the entire summer fishing the farthest corners of Prince William Sound's 3,000 miles of coastline. With only four towns in the whole region, Seward, Whittier, Valdez and Cordova, there's not much choice in shopping opportunities. The *Airedale* was their grocery store and pharmacy, their hardware supply and machine shop.

Prince William Sound is a vast bay rimmed by fjords, mountains and islands. The Chugach mountain range is topped with snow year round and supports over 20 glaciers. The calved ice from the glaciers dots the surface of the sound with stunning blue and white icebergs. In the summer, the surface of the water is so calm that the reflection of the mountains mirrors almost as much detail as the real thing!

The 150-mile long Kenai Peninsula stands between Kenai Packers and the Sound. To get there took us two days. As we approached Montague Island which blocks most of the entrance to the Sound, I was enthralled with the views. I had been smitten with Alaska since our stop in Ketchikan, but now I was in awe. My sense of wonder at the healing power of nature grew with each scenic marvel. I felt joyous in a way I never had. Could it be that part of me that had been stunted for so long, was finally being allowed to wake up? Standing on the bow of the ship, I watched as a salmon rose from what seemed a hundred feet below the surface, jumped out of the water flashing its silver sides, and, splashing back into the crystal clear water, returned to the depths. How incredible is that! I thought to myself. The air temperature was about eighty-five degrees, there wasn't a breath of wind, and the sun was shining. I wondered what it would be like to jump into that glacier-cold water. If there was ever a time to find out, this was it. I asked J.C. if he had ever jumped off the boat.

He looked at me as though to even ask the question was crazy, laughed and said, "No way! That water is way too cold! But if you jump in, I'll run the crane and fish you out."

I kept in mind that J.C. would fish me out and began to figure out how I was going to arrange to make my jump possible. Talking with Tommy, I learned that Captain Dave had been in radio contact with the fishermen and had arranged to meet them in a protected bay or cove near their fishing site. When we dropped anchor, I asked how long before the smaller fishing boat arrived. We had about twenty minutes before they would show up. In my cutoff jeans, bare feet and no shirt, I climbed up to the top of the wheelhouse and looked at J.C., who was manning the crane. I turned my attention twenty-five feet down to the gin-clear, deep blue surface of the water, and the iceberg floating about five hundred yards away that was bigger than the Airedale. I knew that the longer I waited, the less likely I was to jump. Inhaling a deep breath, I took a running start and leapt out like I was attempting a long jump. I held my arms straight over my head and pointed my toes to go as deep as I could. As I was on my way down I could hear J.C. let out a loud "Woo-hoo". It seemed like a long time before I hit the water; but the moment I hit, I began to doubt whether this was such a good idea. Unfortunately, I was successful at penetrating deep into the Sound. I looked up at the surface from what seemed like twenty feet down. I was suddenly so cold, my skin felt like thousands of needles were poking me. The sunlight looked so-o-o warm, sparkling way up at the surface, but refusing to reach me. My ears were ready to burst from the pressure. My mind was calling out, Okay, I've had the experience. Now I want OUT of this water! I kicked and kicked, but it seemed to take forever to get to the surface.

Flailing my arms, I gasped in shock and yelled, "Whoo! Get me out!"

J.C. laughed as he swung the crane over the side of the ship and lowered a hook to just above my head. I grabbed on, slipped off, and tried again. Realizing that my hands were already numb and unable to hang on, I wrapped my arms around the hook just enough, and J.C. lifted me out. I was shaking uncontrollably, but boy, was I exhilarated!

The trawler we were expecting was coming around the corner of the nearby island and in short order we were at work unloading salmon from their hold into ours. Tommy took one of the first salmon from the load and cut it in half. He took a hay hook from me and ran it through the salmon.

Tied to a 100-foot length of light rope, he dropped it over the stern of the ship and tied it to the rail, watching it sink into the depths. We spent the rest of the day emptying their holds of salmon into the large hold of the Airedale. As we finished our work, Tommy winked at me and motioned to follow him. We walked around the wheelhouse to the stern. The thin rope he had tied to the rail was taut.

Tommy grinned. "Halibut" he said, and pulled on his hand-line, feeling the resistance. As Tommy began to pull the line in, the fish pulled back.

"Not very big," he mumbled.

After he had been pulling for a while, I looked down into the depths and saw a huge shadow appear. The closer it got, the bigger it seemed. Taking on shape, it displayed the grayish-brown upper skin and white underside of a Pacific halibut. Five feet long and three feet wide, it struggled to free itself but this huge fish had swallowed the hook. The scale for weighing the loads of salmon was still on the deck. After hauling it over the stern rail, Tommy dragged his fish forward and hung it from the scale. Sixty pounds. "Not the biggest we've caught, but it'll do for dinner," said Erik, while winking at Tommy.

After cleanup, supplies were delivered and a receipt issued to the fisherman. Then it was on to the next rendezvous. En route, we rested. Lying on my bunk, reading a book, I felt an itch on the back of my neck. I scratched it and noticed a small speck appear on the open page. It seemed to move, but it was so small, I couldn't tell what it was. Gently setting down the book, I got out my 35 mm camera and removed the lens. Looking through the small end, the lens became a magnifying glass. The moving speck looked like a small tick. Ticks aren't that small, I thought. It was a louse... a body louse...a crab louse. Oh great, I have crabs! I concluded.

I asked Tommy to take a look. Bending down, he put his eye to the lens and held it over the open book on the desk. "Yup, it's a crab all right. Where was it?" "On my neck," I replied. He walked over to the bunk and picked up the beat-up old feather pillow I had been leaning against. "The guy who had this bunk before you was an old, drunk Polack. I think he left you something to remember him by."

Tommy picked up the pillow and stepped out the door to our bunk-room. He tossed the pillow overboard.

I went to J.C. and asked him if anyone on board had reported or complained about crabs. He eyed me suspiciously and asked why I wanted to know. I told him what had just happened. After some discussion, he looked thoughtful and said, "Tom, when you think about it, you have to agree that no one ever has just one crab. I'm going to have to order special soap and detergent for everyone on the ship. We can't take any chances."

Early the next morning I woke to the sound of turboprop engines echoing off the ship and the surrounding mountains. I had tossed and turned all night, imagining that every itch and sensation on my skin was one of the little vermin. As I went out on deck shaking the sleep out of my head, I saw a mid-sized float-plane, maybe a ten-seater, taxiing up to the *Airedale*. Dave, J.C. and Erik were leaning over the rail, ready to grab the wing and steady it. The engines cut, the prop stopped spinning, and the door just behind the pilot's seat opened. My jaw dropped as five beautiful, fashionably dressed young women stepped out of the plane and onto the pontoon. As they bent over to negotiate the step down from the cabin to the pontoon, each of them treated us to a display of cleavage that sent my imagination aflutter. I could see on the faces of the other men that some version of my thought process was racing through their minds as well. Who were these women? Every one of them looked like they had just stepped off the cover of a fashion magazine. Following the women out the door of the plane was a big, bearded bush pilot whose baseball hat had script above the bill of the cap that said, "The way to a man's heart is through his fly." Over the script was a fly-fishing pole and line with a feathery hook at the end.

Dave seemed to know the pilot and they exchanged greetings and smiles, shaking each other's massive hands. It reminded me of two bears saying hello. The pilot handed Dave a package the size of a shoe box. The pilot asked a question I couldn't hear. Dave glanced my way and pointed. I wanted to say, "Hey, it's not my fault!" It wouldn't have mattered. After a couple more comments and laughs, the pilot got in first, followed by the women, stepping carefully in their high heels.

After the plane had taken off, I asked J.C. who they were. "Working girls on their way to the pipeline," he replied. I thought about the way the women were dressed and wondered where on the Alaska pipeline they would find a need for such clothes. But then, I wasn't a forlorn pipeline worker willing to pay God knows how much money for a prostitute. The clothes must have created a tremendous contrast for them and helped them justify whatever price they were paying for the fantasy.

We all took showers with the anti-louse soap and washed all our clothes and linens with the special detergent. No one ever saw any crab lice besides that one from the feather pillow. The crew was kind and spared me the crab jokes I was expecting.

Our next stop was Cordova, a small fishing town with massive glacier-carved mountains rising straight up behind it. As we approached the village docks, I could see three canneries lining the shore. We tied up alongside the *Ironhead*, which had arrived before us. The crews of the two ships began shouting and laughing, hurling insults at each other, as they worked together to secure the fenders and lines. The boats were cleaned, secured and abandoned as quickly as the crews could finish their chores; the bars of Cordova were calling.

With a larger than usual contingent heading up the hill from the docks to the town, I followed toward the back of the pack. I was, after all, the low man on the totem pole. Looking up from the road in front of me, I saw exactly that; totem poles. Several of them lined the road as we approached the town. Walking up the steep stairs to the bar, we stopped as the door burst open, a young man in jeans and a t-shirt raging out the door. He grabbed the two-by-four railing to steady himself and turned around. Grabbing the screen door, he ripped it off the hinges and threw it down into the street. He marched back into the building and began cruising up and down the bar, cursing the men who sat at the counter, sipping their beers. Not very big, maybe five-foot eight and slender, but angry as a hornet, he challenged anyone and everyone to fight him. Most of them ignored him. He seemed to be a local kid, for some of the older bar patrons told him to go home. As our group of thirsty fishermen combined two tables and brought chairs around, I sauntered over to the pool table and put a quarter next to the two already in line.

Eric told the crew from the *Ironhead* to put away their money; they were going to drink for free tonight. He glanced at me and winked at them. They looked at me curiously. It took a half an hour or so before I had my turn to play, and we had by then consumed several pitchers of beer. I ran the first table, then another, then another. Pitchers of beer were delivered to the table amidst many expressions of thanks, heads shaking in disbelief, and general applause for my pool playing.

Within a couple of hours, I had run six tables playing eight ball and was at least three sheets to the wind. I ran the next game down to the eight ball, and called the easy shot: eight ball in the corner. The eight ball was sitting about six inches in front of the pocket, a routine shot. My opponent was crouching over the table watching, his elbows on the edge, with his chin on his hands. His cue stick was leaning against the wall. He had yet to touch it.

Before I took my shot, he shouted, "Hey!"

I looked at him for the first time through my beer-saturated eyes.

"I've been watching you play, and yeah, you're good. But it's only fun for you. You play and no one else gets as much as a shot. Why don't you just give me one turn? It was my quarter. Whad'ya say?"

I straightened up and thought about it, staring at the table. I could see his point. I shrugged, said, "O.K" and missed the shot on purpose.

He picked up his cue and without so much as a "thank you" proceeded to run the table. Before he took his first shot, I could tell by the way he held the cue he was every bit as good as me. After he finished, he smiled and, sitting down at a nearby table, said, "I'll have Budweiser."

I'd been hustled. Feeling stupid for letting my guard down, I said, "Hey, pal, you just shot your beer."

As I approached him I wasn't quite sure what I had in mind as he stood up. I hadn't really looked at him before. He had brown curly hair down to his shoulders, a neatly trimmed beard and a kind-looking face behind round frameless glasses. He looked down at me. Yes, down. In the moment that I realized could be my last, I waited for his response. I stand 6'2". The internal dialogue going through my head as I looked up at his face, which was at least six inches above mine was simple: Stupid, Tom, really stupid.

The big guy looked down at me and smiled. He put out his hand and introduced himself. "My name's Peter, what's yours?"

I felt an instant rush of relief. Shaking his hand, I quickly replied, "My name's Budweiser and I'll be right back with yours."

I turned on a dime and headed for the bar. Passing the questioning looks of my crewmates, I shrugged. "What can I say, I got beat."

Peter and I sat down and shared the pitcher over stories of fishing and billiards.

The next quarter up was mine. Halfway through the game, the young fighter, who'd been razzing everyone when we had arrived, found an opponent. They were slugging and wrestling each other next to the pool table. The kid was getting the worst of it. A gap opened between them. I took my cue and put it between them, trying to separate them. They locked again, trapping my cue. The bartender came running around the bar. He was bigger than both the fighters combined. He grabbed each of them by the back of their necks and pulled them apart, lifting them off the ground. He tossed the bigger of the two aside and said, "You won, now get out of here!"

To the other he said, "Go home, Mikey."

To me, he pointed his finger and said in an angry voice, "Never get in the middle of a fight!"

I stared back at him. "I was just trying to help."

Shaken, I walked back to the table. J.C. crooked his finger and motioned at me to come over. "Don't ever do that again," he said, as though I had just made the faux-pas of a life time.

"Yeah, I just heard that." I shrugged.

J.C. put his hand on my shoulder. In an older brotherly voice he said, "A friend of mine was walking down the sidewalk in New York City. He saw a mugging and ran up to the mugger and pinned him by the arms from behind. He yelled at the guy on the ground to get up, that he had him. The guy on the ground got up and stuck a knife in the mugger, right up under his ribs into his heart. Then he turned and ran, leaving my buddy holding a corpse." J.C. looked sternly at me and said, "Don't ever do that again."

I had never in my life handled violence well. This experience cemented my intention to avoid it, if at all possible.

By the second week of August, the *Airedale* had made three trips to the far reaches of Prince William Sound and delivered as many loads to Seward and Cordova. The salmon runs were over, so it was time to head back to the cannery at Kenai. On the trip around the Kenai Peninsula, we hit the first serious storm of the season. The chef had chosen this night to prepare a seven-course Chinese dinner to celebrate the end of the salmon season. Just as she was about to serve and call us all to the galley, a rogue wave hit the *Airedale* broadside and almost rolled her over. Every pot on the stove bounced off the ceiling and splattered Chinese food around the kitchen walls and floor. J.C. and Dave called us all into the galley. The chef was still sitting on the floor in the middle of the galley mess, crying. Her beautiful blond hair was tied neatly in a ponytail running down her back, but it was covered in chow mein. As Dave escorted his girlfriend to her room via the shower, he told us to clean it up. Tommy had been looking forward to the feast and was disappointed. Honestly, I was too close to seasick to care.

Back at the docks, the crew began to refit the *Airedale* for king crab fishing. I learned that for the regular crew, salmon fishing in the summer was a way to keep busy. The real money was made king crab fishing. A crewman could make $50,000 to $75,000 or more in as little as a few weeks of crabbing, depending on the catch. I considered the $3,000 I'd be paid when I returned to Seattle. It didn't take me long to do the math and decide I could postpone college for awhile, if I had a chance to go crabbing. I asked J.C. if I could go and crew with them.

He smiled at me and said, "Probably not. Guys wait years to fish crab. Besides, it's not always good. We didn't make any money the last two years. This will be Tommy's third season and he has yet to make any money at it."

I shrugged. College it would be.

The *Airedale* was leaving for the Aleutians in a few days. It was time I said my good-byes to the mates I had spent the summer with. Eric gave me a fond hug and wished me well in school. J.C. shook my hand and said, "You surprised me. You didn't fuck up too bad at all."

Tommy shook my hand and without saying anything, turned and went back into the wheelhouse. Dave waved from the bridge and nodded.

Two weeks after the *Airedale* left for the Bering Sea to fish for king crab, Tommy was knocked overboard by a crab-pot and drowned.

I was re-assigned to crew on the Labrador, the dog ship my brother Phil was on. The Labrador would not be king crab fishing this year and was, instead, preparing to take a hold full of canned salmon back to Seattle. On the way up, the cases of cans had been light. Now they were heavy with fish and ready for the supermarket. By the time the hold was fully loaded, the Labrador was riding low in the water, as she and the other ships had been when full of fresh salmon bound for the cannery. Once the hatch was sealed on the hold, we took on a semi-truck and trailer, a thirty-foot aluminum gill netting fishing boat, five cars and two forklifts. Each of them was strapped to the deck with heavy chains and binders.

Once at sea on our way to Seattle, we passed out of Cook Inlet escorted by a pod of Orca that had at least fifty members. I had never seen so many killer whales at once. With the Aleutian Mountain Range on our starboard side showing off her four snow-covered volcanoes glinting in the sunlight, the forested mountains of the Kenai Peninsula on our port, and all these Orcas, my awe of Alaska rose to new heights.

On the third night out, Phil and I were standing watch at 1 a.m., 500 miles out in the Gulf of Alaska. A storm was raging around us. Swells were cresting up to 25 feet tall, and the wind was howling at 35 knots. There was phosphorescent plankton in the water, making every wave cresting over our bow a show of light. It reminded Phil and me of the scene of the sorcerers apprentice in the Disney movie "Fantasia."

With the full hold and a loaded deck, I was amazed at how stable the Labrador seemed. While she chugged along, deep in a trough, headed into the next swell, I looked out the window at the peaks of massive waves, knowing that the only thing between me and the bottom of the sea was an ancient hull and the will of God. I marveled that I was doing all this for only $3,000. Still, working in the fishing industry in Alaska is one of the great adventures a young person can have. Grateful for the adventure of a lifetime, I smiled inwardly at having had the opportunity, trusting that the plucky little Labrador would carry me safely home.

The long journey back to Seattle was made safer and more enjoyable when, after crossing the Gulf of Alaska, the ship re-entered the calm waters of the inside passage. Looking at the islands, mountain ranges, fjords, and villages from the other direction gave me the feeling that I almost hadn't seen it before. As we approached the Seymour Narrows, I was on the bridge with Eric at the helm. The tide was running against us as it had been when I was on the *Airedale* on the trip up the coast. Eric had the same decision to make as Captain Dave had made. He looked at his charts, then the clock and the tide tables.

Eric mused out loud, "I think we can make it if I give her full throttle. I hope she holds together!" The ship shuddered for a second as Eric accelerated to full power. The bow wave rose as the *Labrador* plowed into the oncoming tide. She was almost halfway through the narrowest part of the channel, when it became clear that Eric had been wrong in his assessment of the timing of the tide change. The *Labrador* slowed as the tide accelerated beyond our twelve knots, challenging our advance. The ship began to drift to starboard and move toward the cliffs as the tidal current took over. Eric ran to the side window, looking down on the dozen or so sport fishing boats that were about to be crushed. Deciding that we weren't going to make it through the narrows after all, he threw the throttle into reverse and hard to port, changing direction, attempting to go with the tide. Maneuvering the ship in a wide u-turn, the *Labrador* just missed the sport fishing boats, whose occupants looked up at us in horror. As the ship momentarily halted in line with the current, Eric throttled forward and down current to a small bay where we anchored until the tide went slack.

An unthinkable disaster had been avoided, but now we were forced to wait six hours for the tide to change and carry us through. While in the small bay, Phil and I double-checked all the binders on our deck cargo to be sure the shaking of the ship hadn't loosened any of the chains. All was well, so we enjoyed a break from crew duties for the next few hours, watching the bald eagles soaring above us and talking about our various adventures of the past three months. The next day, we arrived in Seattle for the last leg of our journey.

Phil and I had planned to visit our childhood home before leaving the Northwest, so we rented a car and drove the ninety miles to Whidbey Island. I had been seven years old when my mother had taken us away, but I had a treasure trove of fond memories to revisit. Phil had been four, so his sense of Whidbey was not as developed as mine; but his excitement level was just as high. The only highway connecting Whidbey to Fidalgo Island, then to the mainland, goes over a span of water called Deception Pass. The bridge over the pass is a quarter-mile long. As a small boy, I had always had a fascination with this bridge and the waterway beneath it. It sits over 200 feet off the water. Looking down through the spaces between the concrete railings, it seemed a long, long way down to the rushing, foaming rapids below. As we crossed the bridge, I told Phil I wanted to pull over and walk out on the bridge to see what it was like to look down at the water again after all these years. We walked out on the bridge's narrow sidewalk, looking around at the fir trees growing on the knolls above the granite cliffs. Seagulls circled below us between the canyon walls that separated the two islands. It was much the same as I had remembered it. The sense of familiarity I felt created a warm, almost sacred smile within me.

When we arrived at the small town of Oak Harbor, I drove straight to the home we had lived in on Walker Avenue, in Penn Cove Park. I was shocked by how small the house seemed. The difference between seeing what appears to be a big house with a child's eyes from about three feet off the ground and seeing a relatively smaller house with an adult's eyes from twice that height creates a remarkable contrast.

The clover-filled lawn of the front yard, where I had abused the honey bee at the age of three, was gone. Where the yard had once been, a chain link fence surrounded a cement patio, where two vicious looking pit bulls stared out at us, growling and launching the occasional warning bark our way. Three Harley Davidson motorcycles sat in the driveway, amid cardboard boxes, clutter, and cast-off appliances. The lot next door, where I had exercised my Herculean strength by pulling pine saplings out of the ground at the age of five, was now a house much like the one my family had lived in, also surrounded by a chain link fence and guarded by dogs. The forest that had surrounded our childhood wonderland was gone. I was deeply disappointed in what I saw.

I looked at Phil and smiled grimly, "I guess you really can't go home, can you?"

The look on his face reflected my disappointment. "Yeah, I guess not, let's go."

We drove up to the Dairy Farm, still owned and operated by Bob and Evee Muzzal. I was happy to see that some things hadn't changed. As we approached the farm, the surrounding pastures and thickets of trees looked about the same. The lower storage lot where the tractors were kept was the same. One of the old trucks, which had seemed so huge when I was small, was still there. It looked ancient, its green paint rusted and faded almost to grey, the wooden bed looking rotted and falling down toward the twisted bumper above the bent, dirt-crusted, unreadable Washington license plate. The tires were still inflated, and I wondered, but doubted that it still ran. As we continued up the road, the milking shed came into view. It hadn't changed at all! I was delighted to see it as I had remembered it. Pulling into the entranceway to the main farmhouse, I carefully kept the rental car tires in the ruts in the dirt driveway, respecting the grass growing on all sides. I stopped the car in front of the red two story farmhouse just as a small woman in her sixties glanced up from her gardening in the yard.

She stood up and looked at us curiously, striding up to us with authority. With a slight frown, she looked at these two rather large, bearded men and said, "May I help you?"

Phil and I had grown beards over the course of the summer. We both weighed about two-hundred pounds and looked like a couple of lumberjacks, or maybe even fishermen!

I smiled at Evie and said, "We're sorry to barge in on you like this unannounced, Evie, but I am Tom North-Beardsley and this is my brother Phil."

She looked me up and down, then smiled back at me and said, "Oh, my God! You sure are, aren't you!?" She stepped forward and gave me a hug. She looked at Phil and said, "Come here, boy!" She hugged him, too, and said, "Look at you! A couple of men now, aren't you! My God! Well, let's go down to the milking shed. Bob is setting up for the evening milking."

As we walked down the road, we told her where we had been, and briefly, that Mom and the family were fine, as far as we knew, having had limited contact with them over the summer. As we approached the milking shed, Bob came around the corner, looking up quizzically, not sure what to make of us. Evie cautioned us, "Don't say anything." She strode out in front of us and said, "Bob, do you know who these young men are?"

We stopped in front of Bob, who was holding a steel bucket in his hand. He looked at us and studied our faces for a moment. Phil and I were grinning from ear to ear. "Well, I'm not sure about this one," Bob said, nodding at Phil, "but I'd know that grin anywhere! Hello Tommy!" He put down the pail, stepped forward and gave me a big bear hug. Bob stood six-foot eight-inches tall, so I was engulfed in his arms. "It's good to see you, boy! And who is this? Must be Phil! Gerry wouldn't be so tall."

Phil nodded, still grinning, and stepped forward as Bob reached for him with those long, strong, farmer's arms. "Come on inside, boys, you can help me with the milking."

As a child, I had loved the milking shed. It had been an adventure of smells, sights and sounds that kept me enraptured, so I was overjoyed at the invitation. Almost nothing looked different to me. The stalls where each cow was milked seemed about the same. The cement floors and the hoses for washing them down were the same. The spiral stairwell to the grain attic was the same. Everything was just smaller, that's all. Of course, it only seemed smaller, because I was bigger; but from my vantage point, it didn't look that way.

Bob introduced us to the laborer operating the milking equipment in the shed, who set to work bringing in the cows. He asked me to bring him a large shovel from across the room. I went over and grabbed the shovel, pivoted and headed back toward Bob. I climbed the three stairs up to the entrance level where the cows came in and ducked my head under two exposed pipes that carried milk from each stall to the shiny stainless steel collecting tank.

Bob smiled at me and said, "You've been working on a ship, haven't you?!"

I smiled back, not thinking about all the enclosed spaces we had been used to negotiating, until he mentioned it. "I suppose we have, Bob." I replied.

I asked him if, when the time came to do so, could I please go up to the feed attic and pull the chain to feed the cows. I had so enjoyed that chore as a child.

He grinned back at me and said, "That's done automatically now, Tommy. Things may look the same around here, but we have made some changes."

Phil and I were invited to stay for dinner; an invitation which we gratefully accepted. We discussed Alaska, the Muzzal children, who had all gone on to live productive lives, and life on the farm. Bob and Evie shared that they could never understand our mother marrying Frank Beardsley. They had visited the Carmel home on a vacation shortly after Mom and Frank were married. When they had met him, their first impression was not a good one. Frank seemed to them to be trying very hard to be charming, and it came off as completely insincere. Their intuition was confirmed when he stepped out of the living room for a moment to talk with one of the children, and immediately became enraged at the child, all out of proportion to the incident at hand. They had thought of him, correctly, as a person who was easy to anger, and feared for Mom's children. But it was none of their business, so they had just shrugged and wished her well.

Phil and I confirmed their suspicions, as we helped with the dishes. After catching them up on our brothers and sisters, we passed hugs and grateful looks all around and said our goodbyes. We stayed in a motel that night and drove back to Seattle the next day for our flight back to California.

Tom – 1975

15

THE MOUNTAIN RETREAT

C ombined with my meager savings, my summer wage from
Alaska was enough to pay for the first semester at Maharishi
International University in Fairfield, Iowa. While applying for
entrance to the university, I had scheduled myself for the
prerequisite Science of Creative Intelligence (SCI) course at a TM
facility in the mountains north of San Francisco. Sitting on about
twenty-five acres of undulating forested mountainside, the new
TM facility had been called Hoberg's Resort before it was purchased
by the TM organization in 1973. It had been a thriving resort in the
1920s, and right on through the 60s, but it needed more maintenance
than the Hoberg family was willing to put into it. So, they sold it
with the proviso that they be allowed to live in their family home
in perpetuity on the property. The TM movement staffed the
"Northern California Capital of the Age of Enlightenment," also
known to TM'ers as "Cobb Mountain," with volunteers who earned
course credit towards meditation courses and attendance at MIU.
There was a spirit of excitement and enthusiasm about the place that
many new enterprises exude out of the promise and hope for growth
and a brighter future.

The main administrative building at Cobb Mountain was a
rambling two-story structure with granite pillars defining the
entrance to the lobby, and a bat-and-board redwood exterior.

This ancient facility was in desperate need of repair. The resort and its varied bungalows, cottages and ranch-style motel structures, seemed to reflect every building style that had ever become popular since its inception. Aside from the stone and redwood main buildings, some of the long multi-room bungalows were bat and board; some of the cottages were stucco; some seemed to be made of plywood; and some, I couldn't begin to guess. A couple of the buildings had burned down and sat in ruins. When the resort was full, it accommodated about a hundred people. The gravel parking lot sat between the buildings and the highway, which wound around the property, allowing almost every building to absorb, or should I say, suffer, from the road noise.

What was called the "Motel Central" section of the resort was situated right along the parking lot next to the highway. My room was in the motel, which was quiet, except for the cars that went by or the motorcycle gangs that roared by, or the pickup trucks with the hot-rod headers that went by with local teenagers hanging out the window shouting, "Go home, you fucking gurus!" The loudest and most annoying noise came from the wall heater that ran along the baseboard on the east side of the room. It pinged loudly, like a hammer being tapped against sheet metal as the elements expanded while it was heating up, and again as the elements contracted when it was cooling down.

The room was about twelve by twelve, with two double beds and a bed table between them on the west wall. On the other wall, partially hiding the noisy heater, was a chest of drawers that dated back to the 1950s. The brown paint was peeling off of the veneer, which was peeling off of the frame. The bathroom off the back of my bedroom was textured sheetrock, which was painted yellow. Rust stains dripped from the exposed nail heads that lined the seams of the sheetrock. Another sort of rust stain came from the water itself at Cobb Mountain, which was heavy with iron; so much so, that all the bathtubs, showers, and sinks were stained orange-red if the water had any tendency to drip or sit for any length of time. And yes, every faucet dripped, because they were all irreparably stained.

It definitely wasn't the Ritz, but I rationalized that I was there to close my eyes, anyway. I sat on the bed and sank down several inches, noticing that the mattress coils squeaked with every move.

I thought, "Well, it's not a cave in the Himalayas; but it's still pretty rustic. At least it doesn't have crabs." Then it occurred to me that maybe it did. I looked at the bed suspiciously and resolved to use the foam pillow, not the feather one. There wasn't sufficient staff to have maid service, so we did our own laundry and changed the beds ourselves. Having just lived onboard a ship for three months, I didn't mind at all. It was actually clean and quiet in comparison.

The food on the menu at Cobb Mountain was vegetarian and quite good. At the first meal in the common dining room, I crossed the creaky oak floor to the steam tables, where I picked up a plate and looked at the offerings under the sneeze glass. I filled my plate with lasagna, garlic bread and steamed zucchini smothered in butter. Turning around and surveying the tables, I saw a mixture of men and women at several tables, and at another there were two attractive women, perhaps my age, sitting by themselves.

My internal dialogue went something like, "Let's see, share a meal with a bunch of guys, or with two beautiful women? Not much of a contest."

I went over and asked the ladies if they minded if I joined them. They smiled and asked me to sit down. Their names were Judy and Lucinda. Judy was blonde and smelled like cigarettes. She seemed nervous and soon shared that she hoped that the meditation course would help her quit smoking. Lucinda had one of the most delightful and genuine smiles I had ever seen. She was on an adventurous road trip, driving around the country in her sky blue Toyota station wagon with her dog, Basho. She had left her home in New Jersey the previous spring and drove through the upper states, seeing the Dakotas, Wyoming and Montana, with stops in Colorado and Utah, before she drove down the coast of Washington, Oregon and now California. Lucinda told us that when she would eventually leave Cobb, she would continue on to Arizona, then New Mexico, and tour the Southern states, before returning home. I was immediately impressed and drawn to her sense of adventure and the courage it took to do this tour alone, not to mention her long brown hair, tanned angular face, warm blue eyes, and her five-foot-ten, very shapely, slender body.

Our daily schedule was kept simple. Before class every day, we were to meditate according to the instructions given to us by the course leaders. I was looking forward to the extended meditations again as I had done at the Residence Course in Pacific Grove. Again, I was to do some yoga to enliven and loosen up the body and prepare it to sit in comfort for twenty minutes. The yoga postures are followed by a few minutes of the yogic breathing, also described earlier, then twenty minutes of meditation. It takes about an hour to do. Then, I was to repeat the process. As with the Residence Course, I did this in the morning and in the evening. The morning program of meditation was followed by breakfast. We were encouraged to go on a "walk and talk" with classmates for a few minutes after meals and before class. TM instructors, one male and one female, were assigned to lead the group in class everyday. Our "classroom" was a library with several couches, recliners, and over-stuffed chairs. Our classroom activities consisted of watching video-taped lectures by Maharishi, who masterfully delved into the subtleties of refined states of awareness experienced during meditation, and how these subtleties of "creative intelligence" were reflected throughout the universe. The lectures were actually videos of courses similar to the one I was on, but with several hundred participants. What we were watching was the Question and Answer sessions, during which, course participants just like me got up to the microphone to ask Maharishi about experiences they were having in meditation. Maharishi would listen, often with his eyes closed. Then he would address their question, helping them understand the abstractions they were trying to articulate and connecting the ideas they were trying to bring together. If he heard a word or concept he was unfamiliar with, he would look to his right or left to someone on staff or ask the audience, "What it is?" in his lilting Indian accent. Meditators from all walks of life found him very endearing. Sitting on a dais in white robes, his black hair flowing past his shoulders into an already graying beard, his explanations became our daily food for thought. I didn't mind at all that we were watching a video and not in the presence of Maharishi himself. I felt like I was in the audience of those previously recorded courses. Their concerns were my concerns. His answers seemed to go right to the heart of my curiosity and satisfy my need of the moment.

One of the course participants asked Maharishi how long it would take them to become enlightened.

"In two to three years of regular practice of meditation, fifteen-to-twenty minutes twice a day," was his response. That seemed like a very short time. I was sure that it would take me much longer, and in fact, time has shown that Maharishi was a bit overly optimistic about that estimation.

In the 1960s, TM had spread quickly, becoming a cultural phenomenon when the Beatles, The Beach Boys, Donovan, and many Hollywood personalities were drawn to this particular type of meditation. Merv Griffin, the popular daytime talk show host, had learned to meditate and had invited Maharishi to be a guest on his show. The media attention given to TM drew more and more people to the organization growing up around Maharishi, who was teaching meditation courses all over the world.

After our viewing of the lecture, our small group of thirty people would engage in group discussion about the material we had seen on tape. Additionally, if someone had an experience in meditation they wanted to share with the group, this was the forum for it.

Morning class was followed by lunch, another walk and talk, then class for another couple of hours, then afternoon meditation program. On walk-and-talk over the ensuing days, Lucinda shared with me that she was twenty years old, and had graduated in three years from Cornell University, with a degree in Psychology. She was also an artist, and drew a picture of a galaxy for me in pastel. Lucinda had been severely dyslexic as a child, and hadn't learned to read or write until she was twelve years old. But at that age, something clicked in her brain, and over the next three years she had caught up with and surpassed her academic age group, going to college at the age of 16 and graduating at nineteen.

As the days wore on, we were enjoying each other's company more and more, and became unofficial course "buddies" for the month. We were required to have a buddy on the SCI course to make sure we were taken care of and that everything went smoothly for us. My official buddy, a thirty-something guy named Mike, was from Palo Alto. In the first few days, Mike and I took our guardianship of each other very seriously, checking that each of us made it to meals, class, and to bed by ten o'clock at night. Mike was late to class one morning, so I told the instructor I would be leaving class to go and look for him. I left the building, walked around the corner toward Mike's room and saw him walking toward me, taking a last long puff on a cigarette, dropping it to the ground and stomping out the butt. I waited for him to catch up to me before turning to walk with him back to the classroom.

He grimaced in embarrassment as he explained, "The reason I'm here is to stop smoking. I've tried everything but this, so I sure hope it works."

I said nothing, but thought of Judy as we entered the room. It wasn't long before Mike got the vibe that Lucinda and I were becoming an item, and that his buddy services would no longer be required, especially on walk-and-talk. Once in a while over the month of October, Mike would wink at me and ask how I was doing. With a nod and a return wink, I assured him that I was fine, and of course, inquired about his well-being in return. After all, I was technically his buddy and responsible for keeping an eye on him. He seemed to be stable and in good spirits, so all was well.

The more I meditated, the calmer I became. My mind seemed to slow down and my thoughts became clearer as I relaxed more each day. I didn't know enough about the process to be able to say whether it was the yoga or the meditation or the combination of the two. Maybe it was the extended meditation each morning and evening. All I knew was that I was feeling less mentally and emotionally encumbered each day. I thought to myself, "So this is what it's like to relax and feel rested." I began smiling at my classmates with sincere good feeling, instead of forcing an insincere smile to be socially correct.

During the day, my classmates and I stayed relatively quiet. However, it was common in the class sessions for spontaneous laughter to erupt with no more provocation than a cough or a sneeze. For some reason, we all thought this was incredibly funny. The thirty of us in the group would chuckle, then guffaw, and five or ten minutes later, we were trying to pull ourselves together, faces streaked with tears of bliss that came seemingly out of nowhere. After the first few laughing sessions, we were on our guard. No sneezing or coughing! Being on alert didn't help, though. An errant sniff was all we needed. When I felt the rumble go through the group, I knew we were in for another session of protracted hilarity.

What I did not know at the time is that laughter is a form of transcendence. There was a whole lecture on that subject. Maharishi explained that when we laugh, our awareness slips through the gap in our thoughts, and ever so briefly, we touch the bliss that is our essential nature. "It is a tickle to the soul," he said, "and so we experience divine mirth."

The course leaders were very thoughtful and made a big deal about honoring the course participants' birthdays. Mine was on October 17th. For some reason, there was a misunderstanding and on the 7th, I was surprised at the evening meeting with a birthday cake and the singing of "Happy Birthday." Perhaps someone left off the 1 from the number 17. It felt good to be singled out and celebrated, even if they had the wrong day. I realized several days later that these people were really into celebrations when there was a group celebration of all October birthdays. I was included, even having already been recognized. Much to my surprise, when the 17th arrived, I was honored again, with another cake and another round of singing. In my sensitive, ultra-aware state, it wasn't lost on me that this just might be an unusual and remarkable healing of an old wound, suffered by an eight-year-old boy exactly fourteen years earlier.

Every single day of the SCI course brought me new experiences of deep profound silence and a steady expansion of my awareness. My thought process continued to slow down, allowing greater clarity in my mind. I began to make connections I hadn't even considered before. One somewhat esoteric example sticks out in my memory. Maharishi continually talked about being in tune with the laws of nature. Now, since TM comes from India, and as this was a TM facility, there was an influence of Indian culture in Cobb Mountain's social milieu. Just about every room smelled like sandalwood incense, and quite often, the conversation was sprinkled with words I had never heard before like "karma" and "dharma." Today, this terminology has worked its way into the common American lexicon; but in 1975, it was still foreign. Pictures of Indian mythological deities were everywhere, and stories from Indian mythology were constantly being told.

As I was relatively new to all of this, I wondered who these characters were: Krishna, Agni, Indra, Saraswati, and the like. Somehow, I had one of those "aha!" moments in class one day.

I had a realization while listening to Maharishi talk about the laws of nature and the various deities of the Indian pantheon, that they were one and the same. It occurred to me that until recently in history, the extreme majority of humans all over the planet were illiterate. One way to explain natural phenomenon is to put these abstract ideas into a form that an illiterate person can relate to, such as another person. In other words, change the laws of nature into people or characters in a story, and the concept becomes that much more accessible. People can relate to people. Even so, I realized that the deities of the Indian mythological pantheon, and every other cultural mythology, for that matter, were simply personifications of the laws of nature.

I'm certain that I would not have made that connection at any time in my life before taking the SCI course. First of all, it would never have occurred to me. Secondly, my mind had been too clouded, confused and stressed. The experience of deep meditation had given me a clarity that allowed me to not only become more coherent, but to observe my own progress toward becoming more coherent.

I was profoundly awed by the growth I experienced during the SCI course. My desire to refine my consciousness was enhanced with each successive meditation. One way I began to think about my desire for expanded awareness was to picture it as a journey of spiritual awakening. Interestingly, a friend once sent me a list called the "Twelve Signs of Spiritual Awakening." Each of these signs is a quality that we would expect to find in a person who has spent some time on the path to enlightenment:

An increased tendency to let things happen rather than making them happen.

Frequent attacks of smiling.

Feelings of being connected to others and nature.

Frequent overwhelming episodes of appreciation.

Tendency to think and act spontaneously rather than from fears based on past experiences.

An unmistakable ability to enjoy each moment.

A loss of ability to worry.

A loss of interest in conflict.

A loss of interest in interrupting the actions of others.

A loss of interest in judging others.

A loss of interest in judging self; a true state of be-ing.

Gaining the ability to love without expecting anything in return,which makes living life a complete state of joy.

Although I felt I was light years from displaying these attributes, still, like Dorothy leaving the land of the Munchkins, I had stepped onto a strange and wonderful path. Having now had a month of SCI, I was anxious to make my way to Iowa. For many of the class participants, it was back to life as they had known it before this magical thirty days. For me, the adventure was just beginning. By the way, by the end of the course, both Mike and Judy stopped smoking.

Tom and Nick North, Whidbey Island, Washington – 1954

16

FROM DREAMS TO REALITY

Maharishi International University (MIU) began near Santa Barbara, California in 1973 and moved to Fairfield, Iowa in September of 1974. Until the late 1960s, the Fairfield campus had been owned by Parsons College, a chain of liberal arts colleges scattered around the Midwest. Parsons had a reputation as a school where the wealthy could send their delinquent or otherwise intellectually-challenged children who couldn't get into ivy-league schools. Adopting a fairly loose academic retention policy, their enrollment skyrocketed and boys outnumbered girls by a four-to-one ratio. In the early seventies, the "Parsons Bubble" collapsed beneath the weight of allegations concerning fiscal abuse and mismanagement, which included a $20 million campus renovation. The TM organization was able to purchase the entire campus for the fire-sale price of $4 million.

Fairfield was and is a small Midwestern agrarian community, with a population of about 10,000 people; most of them earning their living in some way from the farming industry. When Parsons was part of the community, students provided a lot of energy for a thriving trade in the local bars and steakhouses. One of the humorous ironies of the revival of the campus was that when the business owners learned that the university was going to start up again, the bars filled their refrigerators with beer, and the steakhouses with beef. However, they weren't able to move those products, because the community ended up getting mostly non-drinking vegetarians.

The disconnect didn't end with food and drink. The town was situated in the middle of America's Bible Belt and residents came to fear what they didn't understand. The Bible-thumping Midwest farmers and townspeople had been able to understand and at least tolerate the hard-drinking Parsons students, who would act rowdy and dance on top of tables, but it was more difficult to accept the strange, Far Eastern-minded people who were showing up in their midst, using strange words, eating strange food, and engaging in practices that the local natives neither comprehended nor cared to share in.

The new students didn't necessarily look that different. In fact, they dressed more conservatively than most college students. However, because the ideas they represented were potentially alienating to the townsfolk, it was recommended that the men wear suits and the ladies wear simple dresses, to present a proper, less threatening image to the public. That tactic went only so far. As then mayor, Ralph Rasmussen said in his welcoming address to the student body, "Quite frankly, we don't understand you people at all!"

The campus was beautiful and quite large, occupying 185 acres. Many of the buildings were stately old brick, covered with ivy. At the front gates was a sign emblazoned with Maharishi International University, bearing the quote, "KNOWLEDGE IS STRUCTURED IN CONSCIOUSNESS" wrapped around the image of a rounded tree, its branches bearing fruit. Beyond the sign was a long parking lot, which fronted buildings on both sides. On the right side were the classic ivy-covered administrative offices in a red brick colonial motif, some of them replete with white colonnades and trim. On the left was the main lecture hall called the Learning Center. From the street, it looked like a large one-story circular brick building, perhaps 125 feet in diameter. But it had a second, lower level below the ground. It housed a number of lecture halls and some smaller classrooms within its core. Near the high point of elevation on campus, the Learning Center looked down on sweeping lawns, quite a few more buildings, and two ponds that were bordered on one side with tall windblown cattails.

There was a creek running east through the low point of the grounds, surrounded by cottonwood, elm and willow trees. Waterfowl and songbirds made this area their homes, providing that part of campus with a symphony of sound and color. Beyond the Learning Center were "the Pods" or dormitories that housed some of the 600 or so freshmen and sophomore students. Each Pod was octagonal with two visible stories for dorm rooms. The Pods all had basements, some of which had been converted to a student lounge or a kitchen.

Each dorm room opened out onto a central court or atrium. There were about twenty Pods visible from the Learning Center and each one had become home to about eighteen students.

Beyond the parking lot on the left was the Dining Commons. Also brick, it was single story; and although one of the more non-descript buildings on campus, it was extremely popular, for obvious reasons. The Student Union was close by, with a rather modern, somewhat A-shaped roof; and next to that was the gymnasium or "Field House" as it was known.

The Burlington Northern Railway ran on tracks that formed the University's western boundary. This was within a few dozen yards of the Pods on the west side of campus. I made a note to avoid being assigned to those Pods. I had visions of being awakened in the middle of the night by the train on its way to Iowa City, sixty miles north. On the other side of the tracks began farmland that stretched for miles and miles... the kind of rolling cornfields the Midwest is famous for. There were larger frat houses east of Highway 34, a two-lane thoroughfare that cut through campus. On the west side of the highway was the starkly brick and glass Howard Dorm, more classrooms, and the library.

I felt so privileged to be at MIU, like a man who had found water after a long sojourn in the desert. I remember walking through the parking lots after registering, staring up at the ivy-covered buildings and marveling at my good fortune. Another person might have had a ho-hum response to the place; but I was thanking God for giving me the opportunity to be in a truly supportive environment, where I could grow as a person in any direction I chose. Most students are excited about their first day at college; but after touring the campus and enjoying my first meal, my excitement was barely containable. I felt like an immigrant might have felt coming to America and seeing the Statue of Liberty for the first time, full of hope and expectation for a better life.

I had overcome the obstacles in my way and made it to college! And not just any college: this environment embodied my opportunity to re-invent myself. The peaceful and supportive sentiment I sensed in the people I was meeting at MIU gave me a feeling like I was "coming home to a place I had never been before," as John Denver wrote. This was where I could find myself and mend my broken pieces. Earning a degree at the same time was an additional bonus. The anticipation of that growth and the possibility of redemption gave me an enormous sense of gratitude. On the first evening there, I went to the dining hall and saw people of all ages, but mostly young people like myself. I was almost speechless. I felt like a child at Disneyland.

After having had to deal with a steady stream of familial challenges up to that point in time, I marveled at the contrast, with the unconditional acceptance, spiritual equilibrium and even exuberance that seemed to fill the place. I could see my own sense of relief reflected in the faces of the people I was with, and could hear it in the ring of their voices. Love seemed to pervade the entire environment at MIU.

Maharishi Mahesh Yogi had instructed the TM organization leaders in the U.S. to build a university where students practicing TM could experience and enjoy "200 percent of life." He arrived at the 200 percent figure by adding one hundred percent that is "relative," meaning oriented to our daily existence in the material world, (sometimes characterized as "chopping wood and carrying water") to the other one hundred percent of life, that he termed "absolute," referring to the experience of transcendent pure consciousness in and, eventually, out of meditation. In other words, Maharishi was advocating a quality of life with the aggressive goal of embracing both sides—relative and absolute—of our human experiences.

Part of the relative side of the equation for the university was the logistical challenge of feeding 2,000 people a day—faculty, staff and students. The school itself made no dietary regulations or demands on the students, acknowledging diversity and accommodating the American predilection for consuming animal protein.

No one was required to be a vegetarian; chicken and/or fish were served daily. When MIU moved from Santa Barbara to Iowa, they continued their food supply contract with Sunburst Farms, an organic food producer operating throughout the Santa Barbara area. As students, we thought it was great; eating all the fresh organic fruits and vegetables we wanted, trucked in daily from Santa Barbara. Wow!

Walking into the food court of the cafeteria was a mouth-watering experience. On one side of the food service area was a bank of six electric, industrial-grade juicers. Large barrels of oranges, grapefruits and carrots stood nearby, ready to juice into the four glasses on my tray. Giant bowls of nuts, roasted or raw, cashews, peanuts, and filberts, awaited in large stainless steel bowls, all for the taking. On Thanksgiving, several whole turkeys were available, from which we could carve our own portions! The lower-stress environment clearly showed in the enthusiasm of the kitchen staff, who prepared food with the élan of five-star chefs, creating a dining experience not unlike one found at a Whole Foods type of store.

One day I drank six tall glasses of fresh squeezed orange juice… just because I could! I got hives. Maybe I overdid it? Regardless, the food was so good that in 1975 the university was rated second in the country in the Playboy magazine national college food-service poll. I don't know how it managed to beat MIU, but Princeton came in first. Go figure!

Then someone came up with the idea of family-style dining. Bringing people together around the dinner table was a great idea, but only in theory. The food was delivered to the farthest tables first and then the servers worked back toward the kitchen as they served. Somehow platters of roasted chicken or baked fish, and especially the chocolate chip cookies, disappeared on the way past my table. I don't know how that happened. This same thing happened to tables where friends of mine sat. Trust me: family-style dining didn't work. The university's administrative staff was attempting to honor Maharishi's instruction to deliver 200 percent of life, but initially, this wasn't very realistic when it came to budgeting.

Sunburst Farms had very high quality food, but keeping the contract with Sunburst was not a good decision, either fiscally or logistically. The cost of trucking organic food from California to

Iowa every day, 365 days a year was enormous, not to mention
the cost of the high quality, organic food itself. In its third year in
Fairfield, starting to feel the fiscal strain, the university hired a
professional administrator. He quickly made the observation that
money didn't seem to go as far as it should in a two-hundred-
percent-of-life universe. His audit determined that 200 percent of
the university budget was going into our mouths! He put a stop to
that right away. Good-bye fresh squeezed juices! Good-bye juicers!
Good-bye raw or roasted and salted everything! Aw, nuts! Good-
bye Princeton and the Playboy poll!

The enormous change in the menu was a shock and a
disappointment to the students, but was nevertheless, necessary
to save the university from an early demise. It's noteworthy that
students were absolutely free to drive into town for a steak and
a beer, if they wished.

Although not as many of us chose to do that compared to the
Parsons College days, some of the students were actually adept at
consuming beer, yours truly among them. However, the school
fostered a social climate that encouraged development of a healthy
diet. It encouraged us to pay attention to the union of mind, body,
and spirit, rather than maintaining them as separate considerations.
So if I drank that six-pack, I knew I was creating a toxic environment,
dulling the mind, and affecting meditation. But, being a little rough
around the edges, on many occasions, I did just that. The school
faculty considered beer drinking and the like to be activities that I
should someday put behind me; but they were certainly not to be
banned or forbidden by some list of rules and regulations (although
it was not allowed on campus). The students were regarded as
independent beings. It was up to us to find our way to the light,
so to speak.

If I never came to sufficient clarity to modify those things, the
school understood that no amount of regulations would serve to
bring me to enlightenment; these things are always inside jobs,
from the TM point-of-view.

Nobody ever mentioned my drinking except Therese. One of
the several young ladies I became enamored with during my stay
at MIU, Therese had a gift. Actually, she had several; two of them
located just about ten inches below her collarbone. Oh, my god!
It was so difficult to maintain eye-contact! She was beautiful, with

wild blond curly hair, deep blue eyes and a smile to melt my heart. She also had an ability to see "auras," the energy field around every human body. Two days after I'd had just a couple of beers over a pool game at a local bar, I ran into Therese on campus. I approached her for a hug, but she held me at arms' length and looked at me disapprovingly. I asked what was wrong. She informed me that I had a big "A" for alcohol pulsating around my body. It wasn't long afterwards that I came to see the wisdom of controlling and refining my behaviors. If Therese could see the effects of alcohol on my system a full two days after its consumption, it couldn't be a good thing. It was a practical choice, really, because of the need I felt of throwing off hindrances to gaining what I needed and desired, which included Therese.

The campus was permeated by a pragmatic fervor, which was different from any religious zeal. There was an underlying acceptance of the fact that certain behaviors and diets were appropriate for people who were seeking what we were seeking —lending themselves to an optimal support of the experience of meditation. Rather than rules and regulations, this was a tide, a trend that moved among the student body, raising us all by energy created through the sense of connectedness that the school program acknowledged, and, in fact, fostered.

Since Maharishi Mahesh Yogi had been a physics student during his undergraduate studies at the University of Allahabad, he spoke the language of science. When he brought TM to the United States, he attracted many academic people who were at the cutting edge of their own disciplines, including some Nobel Laureates. These educators had been at many of the top universities of the world, including Oxford, Cambridge, Harvard, Yale and Princeton. Having reached the outer limits of their chosen field of study, they apparently found themselves asking, "What's next in our disciplines?" which included such specialties as physics, music, literature, business, biology, etc.

The answer they came to, much to Maharishi's delight, was "consciousness."

Maharishi pointed out at symposium after symposium across the U.S., and around the world, that academic disciplines could be raised to the next level by acknowledging their role in integration of and harmony with the "laws of the universe." Higher meaning and connections, he pointed out, could be derived from an increase in awareness of the place of one's consciousness and of any particular body of knowledge within "the grand scheme of things."

To return to the symbolism of the MIU logo, once again, the totality of knowledge can be viewed as a tree, with its roots representing consciousness itself. As it rises out of the root system, the trunk branches out, with each branch of knowledge taking its place as one part of the entire scheme of knowledge that the tree exhibits when viewed as an overarching meta-structure. In this "tree of knowledge" metaphor, the parts fit together to make the whole because our experience of any and all knowledge is actually based in consciousness. In contrast, mainstream western educational institutions teach individual disciplines as disjointed and unrelated topics, but the MIU curriculum presents them as related and complimentary to one another.

My own discipline, business administration, for example, is connected to biology, which is connected to music, which is connected to literature, math and art. This is not hard to see, really, because many of the expressions of these disciplines can be represented as sine-waves. We see the up-and-down motion of sine-waves in the beat of a heart or the scales of musical notes, the changing of the seasons, or the movement of the economies, as they expand and contract. Leading-edge quantum physicists have been reporting for decades that the overarching structure of the universe reveals itself in such mathematical "laws" as the Golden Mean, sometimes called the Golden Ratio or Golden Rectangle, which shows up in everything from the proportions in a human face to the arrangement of veins in a leaf.

Such things are not aberrations; they point to a fundamental unity of the world, and indicate an underlying matrix of energy and intelligence, expressed in myriad forms, all woven elegantly into the "Circle of Life."

As a new student at MIU, my first academic year began with 36 core courses, which I took (along with 400 other freshmen) at the rate of one course per week, eight hours per day. These were general college courses that included the traditional sciences and liberal arts, such as math, physics, biology, art, music and English literature among others. Every student was required to take the first year of core courses. I was a transfer student, with 30 units coming in. But by taking these courses, I had the opportunity to see the music in biology and the physics of finance. It all made sense in the light of human consciousness, something that I could now more easily point to as the "root of the tree of knowledge."

By the end of the first nine months, I had completed the required core courses and prepared to move on to the next year's curriculum, which consisted of nine courses, each one month in length. These were much more specialized toward the student's major, and in my case included mostly business-related courses. However, the interdisciplinary theme wasn't abandoned after the first year. In that second year, I also took a one-month Western philosophy course and a one-month education course as electives. To say I was getting a well-rounded education would be to put it mildly!

North children in Seattle visiting Auntie on the way to California – 1960

17

A PLACE TO HEAL

When Maharishi Mahesh Yogi came from India, he was accustomed to the monastic experience of meditation, which was, by nature, reclusive. As the first Westerners began going to India to learn meditation, they were given their mantras, told to go to their rooms, and meditate as long as they liked. The experience for each devotee always focused upon the meditation experience; the environment had no sense of time-restriction, nor any imposition of schedules. The devotee essentially became reclusive and people would often remain in a meditative state for days on end. Meals would be brought to them, left outside their door, and sometimes taken away untouched.

However, accommodation had to be made when meditation was exported to the West. The average person's daily schedule requires time to be allocated throughout the day for just about everything, posing a conflict with the idea of freely meditating as long as you like and whenever you wish to do so. In addition to that, Westerners brought various levels of stress and expectation to their experience of meditation. It was discovered early on that too much expansion of awareness too fast can create complications for people who are unprepared for the pace of "purification" of body and mind that comes along with it. Over the years, I have met many people who were part of the early meditation safaris to the Himalayas.

Most of them were perfectly well-adjusted and benefited enormously from their experience. Others, however, seemed quite "spaced out." These unfortunates often had a hard time adjusting to the social environment they attempted to re-enter. Through observing experiences like these, it became clear to me that meditation is a very powerful technique for purifying and refining the mind, body and spirit.

It became clear to the TM movement leadership that unstable individuals could create risks for themselves and for the people around them. As these casualties continued to occur in the early meditation courses, the time allotment for meditation was refined until it was determined that 20 minutes twice a day was an appropriate pace for the Western mind. It's a standard that has continued until the present day. The "risky" aspects of meditation occasionally manifested themselves at MIU. Disassociation would happen to a couple of classmates every year, and we would hear on the grapevine about someone "losing it" and being taken to what was referred to among the students as "The MIU Room" at the University of Iowa Medical Center, sixty miles away in Iowa City. There were people who, perhaps due to infusing pure consciousness "too much, too fast," or perhaps due to some inherent weakness in their nervous system, had lost their sense of individual ego. They went "out there" and never came back.

I learned about The MIU Room very early in my studies at the university. At one of the first cafeteria meals I attended, I noticed a particularly attractive young blonde woman. I learned that she was a second-year student named Gabriella and resolved to meet her some day. Two weeks later, while going through the dining hall, I realized that I had not seen her for a few days.

I asked one of my new friends, "Where's Gabriella?"

A knowing look crossed his face. "You didn't hear? She went to The MIU Room."

It turned out that Gabriella had come into the dining hall, picked up her food tray, and then became "lost" in her mashed potatoes. After 20 minutes, someone realized what was going on, and in short order, the "men in white coats" took her away. She never returned to the campus. I don't know if she ever returned to the world.

The University of Iowa psychiatric ward came to include former students who had experienced this kind of failure at maintaining integration. These "lost" souls couldn't carry on a conversation, and sometimes became incoherent. Or, as in Gabriella's case, they would become fixated on some normal object.

Because the school was experimental, educators from around the country came to visit and to observe classes. Many of them remarked that they wished their own students would display the same kind of enthusiasm and integrated understanding as the students at MIU. A few of them actually chose to remain, learned to meditate and became faculty members. Another group of visitors who came from time-to-time was a small brotherhood of Benedictine monks from Dubuque, Iowa. This was a monastic order of Catholic monks who adhere to the 1,500 year-old rule of St. Benedict by taking a vow of silence and spending their lives in prayer. They loved visiting MIU, because they found an entire community who could relate to the experiences that they were accustomed to in the depths of their own personal silence.

Every third month, for my first two years, all students at MIU went into a specialized course of study called "Forest Academy." The metaphor referred to the time yogis often spend away from humanity in a cave or deep in a forest. During this time, we stepped back from the society of students and faculty and spent an entire month in reclusion and deep meditation; much as I had done in the SCI course I'd taken at Cobb Mountain in California. Staying on campus and limiting interactions with students not on the course was required. The university imposed controls and supervision on the students to limit the "casualties." This was understood by the students, and generally speaking, compliance was not a problem. During the time of Forest Academy, I was amazed at how sensitive my reactions became when I inadvertently interacted with someone not on the meditation course. Even after a short conversation, I could feel an increase in heart rate, and a generally unsettled, uncomfortable influence in my body. Maharishi knew what he was doing when he structured the isolation factor into our activity schedule.

In each month of Forest Academy, the frequency of meditation extended beyond the normal 20 minutes twice daily, with the intention to delve into silence and stay as quiet as possible throughout the month. As I settled down, like most of the students, I looked forward to accelerating "the purification process," permitting my body and mind to slow their pace, to unwind and release the backlog of stress I had accumulated in what I considered to have been a very stressful life. In so doing, I was simultaneously enhancing the clarity of transcendence or pure consciousness in my meditations.

Diving into my own consciousness was a process that, day by day, piqued my sense of wonder as my mind quieted down and my body settled, deeper and deeper. When meditations are experienced sequentially, the second meditation often will pick up where the first one leaves off, deepening with each one. It became common to observe only four breaths and sixteen heart beats per minute. That was between meditations. In the depths of silence during meditation, there was often no perceptible breath or heart beat. It was often the case that after only repeating the mantra once, I experienced my body falling away, with my awareness expanding into sheer, blissful unboundedness.

The only problem with additional meditations was forgetting where I was, what I was doing, and which meditation I was on. When I was doing my asanas, the thought sequence went something like this: "Is it the swan pose next or the lion? Did I just do a sun salute or was that a peacock? Am I on the second set or is it the third? How long have I been doing the breathing? I forgot what time I started. I sure wish I could stop thinking about Lucinda. She is such a wonderful woman and what a body! Tom, get your mind back on yoga! Oh, yeah, now which asana was next?"

Multiple meditations resulted in a cascading effect into greater sensitivity, which carried with it certain risks. Each of us had a buddy, for safety's sake, just like a scuba diving buddy. Each had to always know where the other was. The buddy pairs, in turn, reported into a small group. The purpose was to monitor each other's experience, ensuring that it remained easy, effortless, and as comfortable as possible. That directive could also be translated as: Stay close with your buddy, so that there's no going over the boundaries into behaviors that are not recommended. It's likely we could all agree that doing naked yoga on the grass in the middle of the campus in the middle of the day would qualify as a behavior that is… not recommended. Fixating on and stalking another student or faculty member: definitely not recommended. That will get you sent home or to the MIU Room. One student was feeling so uninhibited, so free of the fetters of social boundaries, that he felt it was just fine to practice his yoga postures on the lawn as previously mentioned (naked).

I arrived just as he was being escorted back to his room by members of campus security. I heard that he was then taken to the medical center for observation and was not allowed back on campus.

Anyone who began exhibiting behaviors inconsistent with the expected range of experiences became suspected of being "OTP," or "Off the Program." Of course, many of us have exhibited some anti-authoritarian tendencies in our lives; so it's perfectly understandable that at 10:30 at night, one might want to go into town for one reason or another. That might not sound like such a transgression; but in such a settled, subtle state, while the body and mind are so-o-o-o quiet, it could actually be a shock to one's nervous system to force it to perform regular activity. We have all had the experience of being startled by someone we didn't know was behind us. Demanding activity of a body in a meditative state can be somewhat like that.

As advisable as it was to avoid going into town, it was even more advisable to stay away from the car dealerships, especially when they were open. We were warned about sudden impulsive "gotta-have-it" feelings; but George, who was on my course, must not have been listening. He went into town on a lunch break during the third week of rounding and walked by the local Ford dealership. He fell in love with and drove back to campus in his new Ford Mustang, which, of course, he could not afford. Well, it seemed that he could afford the Mustang, but then he couldn't afford his second semester of school. After Forest Academy, George said he didn't even like Mustangs. Yes, indeed, George had to go home.

It became apparent to many of us that equally important during these periods of extended meditation was the avoidance of romantic interactions, or what we referred to as "course relationships." Having had an experience of bliss during meditation, it was not uncommon for a course participant to outwardly direct that opened heart… and fall madly in love with another person he or she barely knew, or didn't know at all. Momentarily convinced of the divinity of this new object of affection, all attention would be focused on her or him. It was also common to fall completely out of love again, all in the course of a single meal or class session! Those who stayed transfixed beyond that moment or brought their newly found infatuation with them into normal activity often regretted it. I listened carefully when the course director, Holly, warned us about course relationships. I made sure that the infatuations I fell… or jumped into, stayed temporary…except the one I developed for Holly. I delayed that one until Forest Academy was over.

If I had gone to college just for the academic degree, it might have been to a more traditional university, but long meditation courses were only available at MIU. I recognized early on that in a direct, profound, and systematic way, it helped me to heal. As with the SCI course, laughter was one of the wonderful things about these times. The sensitive state of consciousness we were in provided us with access to the bliss that we (and everyone, for that matter) normally covered with layers of personality; it was the laughter of pure delight. But the un-stressing takes whatever form is specific to the individual. In my case, bouts of depression haunted me as the emotional and psychological traumas of earlier life left me.

There were times when I would go on a "walk and talk" with my buddy and I would not just feel, but re-live the horrible depressions that I had experienced in my adolescence and teen years. What got me through the reliving of those depressions was the understanding that these emotional stresses were unwinding themselves, and exiting…. leaving my system for good. That didn't make them less uncomfortable or easier to experience; but having identified that they were unrelated to any current experience of the moment helped. On a physical level, for example, I had gone through two surgeries on my left knee — one at age six and the other at age 16—to remove ganglion cysts that had occurred and reoccurred. During three consecutive Forest Academies, I experienced excruciating pain in that same knee that was identical to the experience of having those cysts surgically removed. The pain started when I increased the number of meditations, lasted the duration of the course, and stopped when I went back to a normal activity schedule. Following the third Forest, the pain stopped. There was no more pain... ever.

This was not an isolated incidence. One of my classmates, Gary, came to the dining hall for breakfast one time with an amazed look on his face.

"You look astonished. What's up?" I asked.

"When I was 16, I was in a car accident and spent nine months in traction; plus, I had to wear a collar for many months after that. I lost some range of motion and couldn't move my head... like this!"

Gary moved his head from left to right with as much range as I could do myself. That morning, in his meditation, he had experienced the same movements that his head had gone through in the accident. And when the pain stopped, the full range of motion was restored. The lack of mobility that he had experienced for so many years was gone. This kind of "un-stressing" was very common for the students. The pains were physical; the cures were both physical and spiritual, because, I came to realize, they are one and the same.

The benefit of releasing deep-rooted stresses from the body is the corresponding freeing of the consciousness that is bound in the tissues. In her landmark book, *Anatomy of the Spirit*, Carolyn Myss creates a simple comparison of the energy coursing through our bodies to electrical wires. She suggests you imagine 100 wires coming in through the top of your head, bringing all the energy you use on a daily basis. If you have 50 wires bound up with some physical or emotional trauma from the past, and another 40 tied up with some addiction or another, then you are attempting to run your entire physical, emotional and spiritual body with only 10 percent of your energy system. As you unwind the stresses in your body and from your emotions, you free the consciousness and the energy that comes with it to live life closer to that 200 percent number Maharishi talks about. That was my experience; one day at a time, unraveling the stresses in my system.

Tom with Grandpa Elliot North in Ajo, Arizona – 1976

18

VISITING THE SOUTHWESTERN NORTHS

Having been through a month of extended meditations, I felt ready to tackle the next level of academic challenge. I was refreshed, enlivened, and excited about resuming my studies. My first Forest Academy, however, ended with the onset of two weeks of Easter vacation. When I considered what to do with that time, it occurred to me that I had not seen much of my father's family since he'd died sixteen years earlier. I had heard from my mother that Grandpa Elliot North, my dad's dad, had been staying with my Aunt Betty and Uncle Joe in Ajo, Arizona. I had fond memories of visiting Grandpa Elliot and Grandma Iva on their Michigan farm when I was a toddler. Watching Grandpa take his teeth out of his mouth and put them into a glass of water at night was a marvel to me! The shocked look of wonder on my face brought the adults in the room to a collective laughing session.

There were other memories I'd cherished about Grandpa, as well. He had a German shepherd named Bosco, who as far as I was concerned, was the smartest dog in the world. One afternoon, Bosco was told to catch one of the farmyard roosters. He chased it around until he cornered it and held it at bay in his own dog house. Grandpa reached into the dog house, grabbed the rooster by the legs and brought it out, squawking and flapping its wings. He gripped it by the neck, and then swung it around in the air a few times until the body separated and fell to the ground. I watched in fascination as that rooster ran around the chicken yard again, but without its head! Later that night, it became our fried chicken dinner. The next day, Grandpa took all of the kids on a tractor ride. I fell off the bench behind the tractor, and with little more than my grandfather's whistle and a nod, Bosco came running, grabbed me by the nape of my shirt, and dragged me to the farm house, into the waiting arms of Grandma Iva.

Grandpa and Grandma had come to visit us in Carmel on a number of occasions. They were simple, uneducated farm folk, without pretension or guile. They loved their son, and it broke their hearts when he died. In almost every family there is a golden child, and Dick North was theirs. They wanted to visit his children more often, but there was always the complication of Frank Beardsley to deal with. He resented what they were to us, and it showed when they visited. So visits were few and far between.

With the two-week vacation approaching swiftly, I went to the MIU library and got out the World Atlas to find out where in Arizona, Ajo might be. Forty miles from the Mexican border, out in the middle of the Sonora Desert, just about as far away from anywhere as it could be, sat the little copper mining town of Ajo.

My uncle owned and operated a steakhouse called Dago Joe's, right on Highway… well, there isn't a highway even close. The road isn't named on the map, but the locals call it the Ajo-Gila Bend Highway. All I could see was that it was halfway between Gila Bend and Mexico.

After hitchhiking part of the way, and taking a Greyhound from Albuquerque, New Mexico to Gila Bend, I arrived at the local bus station, where my aunt came and picked me up. I hadn't seen her since I was a child, and it was gratifying to see how happy she was to see me. We talked about the family all the way to her home, which was right behind the restaurant just off the Ajo-Gila Bend Highway. Having worked at a steakhouse for four years, I expected to see a restaurant at least along the lines of a coffee shop. Joe had built the building himself, but never finished it. Standing on naked cinder blocks and two-by-four struts, the walls were peeling plywood and what looked like whitewashed sheetrock on the outside with a small, hand-painted sign that read, "Dago Joe's" on the ridge line of the roof. A single spotlight mounted below the sign was all that served to illuminate the entire sand and gravel covered parking lot.

My first impression was, "Oh my god, you've got to be kidding!" but, being a polite grandson and nephew, I kept that to myself. Parked behind the restaurant was my grandfather's old camper. Aunt Betty parked the car next to it and went to knock on the camper door.

"Someone's here to see you, Grandpa!" she hollered.

The door opened and a tired old voice came out, "Oh? Who might that be?"

Grandpa carefully stepped down from the camper and, straightening up, looked me up and down. A tear rolled down his cheek, as he wrapped his arms around me and said, "Hello, boy. It's mighty fine to see you."

We hugged for a long moment. He stepped back and held me by the shoulders to get a better look at me. "You're a man now, Tommy. Gosh, it's good to see you!" he smiled.

Betty suggested we go into the restaurant to see Joe. I went first, and as we ascended the couple of steps through the back screen door, I looked over my shoulder at Betty and Grandpa. He was smiling broadly at her, as he winked and proudly said, "That's my grandson."

His words went straight to my heart, stirring within me all the longing for a family connection that I had felt but had been denied. In that moment, I felt the years I had been away from him and my extended family. The chasm was enormous, but I knew I could only narrow it a little at a time.

We passed into a small lounge next to a counter that seemed to have come out of a soda fountain in the 1950s. The tables in the lounge were red Formica, and the chairs were stainless steel with red plastic backing. The floors were light-colored linoleum that looked like they hadn't been cleaned in… well, since the 1950s!

Uncle Joe was behind the counter flipping steaks on the grill, a cigarette dangling from the corner of his mouth. His pack of cigarettes was rolled up in the sleeve of his sweat-stained tee-shirt. Joe came around from behind the counter smiling and running his hand through his straight black, greasy hair. He held out that hand to shake mine.

After our initial greetings he said, "You hungry, son?" Before I had a chance to answer, he smiled again and said, "Boy, I'm gonna' fix you the best rib-eye steak you ever ate."

What Uncle Joe could not have known was that I had quit eating red meat as soon as I left Alaska seven months earlier.

I thought about this as I said, "Well, Uncle Joe, I don't eat red meat anymore."

The smile faded from his face as the sound of my words went through his ears and sank into his brain. He stared at me for a moment and then it was as if the proverbial light bulb went on over his head.

He pointed at me and said, "I know why you don't eat red meat! You don't eat red meat, because you never had it cooked right!"

He looked around at the others for reassurance. Aunt Betty and Grandpa smiled at both Joe and me and nodded in agreement. I knew it was no use. Joe would never understand. I smiled back at him, "Medium rare, Uncle Joe."

He was right, of course. It was the most mouth-watering rib-eye steak I had ever eaten.

My aunt and uncle's home looked just like the restaurant. Sitting about 75 feet behind the restaurant, it also was constructed of plywood and sheetrock. They were clearly not interested in impressing anyone.

The next day, Grandpa Elliot took me for a drive out to see hieroglyphs near a spring, deep in the desert. It was good to spend time with my grandfather, asking him questions about my own dad, and listening to his war stories.

As a teenager during World War I, he had worked on a supply ship, shoveling coal into the boilers, all the way across the Atlantic Ocean and back. Grandpa told me that as a result of spending weeks at a time below decks, not having any sense of directional reference, he could not tell which way was which. North, South, East or West was all lost on him.

As we traveled through the desert, I sensed that my Grandpa Elliot was a simple, barely literate man of few words. I didn't care if he was a simpleton or Einstein himself. He was my granddad and I was proud to be his grandson. I looked at him and said, "You are a good man, Grandpa. It means a lot to me to be able to spend time with you."

He looked back at me and quizzically replied, "Oh?"

The family mythology had it that during a stint as a long haul truck driver, he had picked up a hitchhiker and delivered him from St. Louis to Los Angeles, paying for his meals along the way. When he arrived in L.A., he gave the young man some money and wished him well. The young man asked him for his address so he could return the money when he got his life stabilized. My grandfather smiled at him and said, "No need, son. Just do the same for someone else someday."

That is the kind of man he was.

I stayed a few more days, talking with my aunt about meditation, chakras and the time-space continuum. She was an avid reader of science fiction, and I found that during our conversations, concepts related to consciousness were not unfamiliar to her. My grandfather was headed back to his home in Albuquerque, New Mexico, so I rode with him as far as the bus station there. The bus ride back to Fairfield was uneventful, except for the clouds of pot smoke that rose from the seats in the back of the bus. I had wanted to leave that era of my life behind, but it seemed to follow me wherever I went.

College logo – 1976

19

GURU U

Back at the university, I continued my studies, taking core courses, one after another. I enjoyed the singular focus on one subject for the full week, which was an MIU innovation patterned after Colorado College's "block system." Whether it was English literature, Vedic studies, or biology, I was enthralled with the environment, the people, and the enthusiasm that the professors brought to the subject matter.

One of the many "visiting" faculty was Dr. Brian Josephson, a tall, lanky man with thinning, light brown hair on the top of his head and a wonderful English accent. He was a British physicist, who won the Nobel Prize in Physics for identifying the quantum mechanical phenomenon of "tunneling," which, among many other technological wonders, allowed for the invention of cell phones. "Visiting" means that these professors aren't really on the faculty, but have a great reputation so the university wanted to maintain an association with them. As luck would have it, I went for a walk one day with my new friend Stellavera, a beautiful lady with a smile as wide as the Kenai Peninsula, where she is from. Stellavera knew Brian, and I found myself walking across campus with the two of them, chatting about one thing and another. It would be ten minutes before we reached our destination, and I realized that, here I was, in the company of one of the great intellects of the day. I had him almost all to myself and I could ask him any question I wanted to; any question at all! I could gain insight into the secrets of the universe! I thought for a moment and a question that had puzzled me for years popped into my head.

I turned to my left, in Brian's direction, and asked him, "Brian, there is something I have been curious about for a long time."

He looked back at me and becoming serious, replied, "What is it?"

"Well," I said, pausing for a moment, "Do we Americans sound as nasal as you British say we do?"

He chuckled and nodded his head, "Yes, as a matter of fact, you do!"

As we walked toward the residence hall we were headed toward, I couldn't believe what I had just done. I had wasted an enormous opportunity, feeling every bit the knucklehead I was.

On another occasion, later that same year, the student body was treated to a lecture by Dr. John Lewis, Professor of Planetary Sciences at the Massachusetts Institute of Technology where he taught cosmo-chemistry. Dr. Lewis was also a leading consultant to NASA on all matters cosmological. We listened intently as he told us a story of the evolution of the universe, starting with the "Big Bang". The story proceeded to run through the periodic table of chemical elements, connecting each one as a necessary result of its precursor, and ending in the ultimate development of human consciousness. Dr. Lewis explained that the universe is teleological, or goal oriented, resulting in the evolution of creatures capable of reflecting on their own existence, as we are.

In simple terms, God was bored, fractured Him/Herself into myriad parts, and then brought those parts back into a form that created a mirror into which God could look. The amazing thing about the lecture was not so much that Dr. Lewis had, indeed, just shared with me the secret of the universe, but it was that he had done such an amazing job of story-telling that I actually thought I believed that I understood what he said! It was for me, the singular, most important lecture from a faculty member of the four years I spent at MIU. I knew from that moment on why I exist. I exist to reflect consciousness back on itself. And so do you. That's it. That's all of it. And according to John Lewis, it only took fourteen billion years to get us to that point.

When it came time to delve into the study of physics, I was completely intimidated. I kept silent and listened intently as Professor Bob Rabinoff, a tall, dark-haired man with very thick glasses; a hawk-bill nose, began his lecture. His wardrobe, tending toward dark suits and dark ties, seemed to match his serious demeanor. I focused on absorbing every word he said as he explained the similarities between the description of the universe according to quantum physics and the description of the universe according to the Vedas.

"The fantastic thing," he said, "is that they are not similar. They are, in fact, identical!"

I was astounded that two scientific, theoretical systems could evolve on opposite sides of the planet, separated by both space and time (the Vedas are thousands of years old, while quantum physics is 150 years old), and be essentially the same. The professor explained that this is because they have one thing in common: human consciousness.

The next day, several of the students interrupted Professor Rabinoff and complained that he did not include enough mathematics in his course material. They were arguing with him from their seats in the lecture hall, then standing, gesticulating and protesting loudly. I was shocked that they had the audacity to confront the professor like that.

But he calmly replied, "This is a core course for non-physics majors and the focus is Physics and Consciousness." Now if you would kindly sit down and follow the course material, you will find enough math to satisfy your lust for the mathematical keys to the universe in the second year course material. Thank you very much!"

For years, I had been telling myself that, contrary to what Frank Beardsley had told me, I wasn't stupid and I could do this work. Proving to myself that I could understand and master the concepts in sciences like physics or math became all-important.

For each core course there was just one exam, which was always held on Saturday mornings. The exam grade was the final grade for each course. By paying extreme attention in class and studying late into the night during physics week, doing well on the exam seemed like a sure thing. When Saturday came, I was nervous, but confident that I had prepared well for the test. I sat down with the other students in the main lecture hall and began my exam. I felt a steadily growing sense of anxiety and fear as I looked over the test. I began to doubt myself and wondered if I even belonged in college at all. I saw Frank's face frowning down at me from the kitchen door at the Rio Road house, screaming at me, "Boy, you're a loser, and you'll never amount to anything as long as you live!" I began to sweat. An acrid, foul odor exuded from my pores. The student in front of me apparently smelled my discomfort.

He turned around, wrinkling his nose, and asked, "Hey man, are you all right?"

Now, I added embarrassment to my miseries. I got up and moved to a corner seat away from everyone. I blinked away the sweat pouring into my eyes and tried to focus on the problems on the forms in front of me, finally managing to calm down enough to finish the test. Later the next week, I found out that I'd gotten a "C' for the course. I had studied hard every night and paid rapt attention in all the classes. I knew I had done my best, but I was still disappointed. Admittedly, the hard sciences, like math and physics, had always been difficult for me; but I vowed to myself, I am going to improve my grades and make it here!

Most of the professors who taught the core courses were highly qualified and demonstrated mastery of their disciplines. But like faculties in colleges everywhere, some were barely qualified at all. The lecturer for the World Religions core course was a lay person whose name was Paul. Another tall, curly-brown-haired, thirty-something lecturer, he wore a permanently impassioned expression on his face. I had been looking forward to this course, hoping that it would connect the dots between all the world religions through consciousness. After two hours of lecture, I began to suspect that "Brother Paul" was taking his material from a Catholic Catechism text. I had heard it all before in grade school. The student sitting next to me was a fellow named Jack, who had attended Catholic grade school in Connecticut. He and I exchanged a knowing glance and rolled our eyes. I leaned over to Jack and asked him if he played tennis. He responded, "Not well, but anything will be better than this!"

I whispered, "I'm not that good, either, but I agree!"

We left the class, played tennis the rest of the morning, and found that we were well matched. We met at the tennis courts the rest of the week as class was beginning, talking about physics, Jack's major, and of course, girls. Jack shared with me that during the previous summer, he had been math tutor to a young lady who was a member of the Rockefeller family, when he was nineteen and she was sixteen. Jack chuckled, "I taught her math and she taught me… well, anatomical topography. I learned far more than she did."

At any rate, we did not to return to World Religions class until Saturday morning for the exam. Lucky for me, I really did know my catechism and got an "A" for the course.

Biology, a subject I have always loved, was taught by Dr. Robert Keith Wallace, the president of MIU and a biologist with a Ph.D. from UCLA. "Keith" as he was affectionately known, was beloved by everyone on campus. He was soft-spoken, articulate, and smiled as he lectured. He was about five-foot six or seven inches tall, thin, and had wispy blond thinning hair on the top of his head, which he kept pushing back in place when it dropped down over his eyes. He was a joy to listen to. Sitting in his class was like being in heaven for me. In that lecture hall pulsed an excitement among the students that was palpable. I anticipated the delivery of the wisdom of the ages and wasn't disappointed. Making it a point to sit in the front of the lecture hall to catch every nuance of his words and expressions, I listened as Keith made biology come alive. He drew connections between the structure of DNA and consciousness, explaining that the embodiment of the energy and intelligence of the universe is at the basis of all life. There is a wonderful saying from the Vedas, which goes, "As above so below; as within, so without; as with the macrocosm; so with the microcosm." Keith showed us how the same laws of nature that structure the relationship between the planets and the sun, structure the relationships between the various tissues in the human body and the mind. His delivery was a joy to listen to and a tonic for the intellect.

One of the more colorful faculty members was Dr. Susan Levin. "Susie's" Ph.D. was in Education, the department which she chaired; but the rumor mill had it that she had spent her early twenties as a singer in San Francisco during the psychedelic sixties.

A tall, voluptuous, beautiful woman with long black hair, piercing brown eyes and a heart of gold, she exemplified what Maharishi wanted us all to radiate, which was "creative intelligence." As she taught the principles of "consciousness-based education," the subject matter sang to me. When we talked about the proverbial "light-bulb" going on in our heads when we get an idea; well, let's just say that Susie was turning lights on for everyone in the room, all week long.

Moving on to the next week, however, I was not so thrilled with the music core course. Not being musically inclined, I had hoped to learn the basics of music theory and perhaps develop an interest in the subject. The professor, Dr. Jones, who had Hollywood good looks and a whimsical air about him, was a concert pianist who had earned his Masters in Fine Arts from Julliard. The most exquisite explanations of the connections between music and consciousness, sound and silence had to be in store. Paul began by trying to explain a fugue. Into the hand-held microphone he said, "A fugue is... well, a fugue is... well, let me show you."

Then he walked over to the piano, put down the microphone and played a beautiful piece for us. We all clapped and smiled, but I didn't have any better understanding of what a fugue was than before. The whole week went that way. When Saturday came around, I was one of the seventy percent of the class who flunked the exam. The other thirty percent were either musicians or had some musical training.

My statistics professor was another interesting character. I don't remember his name, and he doesn't even appear in any of the yearbooks I have. But he was an engineer from Israel, who had spent many years in the Israeli army. Although darkly handsome, his physical features seemed to have been precisely cut from a very linear diagram; square jaw, steeply angled nose beneath square, thick, black glasses, and a dark single eyebrow that went from the extreme end of one side of his forehead to the other. He was soft-spoken, but his demeanor was extremely military, which didn't set well with me. I knew we students were in trouble when he arrived in the classroom wearing a black suit and tie anchored by combat boots. He was another well-meaning and very knowledgeable faculty member who was probably very good at engineering, but he just could not teach. Pointing at diagrams and graphs, bell curves and data schedules, he'd ask us if we understood it and did we have any questions. When one of us (often me) would answer that I didn't get it, he would point at the chalk board or slide and say, "Well, it's perfectly obvious!" He didn't even make it through the first week of class, and had to be replaced.

However, during the short time he was my teacher, I happened to have had dinner with his father, who was visiting MIU to find out what his son was doing in this strange place in Iowa, of all places. His father didn't meditate and had no interest in meditation. But during our meal, he shared with me that he always wondered about something.

"When my son and daughter-in-law go into the spare room to "meditate," are they really meditating, or having sex?"

I laughed, and assured him that even as little as I knew of his son, they were most definitely meditating.

In spite of the few duds among the faculty, most of the core courses were taught well, providing inspiration beyond my expectations.

The idea of consciousness-based education attracted an interesting mix of students as well as faculty. There were a lot of hippies and ex-hippies among the university population, but I couldn't tell the difference outwardly because long hair and beards on men were not just discouraged, but forbidden. The university wanted to project a conservative image and required that its faculty and students convey that conservatism in both dress and hair style. The faculty men and any male students who were teachers of TM were required to wear suit and tie, and the ladies wore conservative dresses most of the time.

Like the professors, some of the students came as transfers from Ivy League schools. Having been told by my mother and step-father that I didn't belong in college, I was in awe of the scholarly rigor and precise thinking I found myself surrounded by. In the company of many of my classmates, I often felt like an intellectual infant in the presence of adults. One such occasion happened during a literature class. The subject was Shakespeare's play, Twelfth Night. Early in the play, the scene is set with a hillside covered in violets. It occurred to me that this was a form of "foreshadowing;" the planting of an idea in the reader's mind before the introduction of one of the central characters, Viola.

I meekly suggested to the class that this might be so, and then looked around for a response. The enthusiastic reply came from the smartest student in the school, Steven Bernhardt, who supported my observation with gusto, slapping his head and exclaiming, "Wow! What a great connection! Of course, it's foreshadowing! Shakespeare never misplaced a word. It has to be foreshadowing!"

I didn't know what to say. I had never been in a conversation with Steven Bernhardt, being completely intimidated in his presence. But I found that he was a good person, with a genuine love of knowledge, welcoming me into a scholarly discussion. All I could say, stammering, was, "I... I guess so."

No discussion of the students would be complete without mentioning the "bliss-ninnies."

As opposed to students like myself, who were at MIU to expand their awareness and purify their nervous system of the intoxicants they may have errantly ingested along the path, there was an entire segment of the broader group who seemed to be genuinely pure, saintly people. Some of them had unfailing smiles plastered on their faces, accompanied by an affinity for the rules and regulations. I, and people like me, who were at times more inclined toward beer and billiards, found this irritating. A common belief circulating among the bliss-ninnies was that having sex was counter-productive to spiritual evolution, causing the energy to travel down the chakra system; and of course, in order to become enlightened, we want it going up, you know! Consumption of alcohol was another impediment to be avoided if one wanted to maintain that sparkling aura. For me, the most annoying characteristic of the bliss-ninnies was the complete acceptance of authority from administrators and course leaders, teachers, or anyone who was rumored to have an inside track to higher states of consciousness.

The odd thing was, and this really bothered me, was that the longer I spent at MIU, the more I seemed to take on these traits myself. I made note of this early on and guarded myself against too much non-specific smiling and engaged in activities like sex and drinking that ensured that I wouldn't evolve too fast. But as time passed and I meditated more, I seemed to drift away from at least the drinking.

The weather in Iowa never ceased to amaze me. Each season seemed to arrive dramatically and all at once. There was a transition that happened almost as if some divine hand pulled down a curtain with a new landscape painted on it. The fall came with its turning of the color of the leaves on the deciduous trees right at Labor Day each year (or so it seemed). Winter came on the day after Thanksgiving, without fail, every year, often with a snowfall. Spring leapt out of winter at Easter, with crocuses popping out of the ground as though someone had snuck in at night and planted them almost fully grown. Summer became instantly oppressive with its heat and humidity, usually right around Memorial Day.

An Iowa winter can be as challenging as in any of the other upper Midwestern states that are famous for extremely cold conditions. The winter of 1976-77 wasn't exactly an ice cave in the Himalayas, but it was so harsh that the austerity we faced made the MIU campus seem like one.

In preparation for the oncoming winter, I had scoured the second-hand stores for suitable clothing to protect myself from the cold. With some luck, and a huge dose of serendipity, I had managed to buy a pea-green military-surplus arctic coat, complete with sheepskin lining and a fur–lined hood, in my size, for twenty-five bucks. With my long underwear, heavy socks and rubberized boots (also purchased at the second-hand store, for five dollars), a pair of down-filled mittens and a large wraparound shawl, I thought I was ready for the worst.

In January of 1977, an arctic storm swept down out of Canada and gripped Iowa and the surrounding states in all-time, record low temperatures for two weeks. Snow drifts piled so high on the freeways that the natural gas trucks that brought fuel to the MIU campus couldn't get through. With the school's stored supplies of gas dwindling, the college administrators calculated how long it would take to run out. It turned out that the disruption of the gas company's delivery schedules left the possibility that the school might be without enough natural gas to heat the buildings for an indeterminate amount of time.

It was left to the students to decide whether to close the school and go home until the spring thaw arrived after the Easter break, or to shut down all non-essential buildings and tough it out. "Non-essential" meant all the dorms, all the classrooms and the gymnasium. The plan was to heat only the administration building and the cafeteria. A meeting of the entire student body was held and the issue was put to a vote. Close the school and go home, or tough it out with unheated classrooms? The vote wasn't even close. Almost unanimously, the students voted to keep the school open.

For several days, the university maintenance crew moved from building to building, filling the water pipes with anti-freeze. Preparing for the moment when the heat was turned off, they wanted to make sure the water in the plumbing didn't freeze and burst the pipes.

While that was being accomplished, my dorm-mates and I were back in the second-hand stores, buying all of the antiquated, electric coffee-makers we could find. We had no idea how long the heating crisis would last; but we knew that we were going to be without showers, if we were caught unprepared when the heat and water to our building was shut off. Fortunately for us, there was a surplus of old, institutional, multi-gallon coffee-makers to be had cheaply. Steve, my dorm-mate in the room next to mine, came up with the idea of melting snow in the coffee-makers, then filling one-gallon water jugs with the hot water.

The cap of the water jug was punctured with several holes, and, by holding the jug upside down over one's head…voila! Hot showers! The air temperature in the shower stall was near or below freezing, however, so trust me, we didn't dawdle while drying off and getting dressed!

For the two weeks that the heat was turned off in the dorms, the classrooms, and the library, I wore my arctic clothes almost everywhere. Outside, the temperature dropped to seventy degrees below zero with the wind-chill factor. Everyone was warned not to go outside alone, or at all, if possible. Just breathing could be dangerous. I sat in classes with a shawl around my mouth, watching the condensation from my breath drift away into the air. Writing was a little challenging with down mittens on, but I managed.

I followed the warning not to go outside in the minus-degree weather until, that is, it became clear that I would have to go out and rescue the duck. What duck? Why, the duck who wouldn't come inside, of course! That duck.

The picturesque ponds in the center of campus were home to a variety of ducks during the spring, summer and fall. We had several large white ducks and a few mallards, with their beautiful blue pin feathers and shiny green heads. One day, late in the month of October, the school's groundskeepers collected the ducks to return them to the rent-a-duck center. It turns out these weren't wild or migratory ducks. The capture technique was rather simple. Grain was put on the grass near the pond. When the ducks came to feast on the grain, a net was thrown over them. They were collected, put in cages in the back of a pickup truck and driven away.

There was one mallard female that refused to fall for the trick. She stayed apart from the other ducks, and when the day was done, she was still out on the little pond, alone. As the weeks wore on and the weather became colder, she could be seen, still out on the pond, stoically carrying on in duck fashion, keeping to herself and refusing overtures of bread or other enticements from concerned students like me. When the snow fell and the pond finally froze over, the little duck was left sitting on the ice during the day and in the reeds at night, not unlike the character from the children's story, Jemima Puddle Duck.

The snow piled higher and the temperatures dropped to levels that would be fatal for a human. The mercury read between zero and a few degrees above for days on end.

Since the pond was between my dorm and the dining commons, on several occasions I stopped to see if I could approach "Jemima," and perhaps talk her into allowing me to pick her up. She would have nothing to do with me, allowing me no closer than about ten feet, before getting up and waddling away. I knew it was just a matter of time before the lack of food and water would wear her down, and I would find her in some little nook in the copse of cottonwood trees, frozen solid, and with x's in her eyes.

When the record low temperatures hit, I suspected that Jemima was probably getting too weak to resist capture. On my walk to breakfast one day, I detoured off the path by the pond to check the spot where I had last seen the mallard huddling among the reed-choked roots of a sapling cottonwood. Sure enough, she hadn't moved since the previous day. As I approached, the crunch of my boots through the three-foot-deep snow drifts made enough noise to cause her to open her eyes. She shifted position and wagged her tail feathers, but seemed otherwise too weak to move. I moved slowly, talking to stubborn little Jemima, telling her it was time to come inside and get warm and have some water. To my surprise and delight, she stayed still as I wrapped my hands around her and lifted her out of the snow and tucked her inside my coat, under my left arm.

I carried the duck to the dining commons, concerned all the while that she might die from the stress of being captured in such a weakened condition. When I got a cardboard box from the kitchen and put the duck in it with a bowl of water and some cornflakes, she drank the water and began immediately eating the cornflakes, which ended my worry.

Having fed little Jemima Puddle Duck, I sought out the head of the groundskeepers and turned her over to him. He smiled and looked surprised, promising to deliver her to the rent-a-duck farm.

Mealtime at MIU, as I'm sure it is at most college campuses, was an important time to share information and rumors, develop and dissolve romantic relationships, and generally facilitate the energy of the community of students. In every group of students, there are characters who stand out as comedians, intellectuals, athletes, musicians, etc. I made a point of sharing mealtime with a variety of people, not getting focused or too attached to any one group and enjoying the diversity and entertainment factor each person and group provided.

One night, sitting at a table with a group of classmates, the young lady at the head of the table decided that she wanted to liven up the evening a bit. Peggy is one of the most outgoing, dynamic women I have ever met. She seemed to be an extrovert, with a sweet soul, an outrageous sense of humor and a penchant for mischief.

This particular night, she suddenly stood up on her chair with her hands full of food that she had grabbed from her plate, and lifting them over her head, shouted "Food fight!"

That is as far as the idea went, because just as the words left her mouth, Professor Susie Levin came out of the faculty dining room, immediately behind Peggy, and shouted in her ear, "Peggy, sit down!"

Peggy was so startled that she complied immediately like a turtle pulling back into its shell. I laughed at the irony of the moment, remembering my antics in grade school when I got caught making faces at Mrs. Baker.

I will admit to having spent a fair amount of my MIU mealtime seeking the company of attractive women; so from time to time, I sat myself down next to one or more of the women I felt fit the description, with the idea of perhaps engaging in connubial behaviors later in the evening if circumstances allowed. However, I must say that I may have occasionally undermined my own chances for the sake of humor or the telling of a good story.

At one evening meal, the menu included artichokes. To make them available to all the diners, the kitchen staff had cut them in half, allowing one serving per person. Coming from California, artichokes were a common vegetable to me, and were nothing out of the ordinary. Some of the students from the east coast or the Midwest had never eaten or even seen one, and asked for guidance in the proper consumption of an artichoke. Do we use a fork? Do we eat the whole leaf? What about the fuzzy stuff in the heart? Can we use our fingers? Reasonable questions to be sure, until one of the young ladies I had sat down with noticed that tucked between the leaves of her artichoke was a worm. Having eaten worm-infested artichokes as a boy, I knew that there was nothing bad about worms in an artichoke, except for perhaps an aesthetic aversion to them. Besides, the worm is just another source of protein, anyway.

The young lady in question, hailing from New York, screwed up her face in a grimace, declaring in disgust, "Eeeew! There's a worm in my artichoke!"

The other girls at the table leaned in her direction to get a look at it, and just as their attention was focused on her plate, I leaned across the table, reached into her artichoke, and removed the worm. With all eyes on my fingers, now clutching the small, cooked, dead creature, I then demonstrated the proper disposal of an artichoke worm.

Enthusiastically telling her, "It's an excellent source of protein," I raised my arm in the air and with an exaggerated flourish, dropped the worm in my mouth, chewing well to make the point.

One girl screamed, "Oh, my god!" covered her mouth, and pushing her chair away, ran from the table.

Two more followed her example, and within a few seconds, I was alone at the table.

Damn! I thought. That prank sure backfired!

North children – 1960

20

THE RAZOR'S EDGE

Maharishi Mahesh Yogi had only one goal when he came to the West and that was to enlighten the world. His spiritual master, Swami Bramananda Saraswati, the acknowledged leader of the Shankaracharya order of Hindu monks, had given him marching orders before passing away in 1953. Affectionately known as "Guru Dev" (divine teacher), he had instructed Maharishi to take the knowledge of enlightenment to the masses, and ultimately, restore the understanding that "the essential nature of life is bliss" to western civilization.

Maharishi began teaching Transcendental Meditation in 1959, and its effects on the collective consciousness of humanity would be his contribution toward the transformation of human experience on a global scale referred to by his master. Having spent the first fifteen years of his quest multiplying himself by training teachers to systematize the spread of TM, and sharing his wisdom with the intellectual elite of the world, it was determined that a university where ideal education would be established was the next step to take.

Beginning in 1973, MIU was a giant petri dish within which Maharishi experimented with spiritual techniques from the ancient Vedic scriptures. He monitored the experiences of students at the university and meditators all over the world. As course participants demonstrated an understanding of the experiences of deep transcendence, and more importantly, began articulating that understanding, Maharishi introduced new programs and techniques. Meditation courses became longer, some of them lasting a year or more (although not at the university).

In 1978, I participated in the first TM-Sidhis (pronounced "cities") training course taught at MIU. The course lasted throughout the entire summer and was Maharishi Mahesh Yogi's first experiment in integrating the Patañjali Yoga Sutras in an academic setting on a large scale, with about 400 students on the course.

Patañjali was a great seer, a Maharishi himself, who lived about 2,100 years ago. He cognized and set down a series of aphorisms or sutras, whose purpose was to advance human understanding of and integration into higher consciousness, specifically that state of enlightenment sometimes referred to as "unity consciousness" (characterized by everything—including all outer, or observed phenomena—being experienced as one with the "divine within"). From the Sanskrit word "sutra," we get our English derivation "suture", which means "to bind." Proper use of the Patañjali Yoga Sutras, according to Vedic record, causes the meditator's pure consciousness to bind with the body or with the emotions or with the environment, depending on the sutra being practiced, thereby enlivening the effects of that specific sutra in one's consciousness and enhancing one's integration of a more "enlightened" state of wholeness. During the three months of what became known as the MIU Summer Course of 1978, I experienced the greatest transformation of my life. After gradually extending the schedule of meditations over the early weeks of the course, I settled into a routine of continuous transcendence. Many of my meditations were non-stop bliss for hours at a time. I would say the mantra once or twice and that was it. I was gone... into the unbounded... into the Light, from beginning to end.

I want to admit here that, for the first month of the course; I "cheated" at meals.

Please allow me to explain. It is a common understanding among people who meditate regularly or pay attention to such things, that the process of digesting food requires a lot of energy. Few people think much about it, but digestion itself is a form of activity. Any activity in the body or mind can inhibit transcendence to that degree. Less food in the digestive system means less blockage of the transcending process; so in order to expedite my experience of transcendence, I fasted. For an entire month, I ate half a cup of yogurt with a teaspoon of honey in the morning, and nothing else for the rest of the day. In addition, I went into a state of self-imposed silence, only speaking when I had to, which was not often.

In order to enact my "secret plan for accelerated spiritual progress," I needed, and got my course buddy's complicity in this. As long as I promised I wouldn't freak out, he agreed to keep my secret. With so little food to metabolize, and reserving the energy I would have spent talking, I was in a state of walking, waking transcendence for the entire month. Bliss, bliss and more bliss! Every day when we assembled in our respective small groups to discuss how things were going both in and out of meditation, I listened to the other group members describe their experiences.

"I slept through the whole thing," one would say.

"I had non-stop thoughts" said another.

When my turn came, I simply whispered, "Light, just pure light."

The others got sick of hearing it. The looks on their faces reflected their disappointment at not having disappeared into the light.

As I continued to sit through the various video-taped lectures of Maharishi speaking on subjects such as, "The Gap Between Thoughts," "Love and the Tender Impulse of Life," and "The Artist and the Scientist," my appreciation for this humble man whose only apparent desire was to enlighten the world grew immensely. Silence became my favorite subject. I watched Maharishi on videotape, as he patiently reminded me that the essential nature of the mind is bliss. What blocks the experience of bliss, he emphasized, is stress, which often accumulates through the experience of daily living. What became clear to me was that prior to coming to MIU, I had become habituated to experiencing not my bliss, but the many layers of stress that buried it. The result was a state of constantly identifying with the stress and not with my true nature. My experience through the regular practice of meditation was that I was steadily unraveling those knots and slipping into that pure and most natural state of bliss.

A remarkable side effect of the continuous meditation I and other students were doing, was our inability to sleep at night. By spending hours a day in meditation, and staying quiet during class time the rest of the day, our bodies accumulated almost no fatigue at all. After a couple of weeks of this routine, what fatigue I had brought into the course had been eliminated. The result was a state of awareness, or perhaps I should say, "awake-ness," that often lasted throughout the night. This became a problem for some students who found it difficult to lie still for eight hours, not sleeping, but not wanting to be awake. If it was mentioned in small group that sleep was difficult to come by, then that student was conscripted into "the walking group." About 25 course participants were seen on a daily walk, with the intention of giving them at least some little bit of exercise that might help them sleep at night.

Personally, I found it fascinating to lie quietly in bed, feeling the body, monitoring the heartbeat and observing my breathing, which became slower and slower as the night progressed. On several occasions, I was able to quiet my awareness, focus my attention on one blood cell and follow it all around my body. Much like the 1966 science fiction movie, "Fantastic Voyage," in which a group of scientists are shrunken to microscopic size and travel through a human body, I traveled through the entire circulatory system of my own body, seeing its structures and functions from the inside! At other times, I was surprised to notice that my heart was racing, far faster than would normally be healthy. I just lay there unconcerned, observing, and knowing that something good was happening.

During one particular meditation, I did my routine of yoga postures and breathing exercises, and then began my mantra internally. After just a couple of repetitions of the mantra, my body dissolved and my awareness was suddenly traveling in all directions simultaneously, expanding in a spontaneous state of tremendous ecstasy. Sitting in that state, I became aware of a light that emanated from a single point. I went towards the point, passed through a narrow tunnel, and came out into a space of golden light.

Continuing deeper into the light, I knew that it was leading me into the presence of the divine — into the presence of God, which was suffused in that golden light. I didn't just see gold light, but actually became golden light. As I approached the source, the only thought that remained in my awareness was a desire to permanently merge into that light, to be with and of the divine. But then I encountered an invisible barrier, and in my awareness received a message that conveyed to me that I could not merge, but had to return into the physical world. The message wasn't delivered orally, but occurred within my own understanding… not so much a voice, as it was a knowing... a divine surmise, which was, "You must go back," which is when I immediately localized back into my body.

It is important to be clear that when I desired to merge into the divine, it was not a death wish. The "other side" that I experienced was not death; rather, it was transcendent, something beyond the concepts and experience of my normal, waking mind. However, in reflecting on it later, it helped me to grasp that, when we leave this world, we don't go into the ground (no matter what the typical burial looks like). We go into another state of non-physical being, or whatever term we can think of to describe the metaphysical reality that underlies the filmy skin of this terrestrial existence.

My return to the body felt somewhat like the starting of a car engine. Although this is a crude comparison, the feeling of it was like an ignition key had been turned on, and all of the bodily functions roared back into action. My heart, which had been beating so slowly and softly as to be unnoticeable, started pumping again. My lungs filled with air in a deep breath. I felt like the meditation had lasted five minutes but when I looked at the clock, I was astonished to see that it had been four hours!

One might think that the response to such an experience would be elation, but I was terribly disappointed at having been denied the opportunity to merge with the divine presence of God. The Ultimate Parent had said "no" to me. I felt unworthy and rejected, which triggered a depression that lasted for days. I suppose my angels watching me might have sighed and shaken their heads, saying, "Ah, these children… never satisfied."

During the second month, we received the majority of the Patanjali yoga-sutras we would be learning, several at a time. My experience with practicing the sutras picked up where the meditations left off. I had better success with some sutras than with others, but those I had success with were remarkable in their clarity. One repetition of the sutra and the result of the correct use of the sutra would manifest. As we learned the sutras, we were kept under close observation during group meditations for body movements, which might signal some instability in the nervous system. Anyone caught with a head twitch or a visible gyration of the body would be interviewed and could be taken off the course. It got to be a joke among the students, as the word was passed around not to meditate during our regularly scheduled afternoon group meditation. I would often sit there, eyes slightly open, watching the course leaders watching the students. To be fair, the people administering the MIU Summer TM-Sidhis course wanted to make this experiment in group consciousness as safe as possible for the approximately 400 students on the course.

Another point of concern was going OTP. Remember "off the program"? Most students were too sensitive to go into town while doing so many meditations, but it did occasionally happen. We were a self-policing group, responsible to ourselves first and then to the TM-Sidhi administrators. As fate would have it, I was cast in the role of sergeant-at-arms, a job I took quite seriously; perhaps too seriously.

One day, rumors began spreading that, if we as a group did not stay on the program and take our opportunity seriously, we would not be receiving any more sutras, let alone the famous "flying sutra," which was saved for last. The flying sutra was the big deal of the day. A mythology had grown up around it. Everyone on the course speculated what it was like to practice this sutra, reputed to develop one's ability to levitate (and ultimately, as Patañjali himself phrased it, "pass through the sky") at will. Do you fly right away? What does it feel like? How long do you stay up? We all wanted to know. Rumors spread that so-and-so had just come back from a TM-Sidhis course in Europe and had levitated all the way across the room. Of course, she was immediately looked at with tremendous awe and respect (even though none of us were aware of any evidence or witnesses to support this rumor).

Chris, a cocky kid from Chicago, suggested that we all go over to the girls' dorms one night for a little hanky-panky visit. I was incredulous and told him that we needed to adhere to the schedules, lights out and be in bed by ten.

He smirked, "Aw, screw that!" while waving me off with a flippant gesture.

Immediately, I was furious. Completely out of character, I stepped forward and grabbed him by the lapels, pushed him up against a nearby wall and railed at him, "Listen, you punk! You may think you're really cool and better than the rest of us, but I take what we're doing here very seriously. You may not care, but I'm not going to have some smart-ass rich kid ruin what I have worked so long and hard for. So, knock off the wise guy crap and get in line!"

He looked at me in shocked surprise, and then sheepishly smiled. "OK, Tom, I get it. Now would you let me go, please?"

We had no problems after that.

One morning halfway through the third month, I heard the sound of trucks moving about outside the pods. I looked out my dorm room window to see campus vehicles piled high with six-foot by six-foot sheets of foam rubber spreading out among the pods. This could only mean one thing. Chris, the kid from Chicago stayed on the program! We were going to get the flying sutra after all!

At the appointed time, the course participants filed into the learning center main lecture hall. The ascending rows of desks had been fitted with earphones accommodating four hundred students. When Maharishi, in Europe at the time, came on the video phone system, each of us could hear him, see him and be connected to him for instruction. He gave us a lecture on Patañjali's philosophy of the Yoga Sutras, extolling the importance of our role in bringing coherence to the collective awareness of humankind. He then told us he wanted to see one hundred percent success from us. Upon receiving the levitation technique, or as it was called, "the flying sutra," we were to go in silence to our assigned groups of forty students, each group assembling in their respective basements of pods scattered around campus.

As I arrived in my group's basement "flying room," I saw that the entire floor had been covered with foam rubber from the trucks I had seen a few days prior. The students tip-toed on silent stocking feet across the sheet-covered foam, and fanned out to sit in a large circle with empty space in the center of the circle, all forty of us. Sitting next to me was a fellow student from Missouri whose name was Louis. We didn't know each other at all, but exchanged excited glances of expectation before closing our eyes. After a time of meditation, we were to begin the sutra. Sitting in full lotus posture next to Louis (who was also in full lotus), I was engulfed in an energy field that had also captured him. At the drop of the sutra, my field of internal vision turned into bright gold light, as both Louis and I exclaimed loudly, "Oh, my God!"

Immediately, we lifted off the foam. I went straight up and Louis went up and forward about four to six feet. I came down and sat there waiting for the hand of God to come again and move me. Louis kept making large hops around the room.

Every time the impulse overcame him, I'd hear "Oh, my God!" from Louis. I peeked, just for a second, and saw his head move back so quickly I thought his neck would snap. Then it moved forward just as fast, with his chin touching his chest, as his body rose up and came back down, again and again.

He went around the entire center of the circle, the only one of the forty of us to do so. As he arrived back at his starting place, he stopped, turned to face me, leaned forward and shouted, "Why aren't you flying!?"

Then he resumed his effortless circles around the foam, shouting, "Oh, my God! Oh, my God!"

I wondered, too, why I wasn't flying. The familiar cloud of worthlessness and self-doubt came back to hover over me. I sat there chastising myself for not flying. I repeated the sutra, but I didn't move. Not a single inch.

After the session, we returned to the lecture hall, resumed our seats and put our headphones back on. Maharishi asked for a show of hands how many had flown. Four hands went up. One of them was, of course, Louis. Brian, another of my classmates sitting next to me, was another. One of the young women and another fellow across the room also raised their hands. I had only gone straight up and then back down and didn't think that qualified, so I didn't raise my hand.

Suddenly, Brian began to laugh as his whole body began to vibrate and shake like a just-caught fish on the deck of a boat. He was out of control as his head moved forward and back. I was afraid he was going to smash his face into the desktop. I grabbed him and guided him out from the desk and onto the floor, where he continued to laugh and flap around. Another student at the far end of the room caught the frequency Brian was on and began to go through the same seemingly ecstatic movements.

I asked Brian if he was okay.

Through his laughter he said, "Yeah! This is great!"

Later, he described it as having been plugged into a warm, delightful electrical energy that ran in and around his whole body. The flying sutra had activated his and the other student's "kundalini" energy (an inner energy force, most often associated with the "awakening" of the chakras—subtle energy centers within the body—and the development of higher consciousness).

When we broke for lunch, I stood outside the learning center with another friend of mine, Willy Mathes. We looked at each other in amazement as students filed past us on their way to the dining hall.

Willy exclaimed, "Isn't this incredible?"

As we turned to follow the others, I replied, "Yeah man! It sure beats the hell out of church!"

From that day of the flying sutra onward, we all considered ourselves "sidhas" (translated loosely as one who has integrated the sidhis into the wholeness of his/her awareness); aspiring sidhas, to be precise, but sidhas, nonetheless. As the days went by, more and more students raised their hands in the lecture hall, until there were only about thirty of us who had not had some degree of success with the levitation sutra. I didn't consider my initial movement to be "flying," because I had needlessly compared myself with Louis, whose levitation had been beyond amazing.

Meanwhile, a conflict was brewing that began to demand attention. The problem was that it was time for academic classes to resume. With only a week to go before the beginning of the semester, we had not fulfilled Maharishi's instructions to achieve one hundred percent success in the practice of the flying sutra. The elected president of our group was an older, outgoing, popular senior named Mark. He had overseen the collection of evaluation sheets as the course had progressed, and generally seen to it that order was kept and everyone was looked after... sort of the "mother hen" of the group. At the final session with Maharishi, Mark was in the unenviable position of reporting that we had not achieved the goal.

Maharishi, visible on the large projector screen of the video-conference monitor, said to Mark, "So, you will make sure that everyone flies?"

Mark casually replied, "Yes, Maharishi, we will make sure that everyone flies."

To which Maharishi repeated, "But, YOU will make sure that everyone flies?"

Mark didn't get it and repeated himself. "Yes, Maharishi, we will make sure that everyone flies."

Maharishi laughed and said, "No, YOU will YOURSELF make sure that everyone flies!"

As Maharishi shifted his mirthful, compassionate emphasis, Mark got it. His eyes lit up and he said, "Yes Maharishi! I will make sure that everyone flies!

We all chuckled and "oohed" at the enormity of Mark's new assignment and responsibility.

The following day, the unlucky thirty were called to a special meeting. We were informed that we were being sequestered in a "pressure cooker" room, where we would stay and meditate and practice the flying sutra until we flew. We were about two thirds men and one third women. We were then led to our respective flying rooms, separated by gender, as we had been for the entire course, and monitored all day everyday. We broke for bathroom and meals only. Truth be told, I loved it.

Since I had first read about the early days of the India meditation courses, I had wondered what it would be like to meditate non-stop for days on end. Here was my chance to find out. I was a veteran meditator, so I wasn't worried about frying my brain or spacing out and not coming back. I knew what it was to sit in bliss for hours on end. Now, I could do that to my heart's content…sort of. The meditations in the pressure cooker were only ten minutes, and then we were told to practice the flying sutra for as long as it was going to take.

On the third day, I realized that the slight impulse of energy at the base of my spine was what everyone had been referring to as the flying impulse. I had been waiting for "the hand of God" to lift me up, like Ali Baba on his magic carpet. The actual experience of incipient levitation is not like that, at all. Rather, it is quite physical.

After all, we're asking the body to do what the mind instructs it to, albeit in a remarkable manner. The impulse is felt at the drop of the sutra, but one needs to actually engage the muscles of the body and go with the impulse as it occurs. As I began to physically engage to go with the sutra, I felt more bliss and greater energy throughout my body. I bounced around the room a couple of times, and then reported to the monitor that I had flown. He corroborated that he had seen me hop around and I left the pressure cooker to join the main student body. I would say that my experience of levitation was anticlimactic, compared to what I had observed Louis do; but then, I finally realized, I was not there to compare.

What I had accomplished, besides getting in tune with the flying sutra, was to fulfill my desire to meditate for days on end. I had even done it in time to have two days to prepare for the fall semester's classes.

While on the summer course, I received news that a close family friend back in California was getting married. I wanted to attend his wedding, but my budget wasn't going to stretch to include a round trip ticket from Iowa to California and back, which was about 200 dollars. It occurred to me that there were enough siblings in the family to spread the cost quite thinly if I could get each of them to contribute a small sum. I wrote a letter to each and every one of my brothers and sisters, asking them to please send me twenty dollars so that I could attend the wedding. Some of the well-employed sent me more than I asked for. One of them sent me sixty dollars. Another sent forty. The younger ones sent five or ten dollars.

Some of the less fortunate wrote back expressing their desire to help, but, unfortunately, they could not. One of the girls shared that she could not even afford to buy a new pair of shoes, which she desperately needed for the wedding. When all responses were in, I had 300 dollars. I could afford to fly to San Francisco and back to Iowa, and send my shoeless sister money so she could buy those shoes. To my delight, I was asked to be one of the groomsmen.

When the MIU Summer Course was over, I made arrangements to fly out to California for the weekend, which was an incredible extravagance for me. Arriving in San Francisco, I was given a ride from the airport to the wedding by a friend of my sister, Jeanie.

Her friend, Gretchen (yes, the same Gretchen that had sat on my lap in the Jeep), had spent a lot of time in the Beardsley household and had been thought of as "the 21st Beardsley." She had been Jeanie's perpetual best friend since high school. It appeared that Gretchen had kept a warm heart for me since my junior college days when we had been occasional lovers. After we got in the car, she smiled and reached over to fondle my ear. As her hand brushed over my earlobe and stroked it, I suddenly realized how sensitive and alert to subtle physical energies I had become on the TM-Sidhis course. An electric impulse surged from my left ear down to my groin and into my genitals and back to my ear. Gretchen's intentions became shockingly clear. I had barely thought about sex all summer long, and now the opportunity was making itself very apparent. I had only been off the course for a day and wasn't ready to jump into intimate social activity quite that soon. I gently explained to her that I had been through "a lot" recently, and wasn't ready to be sexual with anyone yet.

She seemed to understand, and said, "Hey, take your time." When we arrived at the wedding, I hugged everyone, which, in my family took a long time.

I overheard a conversation between the groom and my mother that Cardinal John J. O'Connor, who would be presiding over the Catholic wedding ceremony, needed a ride from the Oakland airport to the Church. I offered to go pick him up and was assigned the task. Cardinal O'Connor had been a close family friend when he was the post chaplain at the Navy Post-Graduate School in Monterey back in 1961. He had risen in the Navy ranks and had become the chief of Chaplains for the entire U.S. Armed Forces, and was stationed at the Pentagon.

On the way back from the airport, he inquired, "So Tom, what are you doing with your life?"

I told him about my studies at MIU and asked him if he knew anything about Transcendental Meditation.

He looked surprised and replied, "Yeah, I know a lot about it! I was approached earlier this year by a couple of bright young TM teachers who want to introduce TM into the military academies (West Point and Annapolis). I asked them to give me a couple of months to do some research, which I did, and was very favorably disposed to their idea. Stress management makes a lot of sense in the military. But these guys never came back. I was ready to write the check and start the program, but I didn't hear from them. I guess they changed their minds!"

I thought about this for a moment, realizing that a huge opportunity had just gone down the tubes for the TM movement. I made a mental note to inquire about what happened when I returned to MIU.

The wedding was a joy to behold. The new bride and groom went on their honeymoon, and I flew back to Fairfield, Iowa to begin the fall semester of my fourth year of college.

Tom's college graduation – May 1979

21

FINDING DIRECTION

Within the business administration major, I had chosen to specialize in accounting at MIU. The title for the accounting text book was, Accounting, The Basis for Business Decisions. The basis for business decisions… it made sense to me, so that was my choice. I was an attentive student and enjoyed the orderly nature of accounting, recognizing that it embodied the orderliness of nature. Credits and debits mirrored the yin and yang, the positive and negative forces of the universe. I had come to the university   to bring greater order to my mind, and I found that the study of accounting was helping me to do that. My professor was a bright-eyed, young MBA-CPA named Andy Bargerstock. Andy had a whimsical air about him. Serious about his work, but infusing course material with humor and profound insights, he made what some people might think of as "boring information" interesting to me. One day, "Andy," as we typically called him, started class with an announcement that Tom Beardsley (yes, that would be me) was going to run for Treasurer in the upcoming student government elections. It was news to me, but having been adventurous in physical activities all my life, I thought it might do me good to take on something intellectual and social. I went right along with the idea, smiling and trying not to look surprised as the class applauded "my" decision.

Quickly, I mounted a one-man campaign for public office. I ran unopposed for the first few weeks, but then another of the accounting students, Richard, felt it was only fair to have two candidates for the office. This meant I had to actually compete and give a campaign speech in front of the entire student body, which was something I was not looking forward to. I sat myself down and thought about all of my job experience and what I might have to bring to the role of treasurer. I then wrote a speech that I thought would communicate the message I wanted to deliver.

On the night of the campaign speeches, I stood on the podium and spoke about my work history, which, as I recalled to the approximately 250 students in the audience, I felt was substantial. In my short life I had demonstrated ambition and diligence, working since I was eleven, holding down at least two jobs, and sometimes three. I had been involved in several aspects of business, including production (making donuts), inventory control (I had loaded bags of flour from the trucks to the storeroom), record keeping (I made change for customers and gave them a receipt) and public relations (as a busboy, I worked the dining room, serving hundreds of diners on any given evening). In addition, I had supported myself since the age of seventeen and was putting myself through college.

Having shared these accomplishments with the student body (but not the items in parentheses), they seemed to agree that I was the right candidate because they elected me their Treasurer. As such, I set up the ledgers and double entry bookkeeping system for the student government, ran the student theatre, sat on the student-government council and gave financial feedback to the student body President, when asked for it.

I was grateful to Andy for having coaxed me into public office. His encouragement helped me develop and expand my social and leadership skills, as well as directly apply the accounting knowledge I was learning in class.

As my third academic year began, some of my accounting classmates wanted to learn how accounting principles are applied in the investment world. One day, they went to talk with Dr. Dennis Roarke, a physics Professor who had taught chemical physics at Columbia University's School of Medicine before coming to MIU. A couple of the guys, Al Coles and Gary St. Denis, had learned that, in addition to teaching physics classes, Dr. Roarke had a long-standing interest in the financial markets and had managed a few portfolios in his spare time. They asked him if he would be a faculty advisor for the investment club that they wanted to form. When he agreed, they recruited several of their classmates, including me. It changed the course of our lives and we began imagining ourselves as stock-market millionaires.

The group of us got together with Dr. Roarke on Saturday mornings or Sunday afternoons to learn the rudiments of investment theory. Over the first few weeks, we were given instructions about creating portfolios, strategies for picking stocks, and methods for analyzing industries. Since we were starving students, we created model portfolios without any money involved; but during some exercises, the earnings we made on paper were pretty exciting and encouraging. As my grasp of the principles of investment strategy became stronger, I decided that this is what I wanted to do for the rest of my life.

One afternoon at the beginning of my junior year, I was inspired to write a curriculum based upon an investment concept called "The Capital Markets Line," which displays all forms of investment categories moving from most stable and safe (treasury bills) to most volatile and risky (commodity futures). I discovered that the concept very naturally broke itself out into four semesters of study. Treasury bills, certificates of deposits and other short term securities, like municipal bonds, etc. comprised the first semester of study. The second focused on the stock market. Then we went on to hybrid securities, like convertible bonds, and lastly, speculative derivatives like options and commodity futures.

I brought my proposed curriculum to Dr. Roarke, to see if he would permit me to do this as an independent study course. I asked him, "If we can get this approved by the Curriculum Committee of the college, would you teach it?"

He grinned, declaring, "I've been waiting for ten years for someone to do this."

We presented my course proposal to the Curriculum Committee and they approved it, changing just one word in the proposal, converting "and" to "or." Some of the committee members expressed an interest in auditing the class, because it looked so interesting. My analysis of the Capital Markets Line became the basis for a specialization within the business administration major. We called it "Financial Markets and Securities Analysis." For a short while it was part of the curriculum, with completion of two years of accounting classes as a requirement for admission. A dozen of us ended up taking the class.

This experience had the effect of helping to quiet the "message" that I had fought and yet subconsciously bought into for years, i.e., that I wasn't bright, that I was stupid, which Frank Beardsley had so completely instilled in me during the time that I was living and growing up in his completely dysfunctional household. And yet, I didn't feel overly proud or attached to the accomplishment. I just felt good that the idea to create an entire course of study within the business curriculum had arisen in my mind. I did recognize though, that it was an idea whose time had come and had simply come through me.

When I was nearing the end of my senior year, I wrote to my mother and invited her to my graduation. She made some excuses about responsibilities to the family and politely declined to attend. I was not surprised, but I was disappointed. I wrote her back with a reminder to her that, several years earlier, she had told me that if I changed my name back to North, she would disown me. It had occurred to me that turnabout was fair play. I told her that if she did not attend my college graduation, then I would disown her. I would no longer consider myself her son. It meant that much to me that she attend my graduation. After all, I had achieved something significant in my life, a college degree, which I had paid for myself.

All I asked was that she acknowledge my achievement. She wrote back and said that Frank had never been to Iowa and it would be nice to see that part of the country. They were coming!

They arrived the morning of the ceremony and left as soon as it was finished. I spent about four hours with them. The culture shock must have made them very uncomfortable. Frank was completely incapable of hiding his discomfort, with a forced smile on his face much of the time. With his face stuck in an inappropriate, outsized smile and talking through his teeth, he commented on how beautiful and green Iowa is in May. I wanted to tell him to stop posing! But I held my tongue, knowing what a challenge it had been for Frank and Mom to even make the trip.

Relatively quickly, I realized that it had been a mistake to invite them and almost felt sorry for them. But hey, they came. That in itself was a minor miracle, and it was what I had asked of my mom.

As I walked across the stage to receive my diploma, I felt proud of the journey I had taken and the goals I had accomplished. I will forever remember the last words Maharishi spoke to the graduating class. He closed his eyes for a moment, as he often did before saying something profound, opened them, and smiling, said, "If you only take one thing with you as you go out into the world, let it be this... stay rested."

Maharishi had visited the MIU campus a week before I had arrived in 1975 and came for another visit a week after I left in 1979. I thought it ironic that I spent four years there and was never in his presence. However, I was not disappointed. Maharishi had said in many of the early meditation courses that he was not going to play the role of guru to each of us individually.

He said, "I am not important. What is important is the knowledge of enlightenment."

Some of the early disciples did become emotionally attached to him and thought of him as their guru, and still do; but there were very few who spent their adult lives in his presence. With over ten thousand teachers of TM and over six million meditators, it was impossible to spread his attention that widely.

The role of guru in India is a very intimate relationship, requiring complete devotion from the devotee to the master. Traditionally, part of the disciple's path to enlightenment is to be in the magnetic or spiritual field (in Sanskrit, "darshan") of the guru as much as possible, thereby enhancing the mental and spiritual coherence that results from the guru's presumed divine radiance of enlightenment. Although many at MIU (and around the world) desired this relationship, it was not forthcoming for the vast majority. I went to the university knowing I was in a very real sense "damaged goods," and intuitively grasped that my agenda did not include personal audiences with Maharishi. Knowing he was not my Guru, I was not unhappy at not having seen him in person.

As I was preparing myself to leave the academic world of MIU that had made such an important contribution to my growth, redemption and integration as a human being, I reminded myself of a short poem that had come to me in a Forest Academy meditation. It went like this:

Don't think you know
Just because you close your eyes
Although it's the Being
That makes you whole
It's the living
That makes you wise

And so I left MIU to go out into the world, with a fresh sense of purpose and hope in my heart.

Helen and Dick North with their oldest four children in Oak Harbor, Washington
(Little Tommy is on Dick's lap.)

22

FROM FAIRFIELD TO FAIRFIELD

I came out of Maharishi International University a changed man. Four years of disciplined meditation had given me the strength and clarity to cope with the conflicts and self-defeating attitudes that I had unfortunately acquired through my association with Frank Beardsley. I had arrived at MIU distrusting almost all of humanity. I came out recognizing that everyone potentially has a dark side that should be assessed and guarded against; but in most people, there is far more good than bad. My cynicism, although still available to me if I thought it appropriate, was matched by a growing faith in mankind; a recognition of the value of each and every interaction with another human being. Where there had been a constant sense of internal conflict, there was progressively an ever-present calm and a growing sense of self-confidence. Where I had been constantly objectifying women, I now saw them as divine beings, to be respected as the miracles of creation that all humans are. I had learned to see the divine and acknowledge it in everyone.

When I finished school, I had almost no money and it seemed for a time, like I had nowhere to go. As luck or fate would have it, while my class was preparing to graduate, Dr. Dennis Roarke, my investments professor, decided to leave the academic world and start an investment advisory firm. One of my classmates, Albert Coles, had the use of his family's beach house in Fairfield, Connecticut.

Along with our friend and classmate, Gary St. Denis, the three of them planned to move there and go into business. Dr. Roarke, though, made the mistake of making an open invitation to the rest of the class to join them. Whether he made the offer out of politeness, or whether he just thought it sounded good, I will never know. He certainly wasn't counting on me joining them, which is exactly what I did.

In spite of being proud of having put myself through four years of college, I had a mountain of debt to pay off from the student loans I had taken out along the way. I was determined, however, to establish myself in a financial career of some kind, pay off my debts and build a life. What kind of life, I wasn't sure.

I knew I had more to learn about the investment world from Dr. Roarke. Besides, I rationalized that, among the three of us students, I could bring to their fledgling firm a deeper knowledge of accounting than they had, and could set up the bookkeeping system for the new firm. I packed my few things and left Fairfield, Iowa for Fairfield, Connecticut.

Immediately upon arriving in Fairfield, I went out to find work in a steak house, which I knew from my Hatch Cover days, meant instant money. I found employment and in a few weeks was able to pay my own way, fulfilling my desire to be as self-sufficient as possible. The steak house that hired me was called Porky Manero's, a landmark establishment in Westport. Porky Manero had been an amateur golfer of some note and a lively, if sometimes shady, character along the Connecticut waterfront. It was a restaurant with enormous personality; a somewhat schizophrenic personality, but colorful. The owner was Porky's grand-daughter. The kitchen staff was all black, while the manager, the bartenders and half of the waiters were white, gay men. I made an effort to fit right into the cultural patois of the restaurant. There I was, a California boy, fresh from Maharishi International University in Iowa, eating no red meat myself, but schlepping steaks and booze in Westport, Connecticut. At the time, I found myself laughing more than once at the contradictions in my life; but the money was good and I enjoyed the cast of characters I worked with. In the meantime, I worked as many lunch and dinner shifts as I could, with a plan to save enough of my wages and tips to buy a car and then begin investing.

The dining room, which seated about 200 people, was an old-fashioned, windowless space that carried a nightclub atmosphere. Just above the level of the patrons' heads was a cloud of cigarette and cigar smoke, through which the wait-staff plowed, carrying loaded trays of food. Several of the waiters had graduate degrees, but made more after-tax income waiting tables than they could have in their chosen professions or areas of study.

Having moved in with Al, Gary and Dr. Roarke, I set up a manual bookkeeping system, which was never used. Since there were only two clients, not much bookkeeping was necessary, anyway. But it made me feel like I had made a contribution and Dennis continued to share his knowledge of the financial markets with me. Dennis focused on managing those two accounts he had brought from MIU, while Al and Gary went out and got waiter jobs, as I had done. We practiced our meditations daily and worked as many shifts as we could to make money, so that we could trade our investment accounts and apply the financial skills we had acquired. Along the way, another of our former classmates, Jack Cross, showed up and lived with us in Al's beach house for a time.

We were the "four amigo waiters"… along with our former professor, Dr. Dennis Roarke, of course.

The firm of Roarke, Coles and St. Denis was slow to get going. We were babes in the woods, financially — sort of like the Keystone Cops of the investment world! Without marketing knowledge, which drives every business, we were dead in the water. Dennis may have known what an account executive was, but I sure didn't. We knew a little about investing, but nothing about building a business in a very competitive financial world. By the end of the year, we had few clients and little in the way of assets to manage. We were reaching a point of desperation, and tried to think of everyone we knew who we might approach and perhaps manage their money. I thought about my old friend, Michael Tancredi, whom I hadn't spoken to in over five years. What I didn't know when I called him was that I was about to learn one of the most important lessons of my life. When Michael got on the phone, I explained to him that I was now a member of an investment advisory firm, and would he like us to manage his financial assets for him?

He paused, chuckled, and said, "Tom, listen to me carefully. I haven't heard from you in over five years. Now you call me and the first thing out of your mouth is can I manage your money? Not, Michael, how are you? Not, gee, how's the family? But, can I manage your money! I'm hurt and disappointed, Tom. I thought we had a friendship. Now, I'm not so sure."

I was dumbstruck. I had been thoughtless and self-centered (again!). I admitted to Michael that he was right, and we chatted for a time, catching up a bit on the previous five years. There was never another mention of money or investment services. When I hung up, Gary and Al asked me how the conversation had gone. I responded, "Really well, actually. My friend just taught me a lesson I'll never forget."

After the first year, Al and Dennis developed a personality conflict that seemed to have no resolution, and it was decided that we would all go our separate ways. As I had been meeting people over the course of the year, at the restaurant and around town, they would often comment that I had a West Coast accent. When asked where I was from, I told them that I was from Carmel, California. Their almost unanimous response was, "So what are you doing here!" I realized that perhaps they were on to something, and eventually I decided to return to California.

Gary had called the investment firm of E.F. Hutton in Santa Barbara, California, and, explaining that he was a partner in an investment advisory firm, landed a job (sight unseen) there as an account executive. I figured that if Gary could get a job so quickly, then it would be easy for me, too.

I began interviewing at local brokerage firms, although I had a very different experience than Gary. During my first interview, at Blythe, Eastman Dillon, Inc., in Bridgeport, I explained to the manager of the office that I was a stock-picker and could do industry analysis, so he should hire me.

He calmly listened, then with a terse, somewhat sadistic look on his face, leaned forward and asked me, "Young man, we pay people a quarter of a million dollars a year to do analysis... what the hell do we need you for?"

Shaken by his question, I wanted to turn into liquid, sink into a puddle on the floor and slide under the door and out of there as quickly as I could. During my second interview, at Merrill Lynch, I explained to the manager how I wanted to train in his office and then move to California to work there. He smiled and thanked me for my honesty, then suggested that in my next interview I not tell the manager I would be moving to California. He explained that no one wants to spend the money to train me and then have me move away. Good point! I hadn't thought of that. After quite a few more interviews and rejections, I decided to postpone my job hunt until I returned to Carmel. I sold my VW bug to one of the waiters at Manero's, said my good-byes, and bought an airline ticket to San Francisco.

Tom and Connie – 1981

23

PATH OF THE HOUSEHOLDER

I returned to Carmel after a five-year hiatus and stayed with some old friends, while I continued interviewing with financial services companies. After finally learning how to play the interview game, I was on my 14th interview when I landed a great job, beginning my career as an account executive with Dean Witter, Reynolds, Inc. It just so happened that on the day I interviewed, the Northern California regional manager was visiting the Monterey office and decided he wanted to do the interview. I had revised my resume so many times, that, at least on paper, I thought I looked pretty good. The interviewer, Steve Miller, thought so, too, until he got to the part about Maharishi International University.

He looked at me over his reading glasses and said, "Your resume is in perfect order, except for this Maharishi thing. Is that some kind of cult or something?"

I replied, "Have you ever heard of Transcendental Meditation?" He hadn't.

I looked him straight in the eye and insisted, "I understand how the name of the college I attended might seem strange to you, but that happens to be the strongest point on my resume. If you put me and any other new financial advisor on the phone cold calling, when the other guy breaks for lunch and heads for the bar to drown his fear of rejection in gin, I will take a ten-minute meditation break and start calling again like it was a brand new day."

I then spent the next couple of minutes explaining to him the concept of stress management and the importance of relaxation. I finished with, "Now who do you want to have working for you?"

He looked thoughtful for a moment, smiled and replied, "You're hired."

I didn't become a millionaire overnight since financial services companies don't pay trainees a lot of money. Managers want to starve trainees, so they'll be motivated to bring in new business. The formula for trainee compensation is to determine how much money would be required for bare survival and then pay an allowance significantly less than that, so the young account executive-trainees stay hungry and work hard.

Having completed training, I began to dial for dollars, seeking clients. As I began to discuss money, investments and people's perspectives on these two related topics, I had to ask myself the same questions I was asking potential clients. How did I feel about money? What is risk and what is an appropriate risk or a reasonable return? Upon reflection, I found that years of deep meditation had done nothing to replace the faulty programming I had received as a child. When Frank Beardsley took his children's money from them, he was demonstrating to them and reinforcing in their little minds that they don't deserve money or the opportunities it can bring. When he worked the children in the donut and nut shops without pay, he was emphasizing that message. Worst of all, he literally told me and my brothers and sisters that we were worthless, that we were "nothing without the other nineteen." That indoctrination stayed with me, percolating throughout my subconscious, waiting for an opportunity to express itself. It made aspects of my early professional life a challenge for which I was unprepared.

By engaging in regular conversations about money with prospective clients, I was becoming aware that I had a bad case of "poverty consciousness." I hadn't made more than ten thousand dollars in a single year in my life, and suddenly I was talking with people who had, in many cases, millions in investment assets. To my dismay, I found myself uncomfortable discussing large sums of money with prospective clients. In one case, a friend of the family had told me that she would need financial help with a stock sale worth several hundred thousand dollars, and as soon as I was registered, would I please give her a call. When the time came, the idea of dealing with hundreds of thousands of dollars intimidated me in a way I hadn't anticipated; so I found reasons not to call the woman. One day, several weeks after I had been licensed as a stockbroker, I watched her walk in the office door with one of the other brokers in the office. She had become his client, not mine, and I had lost my chance.

This very negative tendency took me years to overcome; but my work became a form of therapy and I focused on rebuilding my self-image every day. I began listening to motivational and sales training tapes to re-program my memory with positive messages. I had also taken up distance running, as a means of balancing vigorous exercise with the inactivity of my sedentary desk job as a stockbroker.

One hot sunny day, I went for a 15-mile run and returned to the house I had rented, dripping sweat and high as a kite from the endorphins rushing through my bloodstream. The house sat on a knoll, so I turned around and looked down the pine-covered hill at the distance I had run. I saw the sweep of the forested hills of Carmel below me and the green coastline of Point Lobos State Park, a small, pine and cypress forested peninsula that juts out into the Pacific Ocean just two miles south of Carmel. Local legend has it that Robert Louis Stevenson, author of *Treasure Island*, used aspects of Point Lobos as his inspiration for that story. It was a beautiful scene to behold. I felt elated, but along with that came an odd feeling; a lack of fulfillment. It was not the first time. All my life I have been blessed with having peak experiences; but the curse that comes with that blessing is that I am often alone when I have them. Here I was again, feeling physically and spiritually high, but alone. I made a mental note to start dating. Perhaps, I mused, I could find an athletic woman to share these moments with. I kept that thought in mind and put it out into the universe.

One day, soon after that long distance run, I was visiting with Gretchen, whom I hadn't seen since the wedding a couple of years before, and asked who else was in town from the old days.

She smiled and said, "Connie Willert has come back."

I raced quickly through the hallways of my memory and remarked, "That's the tall, skinny girl."

Gretchen laughed, long and deeply. "Tom, little girls grow up!"

My imagination began to conjure up goddess-like visions that needed substantiation; I decided I had to check her out.

Connie had been a neighbor when I was growing up; literally "the girl next door." I hardly knew her, though, because, for one thing, our houses were separated by an empty lot that was a quarter mile wide. In addition, she was two years behind me in grade school and two years is an eternity to children.

I recalled her as a tall, skinny, unhappy-looking girl. The unhappiness was a projection, I guess, because, well... when I was younger, I was unhappy, and it turned out that Connie had been doing fine. She had been a competitive swimmer in high school and had kept her athletic figure into adulthood. My first sight of her (as an adult) took place at the home of another mutual friend, Tracy, who had been completely infatuated with my older brother, Nick, during our teen years. Tracy invited me over to her parent's home to visit with her and her parents before she was going out on the town with... Connie Willert! So to get a glimpse of "she who had become a legend in my mind," I accepted the invitation. I knew it was to be a short visit, but I would get a chance to check Connie out and see what had made Gretchen laugh at my misguided comment.

I arrived at Tracy's folk's home first, and reacquainted myself with them. We were visiting in the living room when Connie walked in. At six feet tall, it seemed to me that she had been blessed with the best features of her parent's gene pool. She wore high heels, which made her even taller, and she moved like a cat, her long legs swaying gracefully, the muscular calves standing out beneath her nylons. Wearing a tight blue skirt that came to just above her knees and a white blouse, she looked like she could have just stepped out of an office setting of some kind. Her ample bosom filled out her blouse, but she had it buttoned to the top and I admit that I was disappointed at being denied any hint of cleavage. I was stunned by her celebrity good looks. She had a strong, angular but feminine jaw line that was accented by the full lips of her mouth. Her tanned, clear complexion lay over high cheekbones below blue-green eyes with very little make-up, surrounded by wavy brown hair that came down just below her shoulders. My attention quickly moved back to Connie's eyes, which seemed intelligent, but reserved. During our introduction, she was polite, but barely noticed me and then she and Tracy left. I visited with Ig and Kay, Tracy's parents, for a few more minutes, bringing them up to date on my many and various brothers and sisters, and then I went home.

Continuing my re-acquaintance tour of old friends, several days later, I was hanging out with Harry Goulding at his mother's home when his younger sister Kelly showed up, accompanied by Connie, who had been among her friends throughout high school. We sat around chatting, and as I listened to Connie's voice, I sensed a maturity and self-assured demeanor that I found attractive. It came up in conversation that Connie was dating another guy. I was disappointed and realized that she wouldn't have the time of day for me. However, my desire to explore further contact seemed to be taken up by Cupid, because I then ran into her at a Halloween party where, coincidentally, she went as Wonder Woman and I as Superman. Connie did a more breathtaking job of filling out that costume than Linda Carter had ever managed (and I was a big Linda Carter fan), and that night, the eyes-wide thoughts of "the Man of Steel" were drawn to the other superhero in the room.

I thought she was very alluring, so I called over to her, "Connie. Come over here and talk to me." She looked at me with a blank stare, rebuffing me.

"Never mind," I said. "I'll come over there."

I walked across the crowded room, we began to talk, and I discovered that beneath her incredibly attractive and sexy exterior, Connie Willert was a warm, intelligent, unpretentious and sensitive human being. Much to my delight, the evening was cool to the point of chilly, and goose-bumps were forming on Connie's forearms and bare legs. I was wearing tights and a long sleeve nylon shirt, which did little to keep out the cold; so I did the only thing a superhero would do, under the circumstances. Putting my extensive super-skill set into action, I wrapped my cape around her and shared my body warmth with her. She appreciated the chivalry and I was happy for the opportunity to make physical contact. My excitement was short-lived, however, as Tracy, dressed as Cat Woman, came over and stole Connie from my grasp.

They ditched me and disappeared for the night. I was more than a little frustrated, imagining "my" Wonder Woman in the arms of that other guy, whoever he was.

The following week, Harry had an impromptu reunion of Carmel High alumni, again at Alice's. Connie showed up and we spoke again for a while. I asked her out for a date, and to my delight, she accepted. It turned out that at the Halloween Party, she had been in the process of breaking up with her boyfriend, and I was in the perfect position to provide her with a diversion from that unpleasantness.

During that first date, Connie quizzed me about the meditation I practiced. She had heard from Tracy that I was practicing TM. During and after college, she had taken Dale Carnegie leadership courses and had been interested in self improvement for some time. In the parlance of self-discovery, she was what is known as a "seeker." Shortly thereafter, unbeknownst to me, she went to the Monterey TM center and learned how to meditate. But as we talked, I was increasingly attracted to her grounded, "I'm-comfortable-in-my-own-skin" sensibility. There was no pretension, game playing, or ritualistic mating behavior that in retrospect, often seems so disingenuous. Connie and I were instantly comfortable with each other. Although we were just getting acquainted, it felt to me that we were kindred souls that were actually catching up after a time of being apart.

I found that I wanted to spend as much time as possible with Connie. The next weekend, I was planning to drive to San Jose to attend a lecture by a famous stock market analyst, by the name of Joe Granville. As a young stockbroker, I was in the information-saturation stage and was learning as much as I could from as many sources as I could identify. Joe Granville was the "guru" of the day, and, although sitting in a lecture on investor sentiment indicators might not seem romantic, I asked Connie if she would like to go with me. She agreed to go and I had my second date. I couldn't tell you what Joe Granville said that night, but I can assure you that he might have spoken Mongolian and I wouldn't have noticed.

I discovered that Connie's athletic pursuits went beyond the swimming pool, and that included running, so I invited her for a run at Point Lobos. Jogging along the tree-lined paths that snaked over and around granite cliffs that plunge hundreds of feet to the ocean, we shared a trail that provided one of the most dramatic environments for getting good exercise and second to none for sheer enjoyment. We ran the trails at a conversational pace, and at the end of our run, I was exhilarated, as I had been on so many runs before, but I noticed that the feeling of emptiness I was used to having, had been replaced by a new feeling of fulfillment.

I found myself calling Connie more frequently over the next few weeks, wanting to spend as much time as I could with her. Connie was very easy to be attracted to, and to my delight, I noticed that I was displaying all the inward and outward signs of falling in love. Heck, I wasn't falling in love, I was diving in, heart first.

Having had my share of instantly physical relationships that turned into something less than I bargained for, I backed off from suggesting Connie and I spend the night together. I was content to allow the natural forces of attraction to take their course, figuring we would get there in the right time, at the right place. That place and time occurred some time later, after a romantic dinner at one of the nicer restaurants in Carmel.

I asked Connie if she knew of a place that, in my circle of friends and family, had become known as "The Top of the World." The Top of the World was at the end of a long, windy mountain road that rose from sea level to an elevation of about 1,500 feet, several miles south of Carmel. The panoramic view of the coastline and the vast Pacific Ocean gave the feeling that one was looking out over the edge of the earth. On a clear day, Santa Cruz was visible, 45 miles to the north, across the Monterey peninsula and across Monterey bay.

Connie smiled and said, "Sure, I've been there many times."

"The moon is full tonight. Care to go for a walk at The Top of the World?" I asked.

"Sure!" she replied.

Under a cloudless sky, we drove five miles down the coast, and another mile up the steep, winding, sometimes-one-way road. The moonlight was so bright I could have driven without headlights except for the patches of shadow under the overhanging oak trees, until it ended in an unpaved cul-de-sac. This circle of dirt was bordered by a steep cliff on the west side that looked out over the ocean.

On the east side was a fire road that wound up higher still, through a pine forest, and eventually to the top of the mountain with an elevation of about 2200 feet. After parking the car, we got out and walked up the fire road a few hundred feet to the pine forest. The smell of the trees filled the air, wafting by us on the light, warm breeze. The moon was already about three quarters of the way across the sky, sharing its reflection on the ocean with us. I couldn't have asked for a more romantic setting. My heart soared as I wrapped my arms around Connie and asked the question I had been holding inside myself all evening. "Will you spend the night with me?"

Connie smiled and with her wavy brown hair framing her face in the moonlight, sighed and said, "Yes, I will spend the night with you." Then she wrapped her arms around my neck and kissed me so passionately, I had to remind myself to drive safely on the way back home.

I was not the only one diving into this relationship heart first and during the Christmas holidays, within six weeks of our first date, Connie and I were engaged to be married. The night I proposed, I was very focused upon saying and doing what I thought were the right things, and she mistook my intense attitude as being negative. She thought I was going to break up with her.

I'd asked her to go for a walk with me on Carmel Beach, but when we arrived at the first street corner near her house, she stopped, looked me in the eye and completely blind-sided me by saying, "Look, you are barely talking to me and acting really weird! So, if you want to break up with me, just say so, okay!"

I stared at her for a moment, dumbfounded. The chasm between our two thought patterns began raising doubts in my mind.

My internal dialogue went something like this: If she could suggest that I might want to break up with her, perhaps I'm delusional about the whole idea of proposing. But then, who am I kidding! Falling in love is a delusional act, anyway!

I quickly thought back over a dozen failed relationships. I decided to stay the course and slowly, calmly, explained my odd behavior.

"Silly goose, I don't want to break up with you. I want to marry you! I love you! Why would I ever break up with you? I want to spend the rest of my life with you!"

Her reaction was precious. The look on her face said, "O-my-god! Did I just stick my foot in it, or what?"

I had imagined walking to town, buying a bottle of champagne and two glasses, walking to the beach, and then proposing to her. She preempted the little drama that I had planned, but we still bought a bottle of champagne and sat on a park bench beside the beach, celebrating the happy life that we imagined stretching out before us. That was 32 years ago, and Connie is still the best thing that ever happened to me.

Tom and Connie's wedding – September 1981

24

THE WEDDING

Weddings in a small town can be wonderful events; but as anyone who has ever been married in one knows, they create logistical challenges. Families are complicated webs of connection that give new meaning to the idea of chaos theory. We found that out when we put together our guest list. As twenty-something's with just a few pennies to rub together, we wanted to keep it small. My family blew that out of the water right away. Nineteen siblings, their spouses or significant others, their children and the relatives on both Mom's and Frank's sides of the family made it a 'family only' list of about 50. Then there was Connie's family. So without the neighborhood, we were already at 75 guests. By the time we invited our friends and friends of the parents, we were at a modest guest list of 250. Hey, compared to some weddings, that was small, right?

I had asked Harry to be my best man and he responded in epic fashion. On the morning of the wedding, I went for a run with several of the groomsmen, and a couple of my running buddies. We ran in the Point Lobos state park, a fitting place to have a last run as a single man with my friends. I was not concerned about my running partners, Mike Tancredi and Bill Cusack, but none of my groomsmen were runners. In conversation about the run the night before, I expressed concern about running apparel for the guys. In particular, they needed running shoes if they were going to be comfortable on the 5.6 miles of hilly trails we were going to run on.

As we arrived at Point Lobos in the morning, my groomsmen all protested they would be fine, in spite of not having comfortable running shoes. I was not to worry about them, and was simply to enjoy my run. They began the run with Mike, Bill and me and told us they'd catch up in due time or meet us back at the front entrance of the park. I should have sensed that there was something afoot.

I began the run slowly, not sure what to make of my buddies, some of whom had shown up in street shoes. I was sure they would end up with blistered feet, and once more, insisted they not run. However, they started down the trail with me and insisted back that I just keep my own pace and they would follow along. I lost them after the first mile or so, expecting that they would turn around and go right back to the cars and wait. I wouldn't be gone more than a half an hour anyway. When I got back to the front gate of the park, there was Harry, but none of the other guys. Hm-mm...

A family member had a car collector husband, who'd lent us his fleet of two vintage Rolls Royces and a Bentley. This worked out perfectly for our wedding party transportation needs. Harry was leaning against one of the Rolls Royces when I quizzed him about where our buddies might be.

He looked at his watch and responded in a concerned voice. "Yeah, they are kind of late. Well, let's go look for them."

With Harry driving the Rolls, we were waived right by the park's ranger station. I thought that odd, since the rangers usually collect a fee and give visitors a brochure and receipt before letting them in. As we drove slowly around the park, I was looking at the visible portions of the trails, seeing no one, which only increased my concern. I imagined them sitting on a rock somewhere, rubbing their blistered feet and cursing. Maybe one of them twisted an ankle and the others had to carry the injured groomsman.

Then we rounded a corner, where the road passed through a flat meadow with picnic tables arranged next to an ocean cove. There were the other Rolls and the Bentley, parked by the tables, the trunks opened. Three of the picnic tables had been arranged end to end. They were covered with tablecloths, on which were arranged candelabras, fine bone china, sterling silver place settings, silver coffee and tea service, baskets of fruit, breads, rolls and croissants, pastries of all kinds, a chafing dish of hot scrambled eggs and meats, and pitchers of fresh squeezed orange and grapefruit juice.

I was stunned! It took me a moment to grasp the reality of what I was seeing. This bacchanalian feast in such a magnificent setting seemed right out of a Fellini film. I had not bothered with a bachelor party, but this lavish, almost surreal spread made the thought of one pale by comparison. It was ten o'clock in the morning, the sun was shining, and there was not a breath of wind in the air. My friends, all of them accounted for, lined up by the tables grinning ear to ear. I felt humbled and gratefully hugged each of them in turn. We enjoyed our feast, replete with ribald tales, jokes and toasts to the "doomed man."

Later that afternoon, at the Carmel Mission Basilica, Connie and I were married in front of two hundred and fifty of our best friends and family. During the ceremony, we included a candle lighting ritual, involving each of us taking slender tapers and lighting a single candle on the altar, symbolizing the two of our lives becoming one. Having lit the single candle, we turned to walk away. As we did so, I heard a collective gasp from the congregation. Turning back to the altar, I saw that the candle had gone out. My mind raced. Was our marriage doomed? I went back to the altar, deftly lit the candle, turned to the congregation and in an exaggerated pantomime, shrugged and smiled at them all. The crowd laughed in approval.

Having shared our vows and completed the wedding ceremony, Connie and I walked down the aisle of the church, arm in arm, smiling at the congregation, as we passed amidst the applause and nods of approval. Amazed and excited at what we had just done, we turned to each other as we approached the entrance to the church and spontaneously exclaimed to each other, "We did it!" The photographer fortuitously caught our wondrous facial expressions on film.

In the church courtyard, during the required and seemingly endless picture taking after the wedding ceremony, one of the neighbors, who lived across the street from the Beardsley home on Rio Road, approached me, kissed me on both cheeks and gushed, "I was so inspired when you went back and re-lit the candle that had gone out. It reminded me that the candle of love and passion goes out many times over the course of a marriage, and you have to just re-light that candle every time!"

I stared at her in delighted wonder and thanked her for her wisdom.

Through the good graces of a friend of Connie's family, the reception was held at the very exclusive Beach and Tennis Club in Pebble Beach. When it came time for the cutting of the cake (Death by Chocolate), several shouts from the younger guests suggested we smash those ritual morsels into each other's faces. We shared a knowing glance and carefully placed a bite into each other's mouths. The crowd cheered for our care and respect for one another.

Regarding that "care and respect" and general sense of tenderness towards each other, Indian philosophy holds that, in the "householder path" to enlightenment, (as opposed to the "recluse" path), God Consciousness is achieved through devotion to the family, especially the spouse. There is no greater opportunity to grow in awareness, it is said. My sense is that the opportunity is great, because the challenge may be the most difficult on the planet. However, through unceasing and unconditional giving to one's mate, with an understanding that the act of giving is its own reward, the householder achieves divine union, which is the most fulfilling experience a person can have. As the saying goes, "It's easy to be a saint in a cave."

In the time I have been married to Connie, I've learned that a great marriage can help a person to experience and appreciate awareness of the presence of the Divine in all aspects of life. On the other hand, the lack of absolutely loving devotion to one's spouse can harm the ability of the individual to come to or remain in the evolving state that brings happiness and fulfillment.

The beautiful thing about the "way of the householder" is that challenges can be seen as an opportunity to reinforce and increase love in the relationship. Ultimately, the householder path of life becomes a paradigm for all of our relationships.

It sometimes seems that we twenty-first century Americans love to throw around the term "unconditional love," but I believe that the closer I or anyone approaches to a truly enlightened state of being, the more we will love everyone around us with the unqualified love that we ideally give to our significant others.

The growing family – Connie, Elyse (in her lap), Diana and Tom

25

REMINDERS ALONG THE WAY

G etting married and settling down into a career did not in any way change my practice of meditation. The fact is, one can be in the business world and meditate regularly. It is simply a matter of priorities. Connie and I continued down the path of our married life, integrating spiritual practice into daily activity in what the yogis call "karma yoga," or "yoga in action." Not surprisingly, that is why it's called a meditation practice. By taking one deeply inward step followed by one deeply outward step, each day, we infuse the inner into the outer experience, until there is no separation.

Maharishi was fond of quoting his Guru Dev (divine teacher) as having said, "In this universe, to be blessed with a human body is a rare and wondrous thing. If you have not reached enlightenment in this lifetime, then you have sold a diamond for the price of spinach."

With this in mind, Connie and I continued to meditate together as often as possible, finding that our transcendence intensified as a result. Although the rigors and demands of starting a financial services business created stressful circumstances in my life, it was a primary goal for me to manage that stress and make stress management part of the practice and discipline. In fact, I received a reminder to keep the spiritual component of my life in focus in a most unusual way, through an event that proved to be one of the most incredible experiences of my life. Connie and I had been married a couple of years and were living in a single-story house in Carmel. One night, I woke out of a sound sleep to the sound of someone walking around upstairs. This seems impossible in retrospect because, of course, there was no upstairs. But upon opening my eyes, I saw a staircase near my bed where there had been a wall. I ascended the stairs and found myself in a large living room lit by a single standing lamp that filled the room with a diffused glowing light. On the other side of the room was a couch with a coffee table in front of it and a feminine presence sitting on the couch—a being who was not completely defined. I couldn't make out details of her face, except for a beautiful smile and radiant eyes. She was surrounded by a nimbus—an intense golden glow.

In the same sense that I knew I could not merge into the Divine during that meditation back at MIU, I knew immediately and intuitively that this feminine presence was an angel of death who had come to collect someone.

Incredibly curious, I asked her, "Who are you here for?"

What seemed like a long pause ensued, as she smiled at me in an all-knowing, all-loving, completely accepting fashion. "You," she calmly replied.

The implications of that hit me at once.

"If I go with her, I'll get to see what's on the other side again," I reasoned to myself. "But that means I have to leave Connie."

I was fascinated about the prospect of seeing the other side without being encumbered by the connection with my body which had always limited me during meditations. But at the same time leaving my wife after such a short time was just not in the realm of possibility. We had just begun our lives together and had so much to share.

I said to the angel, "I can't go with you. I have to be with Connie."

She smiled at me, tilted her head, and repeated in that same all-knowing, divinely loving voice, "No, you have to come with me."

She then stood up, turned around, and walked right through the couch, through the wall, and disappeared from sight.

Of course, her clear instruction was for me to follow her. But I knew that if I did so, Connie would wake up to find only my cold lifeless corpse. So I turned around, went back down the stairs, and got back into my body.

As soon as I did so, my eyes popped wide open, I immediately leaped out of bed, turned on all the lights, ran into the bathroom, and splashed cold water in my face.

Connie, awakened by my frantic behavior, was a little frightened and asked me, "What are you doing?"

"Connie, talk to me! I don't care what you say," I answered. "Just talk to me. Let me know I'm alive."

The cold water on my face wasn't enough, so I jumped into a cold shower! I wanted to be as awake as I could possibly be. I told Connie about my experience, and then spent the next hour and a half with a tablet and a pen. Skeptics might, of course, suggest that the event was simply a very intense dream. I would counter that it was an astral dream. The experience admittedly contained some confusing elements; on the physical plane there was no spiral staircase, and no upstairs living room. However, alternate realities don't have to follow the logic of our mundane existence. What is more important and what became clear to me is that we have choices about some things. Not many people get to make the choice that was given to me that night. And now, I look back at the experience as a blessing.

I'd like to note that my older sister, Collien, is clairvoyant; and when I shared this dream with her, she made the wise observation that death is nothing but a change since, as she pointed out, "Consciousness is eternal."

"What you encountered was not so much a death angel as a change angel," Collien concluded.

The truth is, I've never been fearful about death. Having been shot and wondering if I would survive, I had felt, at the time, an incredible calm about the possibility of dying. I have also had several close calls during scuba-diving adventures, none of which incited panic; but instead, a calm that allowed me to cope with the circumstances and work them out. I've also gone to the other side in meditation. It's actually blissful. If we think of death at all, most of us imagine it as having a sense of finality. However, it is well documented that those who've come back from that experience have asserted, to a person, that consciousness continues even when they've left the body.

Collien confirmed this, telling me, "Death becomes a call to change, rather than a cessation of life. You were blessed. This angel was communicating to you a message to not get seduced by materialism, but to stay focused upon the spiritual path."

In a moment, I want to come back to Collien's amazing abilities; but before I do, I want to finish this train of thought. It only recently occurred to me that my reaction to the experience that I just described differed significantly from the experience I noted earlier when, during a meditation at MIU, I followed the golden light through the tunnel, was blocked by an invisible barrier from going forward, and was told by an inner voice that I had to return. At that time, I was depressed and angry that I couldn't merge forever into that light; but in the later encounter with the angel of death, I was unwilling to go on, because I didn't want to leave Connie.

Poets and song-writers write and sing about love being more powerful than death. That wasn't precisely true in this case, but my love for Connie certainly proved to be stronger than my desire for what has often been called Heaven or Paradise.

In 1984, Connie and I were invited to attend the Catholic first communion of my niece and nephew, Danny and Katie Murphy in a large church in San Francisco. My sister, Jeanie, Danny and Katie's mother, and I have always been close, having maintained a correspondence throughout my college years. Connie and I were happy to go and be part of their experience. We sat just in front of my older sister, Collien, her family, and several other extended family members. As the church service proceeded and the time for the actual communion ceremony approached, I was feeling a bit drowsy and decided to meditate. I closed my eyes and after a few moments began the mantra. Not long into the meditation, I felt two points of pain, or headache, right in the frontal lobes of my brain behind my forehead. I had been aware for some time that it was possible to eliminate pain by guided imagery, but had never thought to try it. It is rare for me to get a headache, so it had not previously occurred to me to use this technique. But there I was, with not one, but two points of pain in my head. I thought this odd, but decided to visualize the pain away.

I stopped repeating the mantra, and sat quietly. In that subtle state of awareness, which I want to be clear was not TM, but still very silent, I started my visualization. I began by imagining a column of golden light coming down out of the sky, right through the roof and ceiling of the church and into the top of my head. In my mind, I could see this column of light very clearly. As the light reached the center of my brain, I intended it to branch into two intense, laser-like beams, which I aimed at the points of pain and zapped them. In my subtle state of meditative awareness, I actually watched this internal process take place. The two separate light beams went out into the frontal lobes of my brain, the points of pain disappeared, and the headaches went away. I was rather surprised and proud of myself for this accomplishment and made a mental note to tell Connie what I had done when we left the church.

As we filed out of the church at the end of the service, Connie was walking ahead of me, and I leaned forward to tell her what had happened.

I tapped her on the shoulder and in a low voice said, "Guess what just happened!"

She responded curiously, "What was that?"

Just as she was looking back over her shoulder to hear my answer, Collien interrupted and tapped my shoulder asking, "Tom! What were you doing in there?"

I was unsure what she meant and asked, "What do you mean?"

Collien smiled and explained, "Well, I was sitting right behind you and noticed your head bobbing just a bit, and peeked over your shoulder and noticed your eyes were closed; so, I figured you were meditating. Just then, a column of gold light came down from the ceiling and went right into your head. When it got to the center of your brain, it forked and became like two laser-beams and shot out to the front of your head, right behind your forehead…What were you doing?"

Needless to say, I was stunned! I thought I had been so clever and resourceful, but Colleen had actually watched the event that had taken place!

Connie gave me a quizzical look and asked, "What were you going to tell me, Tom?"

I looked at her in amazement, and looked back at Collien's smiling face, and replied to Connie, "Nothing, Sweetie, I'll tell you later."

With an awed expression on my face, I confirmed to Collien that she had indeed, observed my visualization, and told her about the pain going away. I was once again humbled, by how consciousness expresses itself in such wondrous ways.

Several years later, as I was leaving the grocery store one day, I heard a voice in my head say, "Follow that woman and child."

About twenty feet ahead of me was a woman pushing a shopping cart. In the "child- carrying" seat facing her mother, was a toddler of perhaps 15-18 months of age.

The voice continued to talk to me as I walked. "The woman is going to leave the cart at the back of her car and walk around to the driver's side to unlock it. When she does that, the child will stand up and fall out of the cart onto her head... unless you intervene."

My unspoken response was, "I got it... not to worry."

I was energized! After the death-angel experience of several years before, I was amazed to perceive an angelic presence once again. I followed the woman across the entire parking lot to its farthest corner. She had parked her old rusted Plymouth station wagon, the kind that holds about 11 people, as far as she could from the store. As she reached the car, the angel's prediction came true. The woman stopped the cart at the back of the car, turned and walked around it to the driver's door. As she did so, the baby stood up on wobbly legs and fell out of the cart. I didn't even break stride. I reached out and caught the baby just as she went over. Being the father of two daughters, I knew how to hold a child. I drew her into my arms and spoke to her softly. "It's not good to stand up in a shopping cart." I whispered.

Immediately the child let out a bloodcurdling scream. The mother looked up from the driver's side door, already in panic mode.

I smiled at her, gently bouncing the baby in my arms. "She was headed for the pavement," I explained. The way I held the baby and the tone in my voice spoke the truth.

The mom came over and, with an appreciative look on her face gushed, "Oh, what a smart dad! Thank you!" She took the baby from me and began to console her. I walked away, grateful, and grinning a mile wide.

I was high for days afterward. Apparently, when we're the instrument of divine intervention, our physical vibratory rate is raised, however temporarily. The effect, for me at least, is one of being high, elated, energized.

Although completely different, another miraculous event took place about this time in my business career. I had been working hard for four years, building my financial services business in Carmel. It was slow work, acquiring one client at a time, suffering a lot of rejection along the way. To counter the negative effects of all the no's I heard from people, I listened to motivational and personal growth tapes in the car and while exercising.

Among my favorite speakers was Earl Nightingale, the father of the modern motivational industry.

One day, I called the sales department of his company to order a new set of motivational cassettes. As I gave the sales rep my address, she said, "Is that Carmel, California, or Carmel, Indiana?"

I asked her how she knew there were two Carmel's.

She replied, "Because Mr. Nightingale lives in Carmel, California." This great man lived right here in my own town!

Thinking quickly, I offered the sales rep a deal. I asked her, "You are a commissioned salesperson, aren't you?"

She replied, "Yes, I am."

"Good! If you send me ten Earl Nightingale promotional tapes, I will make sure they get into the hands of ten people in my office who would have a high likelihood of purchasing product from you, if you give me Mr. Nightingale's unlisted home phone number."

At first she was reluctant, saying, "Oh, I'll have to think about that."

The next day she called me and said, "The tapes are in the mail. Here's the phone number."

However, I had the inclination to actually not dial the number. I heard that inner voice again, telling me not to call. I really believe the universe moves us towards good things, if we just keep our mitts off the process, earnestly listen, and have patience. Shakespeare spoke the truth when he wrote, "There's a greater hand that shapes our ends, rough-hew them how we will." The less "rough" we are in hewing those "ends," the more signs of divinity we see in our lives. Taking the guidance in this case, had an amazing result.

One day, several weeks after receiving Mr. Nightingale's phone number, I was helping my brother-in-law disassemble a horse corral in Carmel Valley. We broke for lunch and entered a deli still clothed in our paint and creosote-stained coveralls, with hat-hair and unshaven faces. We looked like we had just crawled out from under the bridge.

As I was just about to take a bite out of my sandwich, I heard the unmistakable voice of Earl Nightingale — one of the unique sounds on the planet — coming from a table behind us. Having listened to his cassettes for countless hours, I'd have known that voice anywhere!

In spite of my appearance, I stood up, excused myself from my brother-in-law for a moment, and walked over to where Mr. Nightingale sat with a very attractive woman, whom I learned, was his wife.

I apologized for the intrusion and asked, "Please excuse me for bothering you, but, you're Earl Nightingale, aren't you?"

He stared at me quizzically and in his deep baritone voice declared, "Yes, I am."

I looked at him apologetically and offered, "Mr. Nightingale, I just want to thank you for the great work you do. You have done wonders for my business, wonders for my wife's business and we just think you are a great man who does great work. I'll leave you alone now, but, thank you."

Earl looked up at me from his seat and asked, "Young man, what line of work are you in?"

I responded, "I'm a financial advisor for Dean Witter Reynolds." Nightingale looked at his wife and she looked back at him and smiled. He turned to me and, looking me up and down again, asked, "Do you have a business card?"

One of the habits I had developed at a very early stage of my career as a financial advisor was to always have a business card on my person. One never knows when opportunity will present itself. I reached into the pocket of my overalls and produced a business card, which I handed over.

Earl studied it for a moment and then said, "Tom, would you please sit down."

As graciously as I could, I pulled a chair from another table in the nearly deserted deli and sat down, facing them with my hands on my very grimy lap.

"Tom, in my life, whenever I have needed someone, they always appear," Nightingale said. "My wife, Diana, and I were just discussing what to do with a $3 million stock distribution I'm taking from my company; and now, you have shown up at our table. So, you are now my financial advisor. I will call you on Monday morning precisely at 6:30 a.m. to make an appointment. I look forward to working with you. Good day."

That was in 1984. Earl Nightingale passed away in 1988, and I continued working with Diana, his widow for many years afterward.

Events such as these are examples of what Maharishi called "support of nature." He described in his book, *The Science of Being and the Art of Living,* how, as we clear our nervous system of the stresses stored there for who knows how long, and as our awareness becomes infused with "pure consciousness" (what the Vedas refer to as the "home of all the laws of nature"), one of the amazing results is this "support of nature." When I was a student at MIU, listening to taped lectures by Maharishi, he would talk about this phenomenon. The way I understood it then, and still do today, is that the energy of the universe flows through each of us to the degree that we are in tune with the laws of nature. We are then supported to that same degree. In my experience, it is not so much a matter of getting what "I" want out of life, but of being in tune with what life wants of me and pursuing that.

At the time, it sounded great. I looked forward to observing it in action. As my life has progressed, I have been, quite happily, a front line witness to it.

Connie and I continued to enjoy our married life, sharing the wonders of day-to-day living. However, even a healthy routine of work, exercise, meditation, and sharing daily life can get to seem monotonous as we begin to take for granted that which we are blessed with. I was certainly guilty of this at the time.

In the mid-eighties, I came home from work one day feeling "stuck." The feeling was a sense of spiritual boredom or lack of progress in what I perceived as my personal growth. I got out of my car in the driveway of the small two-bedroom home Connie and I rented, looked up at the sky and thought, God, please send me a guide, a teacher. I need some help.

Connie and I then went on a meditation course for a week at Cobb, the TM retreat facility in the mountains north of San Francisco where I had taken the SCI course ten years before.

When we returned home, there was a message on our phone-answering machine that sent a shiver up my spine, causing Connie to notice and ask me what was wrong. The message was from Stephanie, who had been at MIU at the same time I had. Coincidentally, she had been the girlfriend of my old friend, Harry Goulding, at U.C. Irvine when they were both undergraduate students there. Small world! I hadn't heard her voice since leaving college, but there it was on my recorder.

The recorded voice said, "Hi, Tom, this is Stephanie Lash. I'm answering your "advertisement." I'm in Santa Cruz; here's my number; call me."

I hadn't told anyone, not even Connie, about my request for guidance. Yet here was a friendly voice from my past, responding to my request. I looked at Connie, wide-eyed in wonder at the realization that my prayer had been answered in what seemed a most unusual way.

Connie looked at me, concerned, and said, "What is it?"

I explained to her what had happened. Now it was her turn to look wide-eyed. "You better call her!" she insisted.

I called the number and after greetings and pleasantries, invited Stephanie to come to Carmel to see Connie and me. I didn't know what to think or what to expect, but I was excited, recognizing that it's not every day we have our prayers answered in such a dramatic fashion. I was looking forward to seeing Stephanie, whom I really didn't know very well. We had been acquaintances, not close friends.

When she arrived, I introduced her to Connie. Immediately, Stephanie took one look at Connie, and then looked back at me; and, suddenly, wagging her index finger in my face admonished, "YOU are not better than she is! Do you get that, mister?!" Then she repeated herself. "You are not better than she is!" The "guidance" had begun.

Stephanie stayed with us for four days, during which time she kicked my spiritual ass up one side and down the other. She guided me through a past life regression, helped me understand my family-programmed poverty-consciousness and, toward the end of her stay, shared with me a bit of her own story of transformation that made me grateful it was Stephanie who had shown up at my request for help.

While she was living in San Diego, and supporting herself with a private practice as a re-birther and channel, Stephanie had an experience that accelerated her spiritual growth dramatically. For those who are unfamiliar with re-birthing, it is a therapeutic method for healing birth trauma through the use of breathing techniques.

Early in her spiritual life Stephanie had developed a strong inner awareness, as her third eye opened, giving her the ability to have very real conversations with 'celestial beings" (archangels, guardian angels, etc.). She seemed to have a special relationship with Jesus, who made himself known to her shortly after she became a re-birther. Jesus was the first "higher being" Stephanie had channeled. As a result of her special bond with him, she kept an almost life-sized Sacred Heart of Jesus picture in her meditation room. Stephanie was enjoying her life on the spiritual path, acknowledging the day-by-day, week-by-week transformation of her own energetic experience.

One afternoon in early November, 1984, Stephanie was meditating in front of the large picture of Jesus, with her attention deeply inward. Suddenly she saw Jesus, in his celestial body, step into the room through the picture and walk up to her. There was a tremendous radiation of energy, so powerful that she started crying. One moment she had been deeply peaceful. The next moment she was literally sobbing, tears streaming down her face.

"Do you really want to get enlightened in this lifetime, Stephanie?" Jesus asked her telepathically.

"Yes, of course I do!" was her immediate reply.

"Then you are going to need to make some major changes in your lifestyle. If you continue the way you are going right now, you will not make it."

Stephanie was surprised to hear this, as she had thought she had been doing pretty well.

She became very humble, and grateful for the guidance of a Master.

"What do I need to do?" She asked.

Jesus instructed her, "You are doing 'spirituality' as a business. You need to learn about non-materialism and faith. You will need to do an exercise in faith for some period of time to learn this.

Then, you can return to whatever lifestyle you choose. You will need to give away everything you own and travel for a time, doing your work with people, but not charging money. I will work with you during this time to help you learn your lessons and protect you; God will handle all your needs."

Stephanie remarked to herself, He really doesn't mince words, does he? This was quite a dramatic exercise He was asking her to do. Once committed, there was no going back. She wasn't sure she was ready or able to do something of that magnitude.

In reply to Jesus' guidance, Stephanie said telepathically, "I'm not sure I can do this on my own, without some kind of validation or intermediary help. I want some sort of validation that the conversation I am having with God is not some kind of wild imagining of my mind."

Jesus nodded in agreement, as she watched him with her inner eye, physical eyes still closed in meditation.

After a moment he said, "If I give you some kind of undeniable validation, and also someone to help you make the transition into this exercise, do you promise to do it?"

Stephanie felt her inner self for a moment to see if she could truly promise to do such an extreme exercise, even with help.

"Yes" she replied.

And with that, He smiled, slowly fading out of the room.

Stephanie stopped sobbing, as the energy in the room returned to normal, realizing that she had been crying during the whole, phenomenal, telepathic conversation. Never before had she had an experience of a higher being intervening in her life this way, without prayers or request from her. It had seemed to come out of nowhere. Stephanie concluded that her cosmic clock was ticking and the alarm had just gone off.

Stephanie continued to live her normal daily life, knowing that if the experience were true, then Jesus would somehow provide outer validation. There was nothing more for her to do about it until then.

Around the middle of December, she was looking at the schedule of events for a local New Age church. Stephanie noticed a Christmas caroling evening that she felt strongly attracted to attend, and made note to go.

As she was driving to the Christmas caroling evening, Stephanie clearly heard her angels talking to her, "You have a connection to make at this event. Make sure your aura is clear so you can be sure to connect with this person."

Having prayed regularly to be guided to those people she could really serve in her work, Stephanie was in the habit of receiving direct information from her angels. She was used to being guided to people she was karmically connected with, or people for whom she happened to be the perfect person for them to work with in order to grow or heal. Often her angels would request that she go to certain places in town, or specific events, in order to meet her clients serendipitously. It was the cosmic networking service!

Stephanie did as they requested, focused her attention, and cleaned up her aura. As she arrived at the church, she walked into the foyer and stood at the entry doors, looking into the church. Quite a few people had arrived, and were mostly sitting in the first ten rows. She looked slowly from row to row, trying to see anyone she knew or felt some connection to.

Stephanie thought, "My connection isn't here yet."

The angels responded, "Oh, yes. He's here."

At least she knew it was a man.

"Where is he?" Stephanie thought. "I can't tell who it is."

"Look over to the far left and back." The angels turned Stephanie's head, as they talked with her.

Sitting all alone in the back, at the very end of the row on the left, was a man reading something. He was in his mid-thirties, tall and thin, with dark hair and olive skin.

"Go over and sit next to him," the angels suggested.

"But he obviously wants to be alone and far away from everyone else! It will be really invasive and quite obvious if I go all the way down the row and sit right next to him," she replied.

Stephanie was embarrassed at the idea of intruding on a stranger like this.

"Go sit next to him. It's important," the angels insisted.

Stephanie gathered her nerve and walked into the church, making her way over to the row where the man was sitting. He was looking down; reading some papers the church had placed on each of the chairs; so she couldn't see his face. Ready for rejection, Stephanie walked down the row to the chair next to him and picked up the papers on it.

Somewhat shyly, she asked, "Excuse me, do you mind if I sit here?"

The man looked up from the paper he was reading and looked her directly in the eyes. His eyes were a soft brown, and as he looked at her, Stephanie felt a strong radiation of power from him. She looked into his eyes; they seemed to have infinite depth. Realizing this was no "normal" guy, Stephanie surmised that he was very spiritually evolved, maybe even enlightened. With all the energy coming from him, she started to feel queasy. Expecting to connect with someone she would be acting as teacher for, not someone who was energetically more powerful than herself, she felt off-balance. She was used to being the one in control of these "serendipitous" encounters.

"No, I don't mind at all. In fact, I've been expecting you Stephanie. Please sit down," he replied.

How did he know my name?

Stephanie sat down, not saying a word.

Neither did he.

Stephanie could feel him smiling to himself at her uneasiness. She started to read the church papers as a way of regaining her inner balance. It made sense to remain quiet until she knew what was going on.

As the evening program began, Stephanie's mind was inward, trying to figure this guy out, even as she sang Christmas carols along with everyone else. Again she thought, How did he know my name? Why was he expecting me?

Neither of them spoke, but Stephanie continued to feel a strong radiation of energy from him throughout the program. By the end of the evening, she was nervous to the point of sweating.

When the program was over, the man looked at Stephanie and asked, "Do you have a car? Would you like to go to a Denny's or something and have some coffee?"

Her angels had told her this was an important connection, so the answer had to be "yes."

Wanting to know how he knew her, yet nervous to the point of being frightened of his powerful emanation, Stephanie wasn't sure at all what she was getting herself into. Driving to a nearby

Denny's, they ordered coffee and sat quietly at the table for a few minutes. Knowing he would answer her questions in his own time, Stephanie just waited for him to talk.

"You know, you think you're such a great channel; but it took you a whole month to connect with me."

A blank stare was all Stephanie could conjure. She had no idea what he was talking about.

"Jesus asked you to go on the road on faith over a month ago. Then He asked me to come here and help you get started. I got here only a day or two after He talked with you. I thought I would just call you on the phone, since you're in the phone book. I decided that would be too extreme for you. For this connection to work, I had to wait until you came to me. It took you a whole month!"

Here was Stephanie's validation and help, all in one package. Her mouth dropped as she sank into a state of shock.

He laughed and smiling, said, "Drink some coffee."

Stephanie sipped her coffee, as a thousand thoughts shot through her mind. *Oh my, this means I'm really going to have to give up all my possessions and way of life and travel on faith! Give up my wonderful 2-bedroom condo in Solano Beach, just walking distance from the ocean? Travel without a car, not knowing where to sleep each night?* She was terrified.

Stephanie looked up from her coffee as a wave of peacefulness suddenly came over her. The young man, whose name she still didn't know, was looking at her with a silly grin on his face.

"It's not all that bad, really. In fact, I couldn't live any other way. I'm what you call an American Sadhu. In India there are saints who spend all their time in meditation and prayer and beg for their food. They won't touch money. In the language of India, they are called Sadhus. If people are lucky, they have an opportunity to give them food or shelter and be blessed by them."

He went on, saying, "I am non-materialistic, and I work with Jesus. I receive my marching orders from Him, and work with sincere students on the path. I won't take money for my work, but you do have to take care of my needs while I'm working with you. That means food and shelter. My work with you is to help you get started with your exercise in living on faith. Jesus says you need to learn non-materialism."

Stephanie nodded numbly. What was there to say? This guy seemed to know everything already. Saying anything at all seemed to be superfluous.

"Talk to me!" he said laughing.

"So how does this work, then?" Stephanie asked weakly.

"I've been working with someone else in town and my things are at his house. We could start by having you give me a ride over there, and then set a time for us to get together tomorrow, if you want."

"If I want? Do I have a choice?"

The next day he showed up at her door, duffel bag in hand. Stephanie looked around behind him; no one else was around. She assumed someone must have dropped him off and then left.

As he came into her condo, he said, "This place feels like old people. You have your parents in your space."

"So? Is something wrong with that?" Stephanie responded.

What kind of a greeting is that? she thought. ...Certainly not very cordial.

This guy seemed all business and no heart. Stephanie got him settled into her meditation room and he immediately said, "Well, let's get started. Let's talk about your connection with your parents."

Thus began an incredibly intense two month period of personal growth.

Dave, as he called himself, stayed at Stephanie's home, working with her night and day, helping her refine her channeling, helping her heal emotionally, and to learn the ways of living on faith.

After about two months, Stephanie had become quite telepathic; and although she was already psychic, her abilities had grown tremendously. Her channeling skills became much more accurate and clear. Having sold some of her possessions and having put the rest in a storage locker, she was ready to start her journey. Dave seemed to think that storing her possessions was just fine, as this experience was more of an exercise in non-materialism, rather than a long-term lifestyle.

Stephanie shared with me that for about a year, she lived on the road, staying with friends along the way, doing channeling, rebirthing, and healing work in exchange for a place to stay and food. Many of the people she stayed with referred her to their friends, who lived in different areas, and those people who wanted her to stay with them paid for her transportation to their homes.

When it was time for her to leave my home, Stephanie admonished me, "You have a lot of work to do on yourself, Tom. Good luck with it."

Sometimes we hear someone say, "Be careful what you ask for, because you just might get it." Believe me; I know just what they're talking about.

North family, Camus, Washington – 1993

26

HEALING THE FAMILY

During a busy morning at work in the spring of 1988, I received a phone call from my younger brother, Phil. After saying hello, he said, "Tom, I need your help. You know how whenever we Norths get together, it always turns into a bitch session about Frank?"

"Yeah, I know what you mean. It gets to be a drag." I replied.

"Well, I was talking to Collien and Janette and we agreed that it would be a good idea to get this off our collective backs once and for all. I need you to help me organize a family therapy session."

On my end of the phone, there was silence as I considered the implications of his request. "Do you know what you're asking?" I was incredulous! But at the same time, it never occurred to me to say no.

I went on, "Phil, consider the scale of what you're suggesting. If we had four or five people in our family, that would be one thing. But think about it! You want to get twenty-two people in the same room to talk about things they have been trying to forget their entire adult lives."

Phil replied solemnly, "Yeah, I know."

I reflected for another moment on my brother's earnest tone of voice. "Of course I'll do it."

"Thanks, Tom! Really! Now, how do we do this?"

"Let me work on it. I'll call you later this week."

I began thinking about what an event like this might be like. It could be wondrous in its healing of untold family wounds and at the same time, it would be dangerous. Getting twenty siblings to consciously confront their issues and pent-up emotions in a group format— in the same room—could be nothing short of incendiary. But I had stopped walking away from challenges a long time ago.

I asked a few of my spiritually oriented friends who they would recommend for family counseling. One of them was adamant that the person to talk to was a local pastoral counselor he knew. I called the counselor and shared the request my brother had made. (Due to the sensitive nature of psychological counseling and therapy sessions, only the names of those who agreed to be mentioned are used in this chapter.) Having agreed to conduct the meetings, we settled on a price, which I thought was more than reasonable and would not scare my brothers and sisters away. I relayed the conversation to Phil, who agreed to a date and time of day. Then I set to work on organizing this "event."

With the intention of assisting Phil in his wish to heal at least some of the family wounds and emotional baggage, I wrote a letter that I sent to each of the family members. I had no illusions about the response I might get from those who had a wish to hide behind the "Yours, Mine, and Ours" fantasy, which the public had bought into for so many years. But I knew that I would benefit as much as Phil would.

The letter read as follows:

"Dear (family member's name),

You are invited to the first ever Beardsley family healing session.

Many of us carry emotional burdens we have struggled with all our lives. If you need help, this is your chance to get it. If you feel that you don't need the healing, then come and support your brothers and sisters who do."

The details of time, location, directions etc., were listed. Then the shit hit the fan.

I received letters from family members accusing me of doing "the devil's work."

My mother called me, and in a syrupy, conciliatory voice, suggested, "Tommy, if you have issues with your father and me, then come and talk with us, and we'll help you work out your problems."

As she was talking, all I could think was, Uh, huh… right… like you did when we were kids.

"Divide and conquer" had been their way of controlling us. Not this time. My response to her was, "Mom, first of all, Frank is not my father. Secondly, your husband has created a lot of pain in the lives of his children and your children. If you want to help your children, you can do so in a group session."

She sighed and hung up without another word.

Two days before the scheduled Saturday, I realized I had not yet met the designated counselor. What if this was the wrong person for the job? What if this isn't even a good person? What if? What if? What if?

I called the counselor and expressed my anxious reservations. I was invited to visit the counselor's office immediately and decide for myself. It wasn't far, so I went right away. With a warm smile, I was greeted at the door. I looked into deep green eyes that seemed to go on forever. There was a depth of wisdom there that I instantly recognized. I relaxed and without so much as an introduction said, "I don't have any questions. I'll see you on Saturday."

Eight of us showed up for the counseling session. I remember walking through the parking lot, seeing aloe vera plants along the way. I remarked to myself that aloe is a healing plant, so this was a good sign.

We gathered in the lobby of the counselor's office for greetings and catching up.

The session was begun with a prayer, asking God for guidance. For the next ten hours, the eight of us emptied skeletons from the closets of our souls.

Each of us, in our turn, had an opportunity to speak and ask questions and get answers from our siblings and from the counselor. Many of the events we shared that day were unknown to the others in the room until they were spoken. A pattern began to emerge. Each of us, as children or early teenagers, at some time or another, had been isolated from the others by some lie or deceit, and then abused by Frank. Or we had been publicly punished to the point of humiliation by him. Ashamed to talk, having been punished for speaking the truth, we had been harboring the guilt of it for all of our adult lives. Our counselor shared with us that this is a common method of control and abuse in pathological families.

Phil raised the question of why our mother didn't stop Frank from molesting the girls. We had no answer. Mom was not present for us to ask her.

We kept at it for the whole day, shedding tears and gaining insights into our own pathological adult behaviors. From alcoholism and drug abuse to the inability to hold a job, to multiple family disorders of our own, we made connections to the experiences we had as children and teens.

I shared a story that had significance for me. Not long before this session was planned, I had been enjoying a typical evening at home with Connie and our daughter Diana, then eighteen months old. We had finished dinner. Connie then nursed the baby while I got up and did the dishes. Putting the pots and lids on the counter after drying them, I watched as Diana stopped nursing, slid off Connie's lap and waddled toward me, smiling. She reached up and on her tiptoes, grabbed a pot lid and slid it off the counter. She rocked back and forth on her tiny legs a bit to catch her balance. As she did so, an angry voice in my head yelled at me, "Hit her! Beat her! She could hurt herself doing that! Punish that child! Smack her right now!"

In my mind and in my heart, I knew this was the voice of Frank. The violent programming that I didn't even know was in me had been activated by this simple act of a child. Fortunately, my years of meditation had given me the ability to distance myself from any impulse to follow these horrific instructions. I thought to myself, Leave her alone. Watch her and see what she does.

Diana turned around and walked to the lower cupboard across from the sink. With one hand, she opened the cupboard, balancing the pot lid on her head with the other. She put the pot lid away, closed the cupboard and turned around, smiling broadly at her accomplishment. She had wanted to help her daddy with the dishes. I picked her up and hugged her and kissed her chubby little cheeks. I told her what a good girl she was and we laughed together.

Amazed, I turned to Connie and told her what had happened inside my head. We marveled at the time bomb that had been planted so many years earlier and had just gone off. Fortunately, it did no harm. Had I responded to the negative programming that I could only associate with Frank Beardsley, I could have destroyed any desire my daughter might ever have of being helpful. Had I followed the errant software that had been written in my mind, I could have done the same kind of damage that we were in counseling to deal with.

By the end of the session, we were amazed that we had been at it for over ten hours with little more than a bathroom break.

At home that evening, I tried to explain to Connie what had happened during the family counseling session. It was difficult to communicate; because every time I tried to relate some aspect of the discussions, I started to cry uncontrollably. She hugged me and held me as I poured out my recollections of the day. Eventually, I was able to share with her, that, as bad as I thought my experience growing up had been, there were others for whom my heart broke, as I had listened to their stories. I shared with Connie some of the traumas that they had been through, and as I did so, I couldn't tell whether the tears streaming down her face were for me or for them… or for all of us.

We all came back the next day and resumed our "inner work" which lasted for another ten hours. By Sunday evening, everyone was both exhausted and exhilarated at the same time. Over the course of the weekend, we had spent twenty hours engaged in hard emotional and spiritual work. I had gained enormous insight and understanding of how my brothers and sisters felt, and how they had dealt with the challenges that we had all faced. I felt a new empathy for them that I had never known. Where previously there had been walls between us which we used to protect ourselves, there was now a bond of love and compassion.

We had gotten so much out of the sessions that we resolved to schedule another weekend. A month later, we met again. We spent another ten hours on Saturday and Sunday, allowing each of us to share that which we needed to share. And once again, we felt the bond of shared experience that we had all previously suffered; only then, we had suffered on our own.

One of the pleasant surprises that came to light had to do with me. I had never considered the role I had played in the lives of my younger brothers and sisters. One of my younger sisters, turned to me and said, "Tom, I just want to thank you for taking me with you fishing and hiking and tide pool exploring when we were children.

If it hadn't been for you, I wouldn't have done those things. It meant a lot to me. None of the other older kids did that, but you did."

Then, to my surprise, several other younger siblings spoke up and said the same or similar things. I was speechless and humbled.

The counselor spoke and said, "So, what happened there, Tom, is that without intending to, or understanding what you were doing, you became a surrogate father to your younger brothers and sisters. They didn't have a functional male role model or life teacher to guide them in the world. But, consciously or unconsciously, you saw that void and filled it for them. However, you were not prepared to take on that role in more than a limited capacity. Still, look around you. These are your brothers and sisters, Tom. They love you and appreciate the contribution you made in their lives. Few people ever get to hear the words that have just been spoken to you. This is a great gift."

I began to cry, as I had done so many times in the previous sessions. Only this time, they were tears of joy and gratitude.

Helen and Dick North – Christmas, 1949

27

GRENDEL'S DEMISE

For a third month in a row, we met again; but this time Mom came to the counseling sessions. She had been convinced by Jeanie and Collien that she would benefit from attending. On Saturday, Mom shared with all of us that she had been devastated when she lost the love of her life, Dick North. As she spoke, I felt my heart melt a bit. I was thirty-five years old and it was the first time in my life that I had heard my mother express any sort of sentiment of any kind about my dad. She had so rarely spoken of him at all. I leaned forward, listening intently.

The counselor asked her, "Helen, is there something you would like to say about the grief you felt from losing your husband?"

Mom sat silently for a moment. Then she said, matter-of-factly, "Well, with the children, I never had a chance to grieve."

The counselor leaned forward and looked at Mom with the same look of compassion that an angel had once given me, and asked, "Helen, would you like that opportunity now?"

Mom sat in silence once more, seeming to ponder the question. She began to shift in her chair, the muscles of her hands and face beginning to twitch, as she allowed the memories stored in her body to awaken. She put her hand to her mouth, as her chin quivered involuntarily.

After a moment, the well of her pent-up emotions overflowed, sending a flood of tears streaming down her cheeks. In a last effort to resist, she lowered and shook her head from side to side, as she put her hands up to her face, succumbing to the torrent of memories of the life that had been torn from her. Mom began to sob uncontrollably.

I sat and watched, feeling with her the loss that she had buried for so many years. My brothers, sisters and I cried with her as we had cried with each other during the previous sessions. This time though, it was different. This was Mom.

After the initial release of pent-up energy had subsided, Mom composed herself enough to explain through her tears that she had had no time for herself; that it was so tiring to be always taking care of the children. I could feel the enormity of the task she had undertaken when Dick North died. I could sense the pain and loneliness she'd experienced, suddenly raising her eight children by herself. Raising them alone was nothing new, but raising them with a broken heart was devastating. Knowing that Dick North would never come back from overseas, as he had always done, was too much to bear. I can't speak for my siblings, but as Mom described that experience, my heart was breaking, too.

Then, we sat with her as she grieved her way through the pain of taking on another, even larger set of children and marrying Frank Beardsley. As an act of self-sacrifice, it had been beyond her ability to achieve; a burden too heavy to bear. We could see how it had taken its toll, wracking her body and crushing her spirit. Watching my mother convulse in the memory of her loss, and the acknowledgement of her failures, I wanted to reach out to her and console; but I knew this was something she had to do on her own. There would be time for that later.

When it seemed that her tears were spent for the moment, she began to tell us the story of her love for Dick North, and how he had been everything to her. They had shared so much joy, passion, and adventure in their marriage, and it had all been taken from her when he died. When she had met Frank Beardsley, she was appalled at the emotional state she found his children in. She said she had never before heard some of the foul words he used. She felt like she could not abandon these children to him and that she had to do something. So she did the only thing she felt she could do. She married him.

In spite of the compassion we all felt for her at that moment, many of us felt that she had been complicit in the abuse that we had been subjected to. Phil pointed out to her that when she married Frank, she took her own eight children into an unhealthy, dangerous environment and abandoned them there. Apparently, it had never occurred to her. She reflected for a moment on what Phil had said, put her hand to her mouth and cried, "Oh my god! I did! I abandoned you!" Her face contorted in a grimace, as the implications of the accusation hit her full force. "I'm sorry! I'm sorry!" she cried. Once again she began to sob uncontrollably.

At the end of the day, ten hours later, we were all emotionally spent but relieved, as is often the case when the truth is allowed to be spoken. My mother commented, "It feels so good to get rid of the lie. The whole 'Yours, Mine and Ours' sham is over, as far as I am concerned. I don't have to pretend anymore. I don't have to live the lie."

Hearing her say these words, I felt convinced of the value of our efforts and resolved never to allow the myth of the movie to overshadow the truth.

Again, we all filed out of the room exhausted and elated. We felt more like a family than we had ever been. Mom said that the next day she would bring Frank. With a thoughtful and determined look, she insisted, "He needs to hear this."

I thought about this and wondered what it might be like to have Frank join in these cathartic discussions. I could not even imagine Frank sitting through a session like the one we had just endured. However, I knew that miracles do happen, and I could only hope that he would actually show up. I would just have to see what unfolded the next day. In my opinion, our counselor had been moderating these sessions perfectly, providing insight and perspective when it was needed.

Much to the surprise of some of us, Frank Beardsley did, in fact, show up the next day. The counselor approached me while everyone was milling about, sipping water or tea, and commented, "From what I've heard of Frank, I expected a fire-breathing monster to come into the room, immediately terrorizing everyone; not that diminutive man over there."

On the other side of the room, Frank stood quietly beside Mom, looking straight ahead, saying nothing. Aside from the permanent scowl on his face, he did look rather meek and harmless. It amazed me that what appeared to be such a small man could have single-handedly caused so much pain and misery among those present.

As had been our practice at the beginning of each session, we began with a prayer, asking for guidance and illumination. Afterward, while Frank was sitting there and observing the others in the room around him, the ground rules for discussion were reviewed, insisting that compassionate honesty be the watch-phrase of the day.

Frank wanted to say something, so he was given the floor. "I don't know what the big deal is here," he began, "I raised my children in a loving household the best I could." He continued his defense, "As God is my judge…"

This comment elicited immediate challenges, and an argument ensued that had Frank turning purple with rage. For a dreadful second I expected him to get up and leave. But then Mom put her hand on his arm and said one word: "Frank!"

He settled down once again and remained quiet.

I felt a dark foreboding for what was about to happen. In a mythic sense, the townspeople were at the gates of the castle, shovels and pitchforks in hand, and they were preparing to tear the whole thing down.

The counselor raised the possibility that Frank had, himself, been abused as a child. He had taken part in reinforcing patterns that his family may have been handing down for generations. Frank explained that he had been the second youngest of 12. His father had been a bank teller for Hibernia Bank in San Francisco, while his mother had been a domestic in the homes of wealthy San Franciscans. With all the older children in school, there was no one to take care of little Frankie. So every weekday morning he was put in the cellar, given food and water, and left there alone until someone came home later in the day. Every day, he had banged and scraped his fingers on the door till they bled, trying to get someone's attention; but no one ever came.

"But," he said, "I loved my father and my mother and was a dutiful son, as God is my judge!"

I had heard this story before, when I was a student at Monterey Peninsula College and had been in a typing class with Frank. He was attending junior college to bring in some G.I. Bill money and to keep himself occupied while his sons ran the donut business. Occasionally, he and I would talk over a cup of coffee in the school cafeteria.

Frank had then told me stories about his youth, playing football in the city streets, being a tough guy in the neighborhood, and going into the Navy as a boxer. He told me that he had been quite the physical specimen and one night, he had been picked up by a woman in a bar in Seattle, who took him back to her apartment for a one-night-stand. While looking around her small living room, he noticed that she had pictures of bodybuilders on her walls. When they had sex, he was finished very soon, and then started to get dressed.

The woman lay there on the bed and asked him, "What about me? You've had pleasure. Aren't you going to give me pleasure?"

He said he had stared at her, not understanding or caring what she meant. "As far as I'm concerned, women are for men's pleasure… end of story. Truth be told, I never wanted children. They were just the result of having sex."

I'd looked at him across the table from me, incredulous that my mother had actually married this man. I'd thought, you are such a pathetic excuse for a human being.

Then I told him that I had to go to my next class and left him sitting in the cafeteria.

One after another, issues were raised that addressed the crimes he had committed against the family in molesting his children. Frank tried spinning his sexual misconduct by arguing that he had the right to participate in the sex lives of his female children. To everyone's disbelief, he insisted, "I'm the father. The father has certain rights!"

My older sister, Janette, has always been a very attractive, sensual-looking woman with large breasts. Frank had preyed upon her in particular. When Janette's turn to speak came she told a story about how Frank had taken her to a cabin at a mountain resort and, when he realized she would not consent to intercourse with him, induced her to masturbate him. Janette cringed at the recounting of this and a look of horrified disgust crossed her face as she described how he ejaculated all over her.

The counselor asked Frank, "Is this true? Did you do these things to Janette?"

"Well, she's got those big tits," he retorted, holding his hands, fingers spread, out in front of his own chest. "I'm her father. I have a right."

The counselor stood up, walked behind Frank, and, using fingers like the talons of an eagle, dug them into his shoulders. Moving around his right side, the counselor approached him nose to nose, and declared in a calm but powerful voice, "Frank! There is no excuse on the face of this planet for violating the trust placed in you by a child!"

The shock of this confrontation seemed to break through Frank's defense.

He looked down at the floor and said, "You're right, you're right. I did it," admitting he had done an evil thing.

We had always been confounded by Mom's eventual and increasingly frequent failure to intervene, and to protect us from the terrible things that Frank was doing to us.

The girls had gone to her repeatedly during that period of time. "Don't you know what's going on?" they had asked.

Her response had been that same Catholic defense the priest had used, "Shame on you for saying such bad things about your father. This is calumny. I don't want to hear another word about it."

This issue was about to be raised in a real breakthrough moment when Phil, who had been the child protagonist in the "Yours, Mine and Ours" story, spoke up again, as he had done the day before.

"Where were you when we were being beaten?" he asked her. Ever the calm one, he followed with, "Where were you when your daughters were being molested?" But then, Phil's emotions engaged and his voice rose as he threw accusations at her, "It's just as much your fault as his, that we grew up so screwed up! When you realized that you couldn't change him and that you were trapped, you fed us to him, to protect yourself!"

At that point, Frank realized that he had to take responsibility for his behavior or else the burden would fall upon his wife. And in a remarkable turn-about, this monstrous person showed that he had at least a sliver of decency and genuine concern for his wife.

In a loud, impassioned voice, he shouted, "Now, you just wait a minute! If there is one thing, one person in this world that I have truly loved, it is this woman! I will not have her taking responsibility for what I have done!"

He looked around the room at all of us and openly acknowledged his guilt. "I did it! I'm responsible; she's not! I take full responsibility for myself!"

And then, in one brief moment, the seemingly impregnable walls he had built to protect himself came tumbling down in ruin. Frank began to weep convulsively. "I'm sorry," he cried. "I'm sorry... I'm sorry." With his voice choking with emotion through his tears, he uttered, "You're absolutely right! I did it! I did it all!" Covering his face with his hands, he repeated, "I'm sorry! I'm sorry!"

Watching Frank cry as I had never seen him do, I saw what the result of a corrupted childhood had done to him. With the realization that he had been unable or unwilling to find a way out of the basement that he had been literally and figuratively trapped in for his entire life, my heart broke for him. He had been perverted by an absence of love in his life, and unfortunately, Frank had chosen to perpetuate that pattern of abuse and perversion.

In spite of that, someone had to let little Frankie out of that basement. I got up from my chair, walked over to where he was sitting, bent over in anguish, and placed my hands on his shoulders. He raised himself from his sitting fetal position to see who was in front of him.

Kneeling down in front of him, I looked him in the eyes and said, "Frank, I forgive you."

He stared at me blankly, apparently not sure how to respond.

I repeated myself, "I forgive you, Frank. You have apologized, and at this point in time, that is all we can ask of you."

He smiled weakly and through his tears, replied, "Thank you." Then he broke down again and continued weeping for the next few moments.

Staring at him in his repentant moment, I thought, The gods of vengeance have been denied. When he dies, he will go to his heaven and his God will forgive him the sins of his life.

It was getting toward the end of the day, so the counselor led us in the "Our Father," speaking of the healing power of forgiveness.

Stressing the importance of Declared Truth in the process of releasing each child from the emotional imprisonment of lies, it was suggested we think about how to integrate what we had learned over these three powerful, transformative weekends.

In a sort of concluding discussion, we learned that when Mom had been worn down by time, fatigue, and the unending discouragements of her life, she realized that she could not save Frank's children from him, or save him from himself. Her own pride and emotional turmoil turned on her. She imploded and denied her quandary by becoming complicit in his crimes.

Her problem had no easy solution. She wouldn't confront Frank because she knew that the confrontation wouldn't change his behavior. By exposing his deeds and holding him responsible, she might tear the family apart; Beardsley children supporting Frank; North children condemning him. This is something she was not prepared to face and was afraid to confront. Even though she had failed to create one family out of two, she would not allow herself to admit that she had completely failed in bringing these two families together.

Her dilemma was appalling: she could either ignore the situation or take a gun and put the beast in the ground, as I had once considered doing.

Mom told us that she believed that society wouldn't support her in making Frank's behavior public. The priest who told my sisters and me that we should respect our father probably spoke the majority opinion of society, at that time. By investing so much of her energy in creating an image of social respectability, she would not even think of supporting the truth of the matter. In her mind, either consciously or unconsciously or both, the illusion was of paramount importance.

Of course, times have changed, and whether she would choose to do so or not, today she would have the recourse of sending him to prison for some hard time. While such behavior is and always has been despicable, we learned from the counselor that the incidence of incest in American families is estimated to be somewhere in the range of 20 percent and some experts say, even much higher. I suspect the rates of incest in American families are much higher than official estimates. Unfortunately, from what I have learned from many of my lady friends, incest may be more common than its absence.

Having exhausted ourselves, we gratefully ended our counseling sessions. Some members of the family experienced a tremendous sense of relief. The weight of the hypocrisy of the "Yours, Mine, and Ours" mythology had been a burden to carry. It was marvelous to put the lie of the big "wonderful" family to rest.

For a time, Mom became a major beneficiary of that cleansing experience. She expressed that she felt genuinely relieved not to have to carry that burden for even one more day.

"I feel like a giant weight has been lifted," she told me, her face appearing more relaxed than I had ever remembered it. Unfortunately, this respite proved to be temporary.

An interesting phenomenon that resulted from the "airing out the closets" in the lives of the participants was that it created a vacuum. Relatively quickly, I could sense it. And if the vacuum doesn't get filled, I recognized, then the hollowness of the now vacated spirit would likely be perpetuated. It must be filled by grace, I thought to myself. Negative energy must be replaced by positive. We needed to be able to look at each other and not be reminded of the pain and horror of the past. We needed to create new memories, to fill the void. As mentioned earlier, for the North's, get-togethers had turned into bitch-fests; so in spite of our fondness for each other, we had generally avoided getting together.

For me, the practice of TM was especially valuable for creating the requisite positive energy required for the task. The gaping hole left by the poisonous stinger of past experiences had been removed and was being filled with the clean and wholesome energy of each twice-daily dip into the transcendent. However, I was concerned about my siblings, who were left on their own to fill that void. I began communicating with them more often, taking a more active interest in their lives, with the goal of helping to breathe new life into the family.

My concern, which proved to be an accurate one, was that the two families, Beardsley and North, would go their separate ways.

Helen North – 1948

28

MOM'S HEALTH BREAKDOWN

B y 1990, my mother was approaching sixty years of age and her health was taking a turn for the worse. Having had ten children, along with a genetic disposition to poor circulation, her legs were ruined. They had been stripped several times of varicose veins, and she was headed for a wheelchair. Unfortunately, she was repeating the pattern her mother had set before her. Grandma Brandmeir had given birth to ten children, and had ended up in a wheelchair, also at age 60.

I went to Mom with a challenge. "Do you want to walk?" I asked.

"Of course I do!" she replied, as though I were asking a stupid question.

Then I explained my plan to her. Because of my experience with TM and my four years at MIU, I was aware of other aspects of self-development and holistic health knowledge that had come from India. I proposed taking her to a Panchakarma clinic in Pacific Palisades, California. Panchakarma is a program of restorative healing based on an ancient Indian system of medical care called Ayurveda (Sanskrit translation: "knowledge of life"). The system is legendary in India, and increasingly in the west, for its restorative capabilities. I offered to pay for Mom's treatments, so she would have nothing to lose and possibly her health to regain. Her Western allopathic doctors had suggested she resign herself to living the rest of her life in a wheelchair, which was something she did not want to accept. I may have been her wayward son, but she agreed that she had nothing to lose.

Off we went, then, to "PacPal". Following five days of treatments, consisting of specifically designed and targeted cleansing massage for her legs, marma (pressure point) therapy and a variety of other treatments, she was able to walk again and was spared the wheelchair.

In fact, on the third day of her treatments, we learned that Dr. Deepak Chopra, the famous lecturer, author, and M.D.-turned Ayurvedic practitioner, was speaking at UCLA on the subject of Ayurveda that night. We decided to attend the lecture, arranged transportation, and arrived early so that Mom could take her time getting to the lecture hall. Prior to receiving her Panchakarma treatments, she could not stand for long, and had needed help to simply step up into a car or onto another level, such as a sidewalk or a stair. But we were both in for a treat!

When we parked the van outside the appropriate building, we looked up and were chagrined to see that we would have to go up five flights of stairs to get to the hall.

Without so much as a word, Mom stepped down out of the van on her own, walked up the first three flights of stairs, turned around, and with her fists held up in front of her, exclaimed, "Anybody want to go a few rounds!"

I was flabbergasted. She started to laugh and waved us along, saying, "Come on, slowpokes!"

Those of us in the van who had seen her on the day she arrived at the clinic looked at one another in wonderment.

Dr. Chopra lectured to an attentive audience of several dozen people that night on the rejuvenating aspects of Ayurveda. We sat in the front row, with knowing looks on our faces. When Mom returned home, she seemed to have a new lease on life, regaining full use of her legs.

Unfortunately, in spite of her renewed ability to walk, Mom proceeded to develop a confounding set of physical pains that harassed her for the rest of her life. She visited specialists from every medical field you can imagine, and had every MRI, CT-scan, and blood test known to Western medicine. The results all came back as inconclusive. The medical doctors couldn't diagnose her problem(s). However, that didn't stop them from prescribing every pain pill under the sun for her.

I offered to take her back to the Ayurvedic doctors, but she refused to go see them. As she continued to take a daily cocktail of Vicodin, Demerol, Codeine, Percocet, and Valium, all washed down with bottles of red wine, her physical and mental deterioration began to accelerate. She began to black out, which raised the problem of hurting herself as she fell. Those of us who were paying attention feared for her but felt helpless, given her stubborn streak and insistence that we mind our own business. We could not rely on Frank to watch out for her because, as we all knew, he was incapable of watching out for anyone but himself.

On one occasion, one of us was talking with Mom on the phone. Suddenly, he heard a thump and the phone went quiet. He could hear the San Francisco 49er football game broadcasting in the background, but nothing else. Recognizing immediately that Mom had blacked out again, he called 911 and had a sheriff's car dispatched to the condo where she and Frank lived.

As the story was related to me later, the sheriff knocked at the door, and heard Frank yelling for Helen to "Answer the goddamn door!" After several such shouts, he appeared at the door himself. The sheriff told Frank that he had reason to believe that there was someone unconscious in the house. Frank vigorously denied that anyone was unconscious in his house. The sheriff asked to come in and found Mom lying on the kitchen floor, unconscious. She spent the rest of the day in the hospital, going through a battery of tests, with no conclusions forthcoming.

Seven years before she died at the age of seventy, Helen North-Beardsley left Frank. She left him on my advice… well, not exactly on my advice alone; but I was the first of her children to suggest to her that she'd be better off without him.

Her frequent fainting spells had become intolerable. Frank was his usual bad influence, reinforcing her alcoholism with his own, and dragging her down with his negativity. The restorative Panchakarma treatments had given her back the use of her legs, but she quickly resumed old, self-destructive habit patterns.

One day when we were talking about her health, I expostulated with her.

"Listen, don't you get it? Every night you get into bed with the man who molested your daughters and who beat your sons. That connection is, and always has been, extremely toxic. It's killing you. For decades, your relationship with that man has been poisoning your soul, and now it's destroying your body as well. So, if you continue to live with him, you will die, and soon. It's really very simple, Mom. If you die, you will leave him. Your alternate choice is to leave him now, while you're alive, and try to make some sense out of the rest of your life. Either way, you are going to leave him."

She was completely resistant to the logic I was sharing with her.

With the same stubborn mask on her face that I had seen when I told her I wanted to change my name back to North, so many years before, she replied, "You don't know what you're talking about. Now, I have to go."

I can't even begin to imagine the conflicts that must have raged in her heart and in her mind. What I do know, however, is that it's common for one's ego to constantly rewrite the memory of events to make them more acceptable to one's self. But Helen North-Beardsley had so tragically bungled her attempts to save the Beardsley children from Frank, and Frank from himself, that it seemed that she just couldn't reconcile any of it.

Mom flew to Seattle to visit her older sister, who has been referred to so far as "Auntie", who, without any contact with or counsel from me, told her the exact same thing about the source of her ill health.

While Mom was there, she called me. "You were the first to suggest this, so I'm letting you know first. I'm leaving Frank."

I was neither happy nor sad for her. "Good to hear, Mom. I'm glad you came to that realization."

When Mom returned from Seattle, Jeanie, Gerry, Collien, and I helped her move into a condo in Santa Rosa. She was basically penniless; so, in an effort to help her achieve self-sufficiency, we each contributed money to sustain her. A small sedan was purchased for her so she could be mobile.

For a few weeks, Mom seemed to be handling life on her own. But it wasn't long before she sideswiped parked cars on two separate, but successive occasions, demonstrating that she was a menace behind the steering wheel. We were glad that nobody was injured in the accidents. Against her protestations that she could continue to drive, her keys were taken away.

Shortly afterward, she had another fainting spell and fell over backwards in her garage, hitting her head. The fall landed her back in the hospital, where she stayed for two weeks, unable to care for herself.

This was the county hospital, which was infamous for its crowded rooms and where the staff was horribly overworked. In conversation with my siblings, we discussed the issue of proper care, and we concluded that Mom just wasn't going to get it in the county hospital. It was agreed that Jeanie, Gerry, Collien and I would go and check her out and take her home.

When we arrived at her room, I smiled and greeted her. She looked at me and smiled back, asking, "Tommy, who is that little boy sitting next to you?"

I looked down to my right and realized that she was referring to her purse which was on a folding chair.

I nonchalantly responded, "Oh, that's your purse, Mom."

She exhaled with an exasperated look on her face, shaking her head and correcting me, "No, it's not! It's a little boy!"

I looked at the purse and back at Mom, suggesting, "Mom, keep your eyes on the little boy." I picked up her purse and walked it over to her. As I got closer to her, she could see that it was her purse. She was embarrassed and looked away.

Collien and I exchanged a knowing glance, nonverbally agreeing that Mom was hallucinating and that we had arrived just in the nick of time. God only knew what drugs they were sedating her with.

Jeanie and Gerry had to go to work the next day, and I had more flexibility in setting my own schedules; so Collien and I stayed on to help Mom. For the next four days, we stayed at her condo, trying to help her manage her pain, and get back on her feet.

Insisting on maintaining her illusion of self-sufficiency, she told us, "You two just run along now; I can take care of myself."

We declined to leave and settled in, Collien sleeping on the couch and me on the floor of the spare bedroom.

Mom had a treadmill in her living-room. She said exercise in the form of fast walking helped to lower the pain intensity, so we stayed by her side as she exercised. But in the evening, when she resumed gulping down several pain pills with two large glasses of red wine, Collien and I began to fear she was going to have reactions that we could not anticipate or respond to. Barely able to sleep, we were completely exhausted after the fourth day. What we had hoped would be stabilizing for Mom, was destabilizing for us.

We arranged to have Mom admitted to Stanford University Hospital, where she underwent tests for the next two weeks. Finding nothing physically wrong to focus on, the doctors agreed that she was indeed, suffering, and turned their focus to pain management. My siblings and I rolled our eyes in exasperation, having been down this road for too long already; but there wasn't much we could do.

Mom had already spent several years in and out of hospitals. Legions of doctors couldn't find a specific ailment that could be addressed. By 1994, she had become hopelessly addicted to her daily regimen of narcotics and alcohol.

It was apparent to those of her children and step-children who were paying attention that she was headed down a path of accelerating self-destruction. But Helen Brandmeir North Beardsley was a stubborn woman. She insisted she was fine and, "Would we please leave her alone, thank you very much." She would not listen to anyone; so in the fall of 1994, we held an intervention, moderated by a professional counselor who specialized in that sort of thing.

During the intervention, we each took turns telling Mom how important she was to us. When it was my turn to talk, I pleaded, "Mom, I don't want you to die. My daughters don't even know their only grandmother (Connie's parents had already passed away), and I'd like to give them the experience of having a grandparent. You're all I've got!"

I was hoping to appeal to her sense of responsibility, but it seemed to have no effect on her.

When we had all exhausted our appeals, the intervention moderator beseeched Mom, "Helen, these are your children who love you and want you to be well and happy. Would you like to say anything to them?"

Mom sighed and exclaimed, "But I'm not addicted! I just want to manage my pain!"

Refusing to acknowledge her pain pill and alcohol dependency, she insisted it was only the pain that was the problem. No one disagreed with her, but since dependency was the final result, it had to be dealt with before it killed her. We eventually convinced her to go into treatment.

The next stop was the Mayo Clinic for thirty days of detox and pain management consultation. Auntie, bless her soul, offered to underwrite Mom's stay there. When we prepared her for her flight to Minneapolis, we took containers with six different pain killers out of her purse.

The doctors at the Mayo clinic had more time to focus on Mom than those at Stanford, but were also unable to isolate a specific cause for her pain. They called her symptoms "Parkinson's-like," but didn't diagnose her with Parkinson's. She expressed to me that she had appreciated their concern and attention, but they hadn't improved her condition or her pain management.

When she returned, she lived with several of her children and step-children in their turn, none of whom could tolerate her for very long, in spite of their best efforts to help. She was alternately belligerent and hyper-critical of everyone, wearing out her welcome very quickly.

Mom and Frank were never divorced. Although she became increasingly embittered about the suffering she had experienced at Frank's hands, she felt entitled to half of his military retirement benefits, which would have terminated had she divorced him.

Her words were, "I'll be damned if I'm going to give up those benefits. He owes me that and a lot more."

In 1995, I visited her at her condo in Santa Rosa, California, and she spoke longingly about her life before Frank. She told me she was amending her will so that her remains would be cremated and her ashes buried in Richard North's grave.

Then she looked at me squarely and said, "I once threatened to disown you if you changed your name back to North. You were the first to suggest such a thing, and I just couldn't allow it. Your brothers came along later with the same idea, and, since I was already familiar with it, I didn't give them the hard time I gave you. I'm sorry. I shouldn't have stood in your way. In fact, if I had any guts at all, I'd change my name back to North, too."

I looked at her in shock. "Can I construe that as a blessing?" I asked with a smile.

She smirked, "I don't know if I'd go that far."

Mom remained in touch with all of her children until she passed. In conversation with my brothers and sisters, we agreed that Mom was the farthest thing from what we would call a nurturing human being. In fact, in my experience, she was not nurturing at all. But she had been a light that had shone (albeit dimly) in the social and familial darkness in which we children had otherwise stumbled through during our formative years.

At the age of seventy, Mom's health had deteriorated to the point that we finally committed her to a full care nursing facility. She died six months later.

A week before she died, I visited her in the room she shared with three other women. I had been warned by my sister Jeanie that Mom drifted in and out of coherence the last time she tried to communicate with her. She was sleeping when I arrived, so, sitting down, I used the time to meditate. After about twenty minutes, I opened my eyes and gently looked at her "third eye," that point of extra-sensory perception in the middle of the forehead. She woke up and looked in my direction. It took her a moment to focus.

She finally recognized me, and in surprise said, "Oh, Tommy! I'm so glad you're here. You know, I've been meaning to tell you… I owe you a big mbmbmbmb."

She babbled incoherently, not knowing I couldn't understand a word she said. I nodded and smiled, and after a short time, she went back to sleep. Was it thanks? Was it an apology? What had she wanted to give me? On my way out to the parking lot I had to chuckle. All my life she and I had miss-communicated on just about everything. And here it was again, at the very end. It had become part of what I call the "cosmic joke."

If we look for it, there's humor in the gap between how we humans think and how we express ourselves. That same humorous gap can be found between generations, between couples and in family relationships. It gives comedians endless material to build comedy routines upon. In my case, my mother and I never saw eye-to-eye on much of anything. In my view of things, as I tried to maintain a relationship with her, she was constantly pulling the rug out from under my feet. I don't think it was a conscious effort; it just worked out that way. She did it when she didn't come to my Little League games… refused to give me her blessing as I left home… when she threatened to disown me… when she told me I didn't need to go to college… when she chose not to attend my college graduation, etc., etc.

For most of us, our mothers occupy a special place in our hearts, sometimes whether we like it or not. The mother role, or "archetype" as Swiss psychiatrist Carl Jung identified it, is a powerful one, beyond our understanding. She is the creative channel through whom we came into this world and, as such, she is our primal connection to the universe itself. In spite of the worst a mother can dole out to her offspring, we crave that contact and that connection. Most of us will overlook major abuse and excuse almost anything to stay connected. My desire for love and approval from my mother kept me coming back to try to make that connection, always, one more time.

I shook my head as I got into my car. I had never been able to establish that bond with her, and would have to learn to just be okay with that.

In Loving Memory of

Helen Eileen Beardsley
April 5, 1930 - April 26, 2000

29

THE FUNERAL

When Mom died in April 2000, her funeral was covered as a national news event. As the matriarch of one of America's largest families and the central character in "Yours, Mine and Ours," she received a celebrity send-off. The media from the San Francisco Bay Area were all there, and the story hit the AP wire, broadcasting out to both national and international TV. Having been interviewed in front of the church and asked a few questions by reporters, I later received phone calls from all over the country.

"I saw you on the news," friends and acquaintances said —some of whom I hadn't been in contact with for decades.

Relatives came from both sides of my parents' families; that is, the Norths and the Brandmeirs, as well as from the extended Beardsley family, and many friends from the past. During the service, the eulogy was given by Auntie, Mom's older sister, who had been so kind, generous, and supportive in every way to Mom and her children.

Auntie looked out from the lectern at a church filled with hundreds of mourners and, with a tone of melancholy in her voice, began, "Our mother always said that Helen would be the one who would have all the babies."

Her mother had made a foreboding prediction, and it had come true in extraordinary fashion. Grandma Brandmeir never knew how right she was!

When it was time to share "Helen Stories," I approached the podium to talk about what I felt was important. Looking out at the gathering, scanning all the faces that had been part of my mother's life, either as direct participants or as interested observers, it occurred to me how little most of them knew of her life, and for that matter, how little I knew of her life. How much can anyone know of the life of another? We can know details of events we experienced alongside the person, or anecdotes as they are told to us, from which we form images and ideas of what we think that person might have been like; but how close are those images and ideas to the experience of that person's life as they knew it? Most often, there is little resemblance at all. We have only our perceptions, which may or may not reflect reality, if there is such a thing.

The past is the past, I thought. We both learn from it and set ourselves free, or we become prisoners or slaves to it, forever doomed to carry the burden, like Marley's chains. I chose to read something that Helen North, somewhere in her deeper musings, believed, but found challenging to manifest in her life, as, I believe, most of us do. I shared it because life is for the living, and the forum of my mother's memorial was a fitting place to remind myself and each and every person in attendance what we are here on earth to do. I read from Marianne Williamson's book, *A Return to Love*. She writes, "Our deepest fear is not that we are inadequate. Our deepest fear is that we are powerful beyond measure. It is our light, not our darkness, that most frightens us. We ask ourselves, who am I to be brilliant, gorgeous, talented, and fabulous? Actually, who are you not to be? You are a child of God. Your playing small doesn't serve the world. There's nothing enlightened about shrinking so that other people won't feel insecure around you. We are all meant to shine, as children do. We are born to make manifest the glory of God that is within us. It's not just in some of us, it's in everyone. And as we let our own light shine, we unconsciously give other people permission to do the same. As we are liberated from our own fear, our presence automatically liberates others."

Bringing home the point and making it personal, I read a prose poem of my own, which I had "heard" within me during a meditation years before. It went:

Within each of us
There is a light
A light that shines eternal
It is the light of the rising sun
It is the light of the full moon
It is the light of the stars in the darkest night
It is the light in a mother's eyes, gleaming at her newborn
It is the light between lovers as they embrace
It is the light in the path of souls
On their journey to the other side
It is the light of Love
It is the light of Being
It is the light of God
See the light
Be the light
Shine the light
For all to see.

During the reception following the Catholic funeral mass, my daughters, Diana and Elyse, who were 13 and 10 years old respectively, were sitting on the church steps visiting with some of their cousins.

An elderly man approached them and asked them, "Do you know who I am?"

They replied that they did not. He said to them, "I'm Frank Beardsley."

They stared at him in curious and cautious wonder. Here was the man whom they had only known as "the evil step-father" of their dad. He had not been welcome in our home during their lives. At the age of 84, he looked something less than the mythology that had grown around him. Regardless, they got up without saying a word in response and walked away to find their mother.

30

THE BURIAL AND
THE RESURRECTION

Mom did have her will amended, so that she'd be buried with Richard North in his grave at the Willamette National Veterans Cemetery in Portland, Oregon. As I drove with Connie, and our two children, Diana and Elyse, in our rented sedan through Portland's deep green forested hillsides to the cemetery, I glanced back at the spectacular view of the Willamette Valley below us. Driving past the wide stone entrance, I looked at the reverently manicured lawns, covered in crosses, headstones and brass plaques. As with so many such sites, this one carried with it an overwhelming sense of peace and quiet, and a tremendous sense of history. As we passed by the hundreds of graves, I couldn't help but wonder; who were all these people? What were their stories?

With a mild northwestern storm blowing through, grey and white clouds went scudding across the sky, occasionally dropping cold rain on us. There were not enough umbrellas to share, so most of us simply accepted the rain when it fell.

Everyone, from both the North and the Beardsley sides of the family, had been encouraged to be present for the burial. One of the younger siblings shared with me that the Beardsley siblings chose not to attend so that the North's could bury their mom with their dad. My understanding is that it was a gesture of compassion and respect. I cannot say that all of them felt this way, but regardless, the only people who showed up for the burial were Helen's original eight children.

It was May 5th, 2000, the day of a major planetary alignment (astrologically speaking), and it appeared that the only people whom the Universe had invited were the inner circle of the children of Richard and Helen North. Four brothers and four sisters, together with some of their spouses, Phil's girlfriend, and my two children, were gathered around the gravesite that blustery afternoon.

I felt a sense of destiny lingering about that somber event. Shortly, I came to understand that no one else was supposed to be there. After forty years in a kind of desert exile, Fate or the Divine had conspired to bring our unbroken circle together with no interlopers. If someone else or a person from the media had tried to attend, I believe they would have been thwarted by cancelled flights, flat tires, or the flu. This was the reuniting of a tribe of people who had passed only with great tribulations through a troubled and weary land. It seemed that this event served to re-establish a family that had been denied an identity for far too long. From the beginning, we hadn't been permitted to speak of the North family as an entity worthy of noting or remembering. But now we were reclaiming an identity that the jealousy of Frank Beardsley had stolen away.

After we were done chatting and visiting, and the time for the committing of Mom's ashes to the grave had come, I called everyone to order.

I asked the group, "Does anyone have anything they would like to say right away?"

No one spoke up. Into that silence, I announced, "Good, because I have something to say."

A voice spoke to my heart and told me to take a deep breath and let it out.

I filled my lungs, lifted my eyes towards heaven, raindrops falling on my upturned cheeks, and literally screamed into the face of the Almighty:

"GOD! YOU LISTEN TO ME!
FORTY YEARS WE HAVE PUT UP WITH THIS… SHIT!
WE HAVE ALL SURVIVED!
AND FINALLY, WE ARE FREE!"

I screamed that declaration so loud that the challenge to the heavens literally tore at my vocal cords. I collapsed to my knees and buried my head in my hands. Immediately I began to weep the tears of forty years in the desert.

We had been led, I believe, to this brief opportunity to finally expose the knowledge of what was real and true for us as a family. The shockwave of my unrestrained proclamation served to tear down the barriers that we had erected to protect ourselves. Had I not been so guided, the moment might have been lost forever. As I knelt on the ground, head bent forward, gripping my sides and crying my heart out, my brothers and sisters broke through their own barriers and cried with me.

Then, some of the siblings stepped forward and spoke to Helen or Dick North, our mom and dad.

Collien, the eldest, looked down at the grave and sadly said, "Mom, I just wish you had been a more loving person. I forgive you for not being that."

Janette, the next in line, who had always been Mom's whipping girl, stood at Collien's shoulder and followed with, "Well Mom, they've been long hard years. But now you're where you've always wanted to be… with the one true love of your life."

Gerry stepped forward and looked down at the grave with a scornful look on his face. He calmly and softly said, "Mom, you didn't fool me then… you don't fool me now."

Nick spoke to his dad, at last affirming and cherishing the relationship that for so long had been denied him. Nick, who is a retired Navy Seal, and as tough a guy as you will ever hope to find, had created a lot of emotional armor. The service was especially meaningful for him because, since he was the oldest son, Nick had the clearest memories of our father and having looked just like him, had been cherished by Mom.

This warrior—this man among men—leaned his face against his father's gravestone and wept unabashedly for the man that death had taken from him too soon, and for the bitter years of his life that the locusts had eaten.

When we were children, our dad was usually stationed on an aircraft carrier for six to nine months at a time—coming home only to get mom pregnant again, it seemed. And little Nick would sit on the edge of the lawn, day after day, and stare down the street waiting for the first sign of his father's homecoming. Dick North's untimely passing had left an enormous and unfulfilled need in his young son's heart, and the gravesite service gave Nick an opportunity to reconnect. He continued to rest his face on Dad's gravestone and wept uncontrollably.

As women will almost instinctively do, my two older sisters, Janette and Colleen, moved to console him. They were just about to reach for him, but I tapped them on the shoulders, turned them around, and said. "Excuse me! Leave him alone. He needs this time with his father."

What might have been a 20-minute ceremony became a two-hour catharsis—a true and honest venting and releasing of pent-up energies that we had been living with for most of our lives. There at the grave of our mom and dad, we dispelled that gloomy force by speaking honest and final words to our only true parents.

After the eight of us had gone through all we sensed we needed to, we interred the ashes and left. Fifty-one years before, in front of a priest, Richard and Helen North were joined in life. Now, in front of us, they were joined again, but in death. As I left them, I was joyful.

As I was walking away from the grave, the thought came to me that I could no longer pretend to be a Beardsley. I had made the irrevocable decision to change my name in conversation with my mother four years before. It was now time to make it so. I'm Tom North! I thought. It's past time to get that right.

As we walked up to our rented car, my ten-year-old daughter, Elyse, came up, slipped her hand in mine, looked up at me, smiled, and said, "Hello, Thomas Roderick NORTH!"

She said that to me right at the moment of my thought. I was astonished… and yet, not.

"You know!" I exclaimed.

Then, she mixed her marvelous spiritual insight with an amazing pragmatism, for one so young. "Yeah, Dad, but we'll have to make sure it's okay with Mom and Diana."

So, now I'm Tom North, once again and forever. I was the first to express the intention to reclaim my father's name and the last to carry it out. My mom died in 2000, having lived to see 44 grandchildren. Frank Beardsley remarried again six weeks after her death. He passed away on December 11, 2012 at the age of 97. Other than my mother's funeral, the two of us hadn't had contact for over 20 years. He had become a non-person in my life and in the lives of the extended North family. I do not judge that; it is just the way it worked out. Having embraced the eastern philosophical belief that there is no hell, only God and the bliss of eternity, I know that Frank Beardsley will enjoy eternal life, as we all will, for that is all there is.

My life is wholesome and good, partly because of the healing that took place when our family finally confronted and exorcized the ghosts that had haunted our minds and hearts for so many decades. But if that had never happened, I would have found, through meditation, I believe, sufficient balance to maintain my spiritual equilibrium and joy.

Nikola Tesla, one of the greatest scientific thinkers who ever lived wrote, "The day science begins to study non-physical phenomena, it will make more progress in one decade than in all the previous centuries of its existence." Thank God we don't wait for the scientists. The "study" of "non-physical phenomena" has been carried on by brilliant thinkers and experimenters for more than three millennia.

The hidden realities of the non-physical world that lay around us and within us are like a vast ocean. The shamans, wise men and women, prophets, and oracles of many religions and spiritual traditions have explored this boundless sea and brought back to us reports about the geography and topography of that mysterious realm. Civilization has benefited and continues to benefit beyond measure by such reports.

I have been sailing on that sea myself for three decades, and continue to venture into its vastness every day. It's a place of unceasing wonder, delight, ecstasy, and bliss.

I feel blessed to say that I've discovered for myself the wholesome and healing effects of meditation by exploring the non-physical side of reality, and am constantly reminded of how everything connects with everything else. Ultimately, it is a web or matrix of light and love that provides a power for living which can undo the effects of circumstances and history, no matter how dysfunctional or grim.

Whatever baggage you are carrying around — no matter how powerfully your personal history might work to pull you down— a power that is within us and around us is more powerful still.

My experiences with the realm of the spirit have led me to healing, significance, and purpose. My only wish for you, dear reader, is that you find the inspiration, encouragement and hope you need to walk the path of your own destiny, to discover the wholeness of your own Divine Being.

I wish you happiness and fulfillment in life.

Tom North

RESOURCES

Given that the nature of *True North* is a story of difficulties in childhood that were overcome by seeking out supportive environments, organizations, people, etc., here is a helpful list for those who might be in need of support with their life circumstances. Since meditation has had such a significant and positive impact in my life, I would be remiss if I didn't start there. I have investigated many kinds of meditation, but what I would like to share with you is that they all fall into one of three categories. These categories are: Concentration, Contemplation, and Transcendental Meditation. My own practice has been focused on Transcendental Meditation for the past 37 years, as I have found it to be the easiest and most effective meditation available today. This is, of course, a biased opinion, but you will make your decisions based on what you feel is most appropriate for you. If you prefer to learn more about Concentration or Contemplation, you can find out more by googling these topics.

You can find out more about TM at www.tm.org

Thanks go to Siobhan Greene, Executive Director of Voices for Children for the Monterey Peninsula, www.voicesforchildrencasa.org for the list of child support agencies.

Abuse Watch.net
America's Promise Alliance.org
Casey Family Programs
Casey Family Services
Children's Defense Fund
Child Trends
Child Welfare League of America
National Center for Children in Poverty
National Council of Juvenile and Family Court Judges
National Foster Care Month Coalition
Children Without a Voice USA

Health and Mental Health:
AACAP Facts for Families
AACAP Mental Health

Educational Advocacy:
Casey Family Programs
California Foster Youth Education Task Force Fact Sheets
Judicial Educational Checklist
California Supplement to the Judicial Educational Checklist
Overview of AB490
AB490 for Attorneys and Advocates

www.1800runaway.org

Office of the Attorney General - California Missing Persons. The
legalities....but more importantly where the information can be
found that should be filed when a child is missing.
http://ag.ca.gov/missing/

Chapin Hall Center for Children - Youth Who Run Away From
Substitute Care. A study/paper that was done by the University of
Chicago. Based on Illinois statistics over a ten year period
(1993-2003). While not from our state and done a few years ago,
the information and graphs are really interesting.

www.chapinhall.org/sites/default/files/old_reports/174.pdf

For readers interested in spiritual development, here is a list of
sources, categories, concepts and individuals to choose from.
Thanks go to Diane Brandon, at www.dianebrandon.com, for
the following alphabetical list of alternative topics, which is
meant to give readers somewhere to start. This list is by no means
exhaustive, but is meant to provide a starting place for anyone
who is interested in alternative knowledge.

Acupressure_1 | Acupuncture_1 | Affirmations_1 | African
American_1 | Alchemy_1 | Alexander Technique_3 | Alternative
Healing_45 | Alternative Health_16 | Alternative Health School_2 |
Ancient Civilizations | Angels_15 | Animal Communication_9 |
Animal Health Care_10 | Aromatherapy Incense Massage Oil_22 |
Art Therapy_9 | Ascension_4 | Astrology_137 | Auras and
Energy_2 | Ayurveda_11 | Bodywork_10 | Brain Wave Training_3
| Breathwork_3 | Buddhism_9 | Business Consulting_2 | Candles
Scented and Spiritual_1 | Career Counseling | Celtic Jewelry_4 |
Channeling_16 | Chigong_2 | Chinese Medicine_1 | Christian
Spirituality_1 | Coaching_36 | Codependence_2 | Color Healing_3
| Consciousness Research_3 | Contemporary Spirituality_1 |
Creativity_2 | Crystal Jewelry_3 | Crystal Spiritual Jewelry_3 |
Crystals_10 | Cultural History_1 | Detoxification_1 | Dowsing_2 |
Dream Interpretation_5 | Dreams_4 | Dreamwork_6 |
Drumming_11 | Earth Changes_3 | Egyptian Mysteries | Energy
Clearing_2 | Energy Field Research_2 | Energy Healing_16 |
Energy Medicine_3 | Enlightenment_5 | Enneagram_1 |
Environmental_6 | Ergonomics | Esoteric Traditions_1 | Essential
Oils_5 | Fat-Loss Patch Wholesale | Fat-Loss Patches_1 | Feng
Shui_25 | Flower Essences_10 | Forensic Hypnosis_1 |
Forgiveness_1 | Forslean Patch_1 | Gaia_5 | Goddess and
Women_8 | Grief Counseling_2 | Guided Imagery_4 | Guided
Meditation_5 | Healers_23 | Healing_14 | Healing Centers_6 |
Health Food_3 | Health Information_83 | Health Insurance_1 |
Heart-Centered_1 | Herbal Medicine_13 | Hinduism_2 | Holistic
Health_31 | Homeopathy_7 | Huna_1 | Hypnotherapy_44 | I
Ching_2 | I Ching Classes_2 | Inspirational_10 | Interfaith_1 |
Intuition_10 | Intuition Expert_2 | Intuition in the Workplace_2 |
Intuitive Counseling_8 | Islam_2 | Jen Fe Next Patches_1 | Jin
Shin_1 | Journaling_2 | Kabbalah_6 | Kinesiology_1 | Kundalini_3
| Labyrinths_1 | Life Purpose_1 | Light Therapy_1 |
Macrobiotics_1 | Magnet Therapy_5 | Mandalas_1 | Massage
Therapy_19 | Medical Intuitives_6 | Meditation_21 | Mediums_3 |
Mens Health | Mental Health_28 | Metaphysical Colleges_1 |
Midlife_1 | Music Therapy_7 | Myth_2 | Native American_4 |

Natural Health Products_24 | Natural Skin Care_1 | Natural
Weight Loss_1 | Nature Awareness_1 | Naturopathy_4 | Near
Death Experience_1 | Neuro-Linguistic Programming_4 | New
Age_10 | New Age Art_36 | New Age Audio Tapes_6 | New Age
Books_62 | New Age Centers_9 | New Age Classes_14 | New Age
Directory_20 | New Age Expos_1 | New Age Forums_19 | New
Age Magazines_17 | New Age Music_70 | New Age News and
Media_19 | New Age Organizations_2 | New Age Practitioners_2
| New Age Singles_1 | New Age Speakers_1 | New Age Stores_49
| New Age Videos_1 | New Age Writing_37 | New Science_6 |
New Thought_15 | Numerology_4 | Organic Resources_2 |
Oriental Art_1 | Out-of-Body Experiences_6 | Pagan_19 |
Paranormal_13 | Parapsychology Research_5 | Past Life
Regression_2 | Personal Development_56 | Personal
Empowerment_8 | Personal Growth_6 | Personology_1 |
Philosophy_2 | Power Centers_2 | Power Patch_1 | Prosperity_2 |
Psychic Readings_48 | Psychic Training_3 | Psychical Research_1 |
Psychics_36 | Psycho-Kinesis_1 | Psychotherapy_2 | Radio and TV
Positive_1 | Rebirthing_3 | Recovery_7 | Recreation Therapy_1 |
Reiki_14 | Relationship Counseling_11 | Relationships_4 |
Relaxation Tapes_3 | Remote Viewing_3 | Renewable Energy_2 |
Retreat Centers_17 | Rosicrucian | Runes_1 | Sacred Geometry_1 |
Search Engines | Sensitivity_1 | Shamanism_9 | Singing Bowls_3 |
Sound Healing_2 | Spiritual Churches_2 | Spiritual Cinema_1 |
Spiritual Coaching | Spiritual Counseling_6 | Spiritual Growth_4 |
Spiritual Teachers_15 | Spiritual Teachings_8 | Spiritualism_2 |
Spirituality and Business_14 | Stress Management_4 | Sufi_3 | Tai
Chi_7 | Tantra_7 | Taoism_6 | Tarot_31 | Tellington Touch_1 |
Therapeutic Touch_1 | Trance Dance_1 | Transcendentalism_6 |
Transpersonal Psychology_8 | Travel and Tours_7 | UFOs_6 |
Visualization_1 | Weight Loss_4 | Weight-Loss Patches_1 |
Wholism_1 | Wiccan_15 | Womens_13 | Womens Magazines |
Work and Career_2 | Work at Home_2 | World Peace_6 | Yoga_35
| Zen_1 | Zeolite_1 |

For spiritual seekers looking for a specific methodology, see either the list above or the individuals listed below. This list is from my own experience, and is meant to give readers specific specialists to contact if you live in Central California or are willing to travel there.

Lyndall Demere, PhD., Dynamic Transformation of Consciousness, www.123people.com

Rick Moss, PhD., Precognitive Re-education, www.essentialpathways.com

Janel Wilette, Psychic, Life Coach, www.synergybyjanel.com

Dia Lynn, Holotropic Breathwork, www.dialynn.com

Rabia Erduman, Chakra Balancing, www.wuweiwu.com

Catheryn Bachman, Astrologer, www.creativepathways.us

Gabrielle Mancuso, Hypnotherapist, www.drmancuso.org

Janine Talty, D.O. Osteopathic Surgeon, www.wellness-rehab.com

Robin Yoshida, Energy Medicine Specialist, www.robineiko.com